Financial Inclusion, Innovation, and Investments

Biotechnology and Capital Markets Working for the Poor

Financial Inclusion, Innovation, and Investments

Biotechnology and Capital Markets Working for the Poor

editors

Ralph D. Christy

Vicki L. Bogan

Cornell University, USA

World Scientific

NEW JERSEY · LONDON · SINGAPORE · BEIJING · SHANGHAI · HONG KONG · TAIPEI · CHENNAI

Published by

World Scientific Publishing Co. Pte. Ltd.

5 Toh Tuck Link, Singapore 596224

USA office: 27 Warren Street, Suite 401-402, Hackensack, NJ 07601

UK office: 57 Shelton Street, Covent Garden, London WC2H 9HE

British Library Cataloguing-in-Publication Data
A catalogue record for this book is available from the British Library.

FINANCIAL INCLUSION, INNOVATION, AND INVESTMENTS
Biotechnology and Capital Markets Working for the Poor

Copyright © 2011 by World Scientific Publishing Co. Pte. Ltd.

ISBN-13 978-981-4329-93-4
ISBN-10 981-4329-93-2

Typeset by Stallion Press
Email: enquiries@stallionpress.com

Printed in Singapore.

Foreword

*Muna Ndulo**

This volume chronicles the paper presentations made at the international symposium on "Financial Inclusion, Innovation, and Investments: Biotechnology and Capital Markets Working for the Poor" held at Cornell University from April 20th to 21st, 2007. Individuals came from across the campus, the United States, and the world to help explore issues relating to financial markets, innovation and investments. We at Cornell, as President Skorton stated, like to contextualize our activities in the land grant philosophy where service is a priority. This symposium at Cornell did exactly that. The symposium aimed at bringing knowledge and analytical skills to addressing the world problem of poverty and economic development and the role the market and technology can play in providing solutions to the problem. As the conference papers noted, the strong

---

*Muna Ndulo is an authority on African legal systems, human rights, constitutions, election monitoring, international development, and legal aspects of foreign investments in developing countries. He has worked as Public Prosecutor for the Zambian Ministry of Legal Affairs, was Dean of University of Zambia School of Law, and from 1986–1996 served the United Nations Commission for International Trade Law (UNCITRAL) as Legal Officer. From 1992 to 1994 he was Political Adviser to the UN Mission in South Africa. He joined Cornell Law School's faculty in 1996, and served in UN Missions as Legal Adviser in East Timor (1999), Kosovo (2000) and Afghanistan (2003). He teaches international organizations and human rights institutions, the legal aspects of foreign investment in developing countries, and the common law and African legal systems. He is also Director of Cornell University's Institute for African Development and Honorary Professor of Law, Cape Town University, SA.

Ndulo holds a D. Phil. from Trinity College, Oxford University; an LL.M. from Harvard Law School; and an LL.B. from University of Zambia.

negative response by many civil society groups to the globalization process is indicative of widespread concerns about its impact on the poor. In our discussions we focused on addressing the challenges of inclusion, and highlighting innovative institutions and strategies of improving access to capital and biotechnology for the poor.

Several papers in this volume highlight the importance of technology. Technology contains both opportunities and threats to developing countries. The major threat is that developing countries will not be well integrated into the new technology early enough; the major opportunity lies in the capabilities of technology to better connect communities to resources within their countries and elsewhere and to better exploit their resources and empower the poor communities and enhance job-creating skills.

Many parts of the world have made progress in meeting the challenge of development, security, and governance. However, for most, especially those in Africa, the progress is still too slow and is too little to make a significant impact on poverty alleviation. Still, far too many people are living under conditions of extreme poverty. In recent times, no country has graduated from least developed to developing middle-income country status. At the very least, I think this implicates policies. As has been noted by several speakers, we now have the millennium development goals. The prospects of achieving the millennium development goals depend largely on the extent to which developing countries are able to transform their economies and increase their participation in the global economy. The widening gap between the rich and the poor which several papers noted, poses a serious threat to security. A system that does not offer some hope and benefit to the losers is liable to be disrupted by acts of desperation.

To transform developing country economies, especially those in Africa, we need action on a number of fronts: (a) governance, (b) trade front, and (c) empowerment of women. Trade and development are mutually supportive. People who work on trade and those who work on development must work together. At both national and international levels, policy communities have been standing with their backs towards each other for far too long. Policy and implementation are still too fragmented and incoherent especially at the national level within governments. Global coherence and better international governance begin at home. Investment policies should be more geared towards strengthening supply capacity and creating the enabling environment in developing states. We must also ask why, despite the investment return on investments to Africa being some of the highest in the world, the African continent attracts the least FDI inflows by region in the world. At the very minimum it should suggest a need to reexamine our strategies for attracting investments.

The differences among developing countries are significant and growing. How should this diversity be addressed in political, economic and institutional terms? We need both trade liberalization and fair ground rules that take account of special and differential needs to a country's level of development. Clearly, developing countries should open access to their markets. Richer developing countries should also open their markets to the least developed countries. We know that many economic studies have shown that those who liberalize and reform effectively gain the most from trade and in economic growth. Many developing countries recognize this. What they seek is equal opportunity to participate and compete in accordance with fair rules that take adequate account of needs related to different levels of development. Where fair rules are needed, two areas stand out: (a) agriculture, and (b) labor-intensive products and services. These sectors are crucial for industrial development and poverty reduction. Agriculture is the major activity in rural areas where a large number of poor people live. In the service area, developed countries should try to help enhance the efficiency of service sectors in developing countries by opening up their markets.

To transform African economies, we need to move from agrarian-based economies towards more industrialized ones. We need to do the following: (a) improve the investment climate which is essential to reduce the cost of doing business, (b) invest heavily in infrastructure — roads, energy, etc., (c) increase the competitiveness of products from developing countries, and (d) invest heavily in human resources development. Former President Mbeki of South Africa wondered why Telkom SA charges many hundreds of percent more per unit than is being charged elsewhere in the world. A key to increasing competitiveness in a global knowledge-based economy is innovation through the applications of and advances in science and technology, and investments in higher education. A word of caution, though, that as we promote the role of the market, we must remember that markets to a large extent reflect the existing distribution of assets; they are not designed to redistribute those assets according to principles of social justice. It follows that there is a need to establish checks and balances designed to blunt the disruptive effects of self-interest. We discussed the question of credit. Credit plays an important role in economic growth. The ability to borrow greatly enhances the profitability of investments. But we must remember that every financial crisis is preceded by an unsustainable expansion of credit. If credit is available, it is too much to expect the debtors to exercise self-restraint.

During the course of the two-day symposium, we discussed not only problems but also what has been achieved and what lessons have been learned. The question for us now is how do these inform new areas of research and for those of us who teach, our teaching? For the policymakers and practitioners, how do they inform our practice and policy making?

Reflections

Clifton R. Wharton, Jr.*

For me personally and for Dolores, it is great to be back at Cornell. Many years ago we spent a mini-sabbatical here on campus in the Department of Agricultural Economics. My last visit here was about 11 years ago when I delivered the Messenger Lecture on April 18, 1996. You know today is April 20th — it was then April 18th — must be something about April that brings me back here.

But I could not resist because the subject of poverty and subsistence agriculture used to be a central focus of my very first career. Now I will admit that my career in this area began almost 60 years ago in 1948 — dealing with Latin America and then with Southeast Asia. Hence, I welcomed the opportunity to revisit my professional roots.

I have selected four topics which I believe have been continuing general issues that span that 60-year period. I am focusing primarily on the programmatic approaches to development.

*Clifton R. Wharton, Jr. is the former Chairman and CEO of TIAA-CREF, President Emeritus of Michigan State University, former Chancellor of the State University of New York, and US Deputy Secretary of State in 1993. Chairman of the Rockefeller Foundation (1982–1987), he was an officer with the Agricultural Development Council (1957–1970). Acknowledgement and remarks made on the occasion of the inaugural presentation of the "Dr. Clifton R. Wharton, Jr. Emerging Markets Award".

ix

1 The Preference for Univariate Solutions to Solve Multivariate Problems

One of the things that has struck me over the years is the fact that most of the problems that one deals with in development are the result of multiple forces and multiple factors. Too often, however, people in the past have tended to initiate programs which have a single focus — they see it as developing the "magic key." They do not recognize or at least will not acknowledge that there are multiple forces and how those multiple forces interact to create the problem that you are dealing with.

I am reminded of an instance which a couple of you here will remember. When the Green Revolution first began, at that time the focus was exclusively on science. There was quite a battle over whether or not to include or introduce the social sciences into the effort. Science was judged as the sole magic solution, the magic key.[1] But science to be fully successful needed to have the broader focus — to include or recognize the multivariate nature of the problem of increasing rice and wheat production. (Regrettably, the same mistake appears to be repeating in African agriculture today.)

Another aspect of this is what I call the "faddism" of the magic keys. When I first began working in the field of development assistance, believe it or not, the first fad was that the United States already had the technical assistance that could be used abroad to alleviate poverty. Because we in the US had the technical capacity, we could just take American technology and transfer it overseas.

Then what followed? The next magic key was "basic needs" — we were going to solve LDC growth by having programs which concentrated on basic needs at the grassroots level. The next fad was "integrated agricultural development." The next was to attack foreign poverty by working with the "poorest of the poor." The next was "sustainable development." The latest is the "millennium challenge" approach. All of those are part of that faddism process.

---

[1] This clash mirrored an earlier conflict within the Rockefeller Foundation that led its then chairman, John D. Rockefeller III, to create the Agricultural Development Council, dedicated to strengthening the rural social sciences in Asia.

I want to emphasize that I am not arguing or criticizing single-focus activities, but the importance of recognizing the need to place them in the wider context of total solutions. The research that some of you have been discussing today and probably will tomorrow, are brilliantly adding knowledge of technology, innovation, markets, capital, etc. But always keep in mind the broader dimensions in the development process that may relate to those particular single-focus efforts.

2 Recognizing the Uniqueness of Problem Settings and Forces

I would argue that you always must recognize the uniqueness and the diversity of the settings where development programs and projects are undertaken. There are local, regional, and at times even national levels where there is important variation. You need to avoid what I used to call the "cookie-cutter" approach — some people talk about the "one-size-fits-all" prescriptions. There are ecological micro-climates and there are also human micro-climates. Haiti is not Nepal. Laos is not Sri Lanka. Yet too often we develop programs as though they were alike. We need to and must appreciate these diversities and their implications for approaches and for programs.

Let me quote from a recent Rockefeller Foundation paper which emphasized this point: "We need more varied specifics and finely tuned range of strategy and policy responses tailored to particular situations."[2] Fifty years ago, the same flexible approach was developed by Art Mosher in the Agricultural Development Council, and that was one of the reasons why ADC was such a tremendous success.[3] He allowed for that variation country by country, region by region.

---

[2] Keith Bezanson and Francisco Sagasti, "Prospects for Development Thinking and Practice," submitted to the Rockefeller Foundation, August 2005.

[3] The best history of ADC is Russell Stevenson and Virginia O. Locke, *The Agricultural Development Council, A History* (Morrilton, Arkansas: Winrock International Institute, 1989).

3   Appreciating the Roles of Values and the Impact of Political Influence on Development Execution

The conflict between values that facilitate and sustain lasting development versus the negative ones has been a constant problem. Let me give a few examples. The influence that the status of women or those that create tribal and ethnic conflicts can often impede or prevent projects intended to achieve economic development. There are also political forces. Professional politicians often approach development issues differently from agricultural development professionals, such as the immediate calculus of politicians versus the longer-term broader views of development experts.

In 1976, I gave a speech at the World Food Conference at Iowa State University. Let me quote the concluding paragraph of that speech:

> "When I look at the key world developmental issues of the next 25 years — food policy, population policy, distributive justice, resource wars — I have concluded that most solutions will be rooted in the ability of the political process, both national and international, to deal with them effectively and remember that if the political process and political will fail to deal with those basic human issues of hunger and survival, the inevitable alternatives will be growing interpersonal violence, domestic upheaval, and wars."[4]

Looking at the world today — not 25 years, but 30 years later — my comment is still valid!

4   Promoting the Centrality of Human Capital in the Development Process

I have always believed that investment in human capital — education and knowledge discovery — is still one of the most critical forces in reducing poverty and achieving self-sustained growth. It sounds so simple and so

---

[4] Clifton R. Wharton, Jr., "The Role of the Professional in Feeding Mankind: The Political Dimension," World Food Conference, Ames, Iowa, June 28, 1976.

obvious. Yet when it comes to setting priorities, many nations including our own continue to short-change funding human capital creation. Education is seen as an expenditure and as a consumer good, not as an investment that produces a vital ongoing return, both to the individual and to the nation. The adequacy and quality of national indigenous human talent — human capital — can be one of the most effective tools in the arsenal of development. I know this is a view that is undoubtedly held by all those in this room, but you are the "choir," of course. You need to be reminded and speak out to the non-believers.

Conclusion

In conclusion, I think that we must constantly remind our audiences that the problem of poverty is a central global issue, domestically and internationally. This is true whether it is the ugly underbelly of poverty in New Orleans that was revealed by Katrina, or the poverty of the hillside *favelas* overlooking Rio de Janeiro which have spawned horrific criminality with huge social and economic costs in Brazil, or the endemic poverty in Darfur, exacerbated by genocide that threatens political and economic stability in Africa.

One conclusion is clear. Poverty, however measured and defined, is still with us. Gaps between nations and within nations, including our own, are persistent and too often are growing. This has been a long-run issue that unfortunately continues to gather negative strength as technology, communications, and economic linkages increasingly shrink the world's global village. Dealing with this issue is in our national interest. It is an economic imperative, a political imperative, a moral imperative, and a human survival imperative. Therefore, in my view, your symposium topic is right on target.

I wish you every success in your symposium because I am confident that your efforts will contribute to its solution.

Thank you.

Contents

Part II: Biotechnology and the Poor   101

6. Overcoming Poverty Through Improved Agricultural Technology   103

Robert W. Herdt

Chapter One

How Can Financial Markets and Biotechnology Help the Rural Poor?

*Ralph D. Christy, Mark Wenner, Emelly Mutambatsere and Willene Johnson**

1.1 Introduction

To gain greater insights into the impacts of markets on economic development, the Emerging Markets Program, in collaboration with the Institute for African Development, and Cornell International Institute for
Food, Agriculture and Development, organized an International Symposium, *Financial Inclusion, Innovations, and Investments: Biotechnology and
Capital Markets Working for the Poor*, in April 2007 at Cornell University, Ithaca, NY. This Symposium explored alternative strategies in
rural development to address the impacts of financial markets and the

*Ralph D. Christy is a professor in the Department of Applied Economics and Manage-
ment and is also the Director of Cornell International Institute for Food, Agriculture and
Development (CIIFAD), Cornell University, Ithaca, New York. Mark Wenner is Senior
Financial Specialist at the Inter-American Development Bank, Washington, DC. Emelly
Mutambatsere is a former Research Associate with the Department of Applied Economics
and Management at Cornell University, and is currently with the African Development
Bank, Tunis, Tunisia. Willene Johnson is the former Director of African Development Bank
and Vice President of the New York Federal Reserve Bank.

1

transfer of biotechnology on the rural poor. The goal of the symposium was twofold:

- identify and assess the key processes through which markets affect the livelihoods of the rural poor, and
- propose micro- and macro-level policies and innovations to address the problems of inclusion that arise.

The symposium brought together leading scholars and practitioners working in those areas who focused on major cross-cutting issues across the developing world and on country-specific case studies.

In line with the mandates of the organizing institutes, the Symposium sought to illuminate the state of the poor *vis-à-vis* emerging global trends in capital and technology movements. With increased integration of capital markets and larger technology flows to the developing world, a central question remains to what extent the fate of the poor will rise or fall and, to the extent that marginalization occurs, what public and private interests will do about it. Can new institutions — public-private partnerships, innovative investments, and scaled-up successful financial projects — be designed to ensure inclusion and help manage the negative consequences?

The Symposium confirmed that the concern for the poor, whose livelihoods are influenced greatly by global capital and technology flows, is currently being translated into a quest for "institutional innovations" in capital and financial markets that better manage risk and improve access. This volume is organized to review and evaluate promising innovations and connect those institutional alternatives to positive impacts on the poor.

1.2 Capital and Technology Flow to Developing Countries: Implications for Growth and Development

Global flows of capital and technology to developing and transition economies through foreign direct investments (FDI) grew exponentially over the two decades between 1980 and 2000, from a total annual average of about USD10 million in 1980 to over USD400 billion in 2006 (UNCTAD, 2007). In Figure 1.1 we map the arguments that trace the

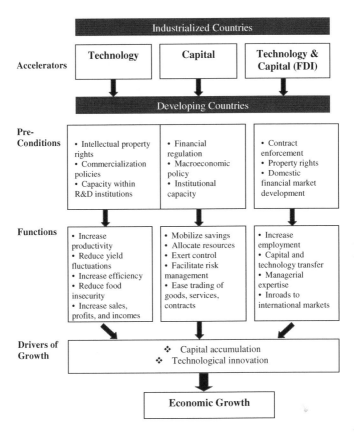

Figure 1.1: Capital and technology flow to developing countries: Implications for economic growth

global flows of technology, capital, and the combined effects of technology and capital — foreign direct investments — on economic progress in developing countries.

The economic theory linking volumes of investment capital and technology to economic growth is well-developed. On capital accumulation, the traditional neo-classical argument is that increased savings and investments generate economic activity and lead to higher domestic output or steady GDP growth (Solow, 1956). Foreign capital flows therefore are thought to fill the finance gap in developing countries, between domestic savings and investment-capital demand, thus enable greater economic efficiency in resource utilization. With regards to technology, the argument is that innovation improves factor productivity, and hence output and domestic income (Kuznets, 1966; Landers, 1969; Rosenberg, 1982; Mokyr, 1990). Endogenous growth theorists model output and productivity growth as a function of the traditional capital assets plus technical progress, asserting that with innovation, the productivity of factors of production such as land, labor and capital is enhanced and more output can be generated from a given set of resources. The theoretic argument for foreign direct investments follows-on: when economies are able to attract foreign investments they benefit through productivity gains from increased capital resources; accelerated diffusion of new technologies, managerial skills and know-how; integration into international production chains; and improved market access (Stiglitz, 2000; Alfaro *et al.*, 2004). Empirically, these relationships are much harder to confirm, and the subsequent implications on poverty and inequality much more ambiguous.

Among the most striking empirical economic relationships uncovered in recent decades is the link between financial market development and economic growth (McKinnon, 1973). What is unclear is how to make financial systems more accessible and inclusive without sacrificing soundness so that levels of poverty and income inequalities within nations can be reduced. The challenge to conventional economic frameworks in analyzing possible impacts of globalization on the poor is explained eloquently by Eloundou-Enyegue (2004), who points out that globalization is an asymmetric process in both direction and coordination. Eloundou-Enyegue argues that globalization involves a series of uncoordinated processes and can be understood as an uncoordinated flow across national borders of: (a) values and aspirations, (b) capital and technology, (c) labor and management, and (d) global and non-governmental institutions. Much of the impact of globalization on growth and development depends on the coordination of these flows: to the extent that any of the flows are not mobile, potential exists for unintended, mostly negative, distributional consequences. Those negative consequences fall disproportionately on the poor.

The growth benefits of technology, theoretically well-established, have been empirically validated through the experiences of most present-day industrialized nations, where innovation was central to both the agricultural and industrial revolutions. Here, the centrality of agricultural biotechnology in economic growth is confirmed by the fact that success in agriculture tends to always precede industrial growth. In developing countries, however, the many advances in agricultural biotechnology observed in the past 50 years have resulted in limited impact on the poor, particularly those living in Sub-Saharan Africa where agricultural productivity is still low. To understand the reasons for low adoption of biotechnology by poor farmers requires an understanding of the following issues: government policies and regulations, intellectual property rights, private sector involvement, public-private partnerships, and socio-economic factors.

The inter-linkage between capital and technology flows in a globalizing world is another critical piece in understanding the effects of foreign investments on the poor. Relative to pure capital flows, FDI represents the longer-term and less volatile types of investments that also are potential avenues for transfer of technology and skills directly to the labor force in recipient countries. However, the observed impact of FDI growth on the poor, or its ability to promote transfer of technology and know-how, remains an open question. Empirical literature finds mixed evidence on the relationship between FDI and micro-level aspects of economic progress such as technology transfer, productivity, and human resources development. On technology transfer, for example, Aitken and Harrison (1999) and Haddad and Harrison (1993) find no evidence of positive technology spillovers in different countries; whereas Blomström (1986) found that Mexican sectors with higher foreign ownership exhibited higher productivity. Recently, Blalock and Gertler (2001) find positive results associated with foreign ownership in Indonesia. Arguably, because growth through FDI is more stable, it also has more positive than negative impacts on the socio-economic status of disadvantaged groups in recipient countries, when compared to other types of foreign financial flows (Stiglitz (2000), among others, argues that large financial flows are more positively correlated with instability than growth).

Therefore, with each type of investment flow, certain pre-conditions exist for expected growth benefits to be realized. Indeed, area-specific innovations are necessary to ensure that growth positively filters through the economy to all social groups, and that the potential negative consequences are adequately managed. In the following sections, and in subsequent chapters of the book, some of those innovative arrangements are highlighted.

1.3 Biotechnology and the Rural Poor[1]

With respect to the poor having access to biotechnology, what has yet to be determined is how to best advance institutional innovation in the presence of market and government failures. For example, consider a small-scale farmer in Malawi. To engage in commercial farm activity, that farmer needs to first address supply-side constraints to increase productivity and marketable surplus. She needs to mobilize financial resources to buy fertilizers and improved seeds; invest in commodity marketing; and assure a stable and healthy supply of labor. To simply participate in local markets requires contending with a mode of transportation possible in the absence of well-developed road networks. Those are the circumstances faced by small-scale producers located in the vast majority of geographically dispersed rural villages in developing countries, villages that often are poorly linked to the major towns and cities.

Biotechnology, ideally, has significant potential for small-scale farmers to address some of those issues. However, investments into agricultural biotechnology in developing countries have been restricted by perceived and actual low market returns for those investments, poor distribution channels, a lack of appreciation for agricultural research-oriented growth, parallel importing, compulsory licensing and high fixed costs of biotechnology research. Prices of improved varieties and complementary inputs are too high, limiting both production and sales of technology research products. Inadequate funding for research and development, partially resulting from the changing structural make-up of the biotechnology industry in the past few decades — shrinking public sector funding coupled with slow private sector growth — has negatively impacted on progress and has increased marginalization. With respect to genetic engineering, biosafety

---

[1] Arguments in this section are drawn from S. Roy and R. Christy, 2005, Agricultural Biotechnology Risks and Economic Development: *A Call for a Public-Private Partnership to Stimulate Investments into African Biotechnology Industries*, Cornell University, Department of Applied Economics and Management, Staff Paper 2005-05.

concerns also have contributed to creating disincentives for both public and private sector investments.[2]

Therefore, in those instances where technology could play a role, questions arise on how best to invest, and to target and reach those farmers that would benefit from improved access. Specifically, what public policy measures can best take advantage of the innovations in biotechnology to spur agricultural development in low-income countries, given the high risk, high cost and low returns of these projects? And, what role can the private sector play in ameliorating some of the constraints faced by farmers in accessing technology for improved productivity? Empirical evidence suggests that solutions focused on bridging the gap between potential and realized returns on investment, through choice of an appropriate economic model coupled with innovative partnership arrangements, hold greater potential for success.

1.3.1 *Public Sector Policy and Funding*

Some of the major innovations in biotechnology R&D were observed in the strategies that drove success in Southeast Asia during the Green Revolution. During the 1960s and 1970s, introduction of improved seed varieties was possible with a well-integrated institutional system and adequate public sector funding. Appropriate resource management techniques and introduction of complementary inputs dramatically increased agricultural productivity and stimulated economic growth within a span of 20 years. Institutions were able to manage costs and risks of long-term projects in areas with high degrees of uncertainty and allow for wider dissemination of knowledge through a vertically integrated system and an enabling public policy regime (Byerlee and Fischer, 2001).

Agricultural R&D investments had strong public sector support in accordance with the development thinking of the time. The Consultative

---

[2]Some developing countries, for example, have been hesitant in promoting research into, or adoption of, genetically engineered foods due to a general lack of information on the long-term health and environmental implications, or for fear of straining trade relations with the European Union, where a moratorium on importation of any genetically modified products is in place.

Group on International Agricultural Research (CGIAR), and the Rockefeller Foundation, facilitated the introduction of high-yielding rice and wheat varieties through financial investments into seed development in Asian and Latin American countries. National agricultural investment centers in recipient countries have grown tremendously, and in the emerging economies such as Brazil and China, are now capable of providing an international network of field experts who act as conduits between farmers and technology, by addressing production constraints and guiding programs that maximize public benefits from technological innovations in agriculture (Barton, 2004).

It is estimated that the public sector still finances around 90% of total agricultural research in developing countries, though research capabilities vary between national agricultural research systems (NARS) (Pray and Umali-Deininger, 1998). The range includes those national systems that possess capacities in molecular biology to develop new products for specific needs (so-called type 1 NARS), to those that possess the capacity to borrow and apply molecular tools (type 2), and those with simply the capacity to borrow and apply technologies (type 3) (Khush, 2002). In the third case, national research centers have no regulatory framework in place to even import and test transgenic products (the case for most of sub-Sahara Africa). In each of these scenarios, different appropriate responses have emerged in the form of private and quasi-private investments.

1.3.2 *Private Sector Investments*

Contrary to the public-sector driven research sector in the past, today the private sector is best poised to lead and finance agricultural R&D. With changes to the industrial structure of the sector, particularly deregulation of the biotechnology industry in most emerging markets, private corporations have an opportunity to invest in more risky biotechnology projects such as crop improvement and disease mitigation. The challenge to development posed by this new trend is that unlike the public sector — driven by social welfare objectives — corporations are driven by shareholder expectations, thus evaluate projects based on profit margins. As a result, much of the agricultural genomic research aimed at developing countries is still marginalized.

Although private corporations' entry into the biotechnology industry in developing countries has in many ways contributed to market development, through policy advocacy and investments, acquisition of local firms has also been high, perpetuating the pre-deregulation structure of the industry. The trend towards consolidation, in some respects, "synergized" research capabilities with local start-ups and public firms, and allowed for economies of scale and scope to override the high fixed costs associated with R&D. Benefits from forward and backward integration not only bypass transaction costs of entering risky markets and initiating field tests, they also provide firms with leverage for innovation despite inefficiencies in the market.

The private sector also has the ability to import technologies with greater efficiency because in addition to pure research goals, profitability and cost-efficiency goals improve the selection process of various investment opportunities. Currently, the international seed industry, for example, has been the largest investor of seed research in commodity export-oriented countries such as Brazil and Argentina; and most field trails of new biotechnologies are conducted by private multinational corporations (MNCs) (Pray and Umali-Deininger, 1998). Although the private sector may seem irrelevant to meeting the needs of the smallholder, opportunities for idealistic market exchanges exist; for example, offering technology products at marginal cost to small farmers, while recouping research expenses by selling to large-scale farmers at market prices (Barton, 2004). Thus, some economists have advocated a pure private sector approach to accelerating technological growth in the developing world, arguing that the private sector offers the best opportunities for technology transfers and commercialization (Barton, 2004).

With increased deregulation of the biotech industry in developing countries — implying a diminishing role for previously monopolistic state-owned research centers, and entry by an increasing number of small firms — the case for strict market power *per se* is no longer sufficient. New entrants have been shown to have the potential to aggressively experiment with new technology, as they are not overburdened by corporate goals and large management structures. Competitive pressure thus is recognized as a reliable mechanism for industry growth, with the power to stimulate innovative activity, consumer surplus, and firms more apt to increasing productive efficiencies. In most of Africa, for example, locally-owned firms are playing a significant role in bridging the technology gap and producing products suited to the small farmer, particularly in the seed industry. The competitiveness of such firms stems from an ability to exploit the "benefits" of market imperfection such as knowledge spillovers, to reach a dispersed consumer group, and to form partnerships with research-generating institutions. Nonetheless, competitiveness is still restricted by inadequate capacity to address all genomic research questions.

1.3.3 *Public-Private Partnerships*

Although most genome research nowadays occurs in the private sector, focus on agricultural production needs specific to the developing world has been limited. Crop and livestock species associated with lower or nonexistent comparative returns on the world market, yet are important to developing regions, have low potential for attracting research-oriented activities from profit-oriented firms. Beyond that, the basic technologies introduced to the market tend to focus little on regionally important foods and improving agronomic traits such as yield and insect and disease resistance. In crops, for example, while cereals such as maize, wheat and rice that are traded on international markets have received substantial attention, others such as sorghum, barley and millet have been subject to significantly less R&D expenditure from foreign public and private sources. For the small local firm, low purchasing power and/or low absorptive capacity in the prospective market, in conjunction with internal capacity constraints, an inability to gain access to complementary inputs such as credit and formal distribution channels, and a still substantially oligopolistic market, sustains barriers to competition and encourages higher price of technology. As a result, most genomic research of particular importance to developing countries has been led by local public institutions such as universities and agriculture research centers, or by "public" international institutions such as the Consultative Group on International Agricultural Research (CGIAR) centers.

As public sector research works toward addressing smallholder farmer issues through biotechnology, it finds itself downstream relative to private sector research. Falconi (1999) found that only a few public-sector research institutions use advanced biotechnology techniques and that in a lot of cases, technology products from the private industry are simply adapted to the local context. Most local firms that could potentially enter into strategic alliances with public sector research institutions are only in the first stages of developing research capacity.

Given the opportunities available to and constraints faced by all players in the developing world's biotechnology industry, a strong case for partnerships can be made. The public sector essentially works as a counterbalance to the private industry in the presence of inefficient agricultural market structures. Varieties developed in the public sector can be introduced to the market at competitive prices, and public sector assets such as a wide range of evaluation networks, expertise in breeding, familiarity with local growing conditions and access to technology delivery systems, can be adequately exploited. The private sector contributes cutting-edge technologies and/or financing.

Collaborations between the private and public sectors may involve private firms simply donating technology, institutions building upon existing biotech tools, or genuine information and knowledge sharing. One of the partnership success stories from Africa is the case of the virus-resistant sweet potato in Kenya, where the Kenya Agricultural Research Institute (KARI) and Monsanto, along with research support from Agricultural Biotechnology for Sustainable Productivity (ABSP) and the Mid-American Consortium, formed a partnership through which Monsanto donated a royalty-free license to virus resistance technology for application to sweet potatoes. Training and internships were provided for Kenyan research scientists and the establishment of biosafety structures, intellectual property rights (IPR) protection and technology transfer mechanisms; it also made possible the very first field test of a transgenic crop in any Eastern or Central African country.

Despite these potential gains from public-private partnerships, many developing countries, especially those in Africa, lack strong public-private partnerships to aid technology development. They suffer from burdensome trade regulations, institutional deficiencies, and regulatory barriers to entry due to biosafety or genomic purity concerns. Hence, the greatest potential impact will likely be observed in economies with the absorptive capacity in terms of infrastructure, regulatory scheme and institutional support.

It has been argued that the best way to stimulate foreign investments into agricultural research is to focus on enabling countries to accelerate partnerships with private seed research companies, with a specific focus on projects with interregional impact. Public policy should thus facilitate collaborations by:

- Strengthening intellectual property rights laws that protect research conducted within the country, and put in place provisions to protect distribution and marketing, as well as clear penalties for violations.
- Increasing administrative resources in regulation and biosafety departments to improve efficiency and reduce regulatory clearance time.
- Improving research networks between countries through harmonization of biosafety and intellectual property laws.

1.4 Deepening Financial Markets

Finance is critical in facilitating and promoting long-run technological adoption, economic growth, and economic equality. Much evidence exists underscoring the strong correlation between the depth of financial markets as measured by M2 as a ratio of GDP, the efficiency in financial markets as measured by the spread between lending and deposit rates, and the ease of access to credit as measured by number of active loans per 100,000 or the average loan size divided by GDP per capita, to the levels of economic growth attained (Levine, 1997, 2001). Countries that have better functioning financial markets tend to grow faster than countries that do not.

The challenge is how to build inclusive, efficient, and robust financial structures. While financial markets in OECD countries for the most part function fairly well, financial markets in emerging and less developed countries are more prone to higher levels of volatility (banking crises, credit crunches, and massive outflows of capital), have considerably higher real average lending rates of interest, and exhibit more limited credit access. Only the better established businesses and the upper middle-class tend to enjoy easy access. For example, while private credit as a share of GDP was 96% for the US in 2005, it was only 30% for the average Latin American country in the same year. Worldwide, it is estimated that between 5%–8% of micro and small business entrepreneurs have access to formal credit. Despite substantial progress and growth in microfinancial services, Microcredit Summit reported in 2004 that 92 million persons received microloans (i.e., loans approximately less than USD5,000) even though the unserved but "bankable population" was 400–500 million. While the basic elements needed to build solid financial systems — legal protection of creditor rights, strong contract enforcement, transparency and disclosure, competent supervision, adequate regulatory frameworks, competition, and solid information and high-quality and low-cost telecommunications infrastructures — are well-known and empirically documented, how to implement the elements in a logical and coordinated fashion is proving to be a dauntingly difficult task in many countries.

Progress in financial institutional development is being made in most emerging countries but in a slow, fitful and painstaking manner. The difficulties of building inclusive financial systems have two dimensions: the macrolevel and the microlevel.

On the macrolevel, the process of opening economies has led to not only trade liberalization and integration but also financial liberalization and integration. Financial markets with flexible exchange rates, few or no capital account restrictions, lower barriers to foreign bank entry, growing adherence to international standards for financial regulation (Basel I and II) and accounting standards, market-determined interest rates, and the advent of more sophisticated and reliable communication technologies have generally improved allocative efficiency, competition, range of products offered, and quality service to clients. More importantly a number of equity and commodity exchanges have developed in emerging markets, giving business people an alternative means to raise capital, trade goods, and for savers to reap higher returns. A large, well-established firm in an emerging market now has better access to cheaper cost of funds than 20 years ago and the average upper middle-class consumer probably has greater comfort in the safety of savings deposits held in an international bank that was not allowed to operate 20 or 30 years ago in their home country, when many countries nationalized banking systems. A whole set of new banking products and conveniences exist, that hitherto were not available — internet banking, smart cards, wire transfers, and hard currency accounts. However, the demise of financial repression that was so commonplace has not yielded a financial utopia. Many of the expected benefits of financial openness and liberalization have not been met, namely improved access and spread reduction. Commercial banks still tend to be extremely risk-averse, oligopolistic and segmented in emerging markets. They still tend to operate with very high spreads and to demand real property for loan collateral. In many countries where the government has severe fiscal deficits, banks find it less risky and quite profitable to finance the government's debt and to restrict lending to private entrepreneurs, especially to the micro and small business sectors. In other cases, banks pursue a strategy of "grabbing the lowest hanging fruit", i.e., focusing on consuming lending. In the burgeoning urban areas of the emerging countries, salaried workers are a very attractive risk-return proposition, especially if their paychecks can be automatically deposited in the lending bank and automatic loan payment deductions made. Therefore, it is quite understandable why a boom in consuming lending is occurring.

The question becomes then why, in spite of significant macrofinancial opening and liberalization worldwide over the last two decades and generally more macroeconomic stability in fundamental variables (inflation, international reserves, real positive interest rates or slightly negative real interest rates on deposits, and sustainable debt management), many of the desired economic and social impacts are not evident at the microlevel. What is the problem with the link?

The short answer is that institutional and policy imperfections impede full realization of benefits. Benefits have been realized only by those that are the least risky to serve and the ones wherein current delivery mechanisms can most economically reach. But they are a tiny minority. The majority are financially excluded.

On the microlevel, a host of factors exist that explains why financial exclusion persists — why access has not improved for the majority and why the cost of financial services is high. The main demand-side factor that makes serving the low-income expensive is that it is a business model based on a high volume of small valued transactions. The poor demand small loans, can only afford small amounts of insurance coverage, and can only deposit small amounts of money. The main supply factors can be summarized as severe asymmetric information, high degrees of unmitigated risk, and high transaction costs. Low-income, small business owners and self-employed operators tend to operate in a world of informality. No financial records are normally kept let alone financial audits prepared, few or no credit bureaus exist, and precious few fixed and titled assets can be pledged as security. The small businesses and farmers are widely dispersed and operate in very heterogeneous conditions. The clients in this segment tend to have the lowest levels of educational attainment and tend to use rudimentary technology, resulting in low productivity and difficulties in effecting changes. The quality of physical infrastructure, especially in the areas of road transport, electrical service, potable water, sanitation, and telecommunications, is wanting in most circumstances. These deficiencies raise the cost of doing business and can impact the quality of products being produced or sold. Lastly, a number of government tax, regulation, and investment policies tend to be biased against the small entrepreneur and the farmer. Taken cumulatively, these factors make small and micro enterprise lending extremely high cost and very risky. The high degree of poverty and the irregular cash flow patterns in this excluded population also make the provision of other financial services — deposit mobilization, insurance, and transfers — complicated and difficult. The operating costs of providing financial services to the poor soar.

The factors even combine to make a vicious circle of underdevelopment. The high average level of operating cost for a financial intermediary specializing in low-income clients, which by far is the most significant challenge, combines with three other reasons to make lending rates even higher.

First, domestic savings tend to be very low in emerging countries outside of Asia. Without a large cushion of domestic savings, financial intermediaries often have to depend on expensive external source of funds. External savers and investors expect a higher than average rate of return compared to what is available in their home markets, thus the cost of funds increases for financial intermediaries, pushing up the final lending rate.

The second reason for high level of interest rates is the lack of good risk management techniques. Individual credit clients generally lack access to insurance and the intermediaries themselves generally do not have access to portfolio insurance or other means such as securitization to transfer the credit risk to third parties. The four main ways micro, small and medium enterprise (MSME) lenders manage their risks are through time-consuming and rigorous credit evaluation processes, loan size limits, portfolio diversification, and excessive provisioning (Wenner *et al.*, 2007). If the intermediary contracts financial obligations in a hard currency, and deficit and currency exchange management policies are weak within the country, there could be additional risks of currency devaluation that again increases the margin of intermediation in the absence of hedging instruments.

The third main reason lending rates are so high is because property rights and contract enforcement is weak. Most clients have limited amounts of titled real estate that can be pledged as surety and the public registries and court systems tend to be not very effective in quickly creating, perfecting, and enforcing security interest in moveable property. Most Napoleonic legal systems favor the debtor over the creditor, thus the need for even more margin.

Despite the formidable array of challenges and problems, uneven progress is being made in providing services to the working poor and to small-scale entrepreneurs. First, microfinance has gained wide legitimacy with conventional bankers, politicians and philanthropists and has matured sufficiently to even be recognized as a separate asset class among investors. Muhammad Yunus, the founder of Grameen Bank, the original pioneer of making unsecured small loans to poor people, was awarded the Nobel Peace Prize in 2006. Compartemos, a specialized Mexican microfinance institution, issued the first initial public offering (IPO) in this class of banking in 2007 with great success. To date, approximately 93 equity investment funds exist that focus on investing in the leading microfinance outfits. More tellingly, several web-based schemes exist wherein someone with surplus funds can directly fund a small loan to a microentrepreneur desirous of funding worldwide.

Looking to the future, one may ask where the field of financial services for the poor is heading. Will and can the current imperfections be satisfactorily addressed to allow a radical improvement in access and hopefully a large positive impact on client welfare, especially those who live in rural areas and depend on agriculture for their livelihood? In this particular case, one may ask will credit be readily available for R&D outfits, seed companies, and farmers desirous of purchasing improved seeds?

The future of finance for the poor needs to be deconstructed. Some areas are progressing well and much hope exists. In other areas, advancements are slow and new technologies, new models of service delivery, and reforms in legal and regulatory frameworks are desperately needed.

Microcredit has three proven lending technologies (group, individual, and village banking) that have been shown to be able to achieve financial self-sustainability if well-managed. However, there are two divided camps. One camp is more poverty-oriented and seeks to reach an increasing number of poorer clients and to even use microfinance as a point of entry to build platforms for the delivery of other vitally needed services such as improved health care, education, renewable energy, and telephone service. The most articulate proponents of this maximalist, social entrepreneurship approach are Grameen Bank, Grameen Foundation USA, BRAC, and Opportunity International. To make progress, however, these groups need access to public subsidies and justify them in cost-benefit terms. The other camp advocates a minimalist approach and seeks to strongly link and connect microfinance with other formal financial services — savings, insurance, remittances, etc. This camp wants to resolve funding issues through savings mobilization and equity investment. Three of the main advocates of this approach are Accion Internacional, Women's World Banking, and Citigroup Foundation. A number of regulated commercial banks are increasingly coming downmarket, lured by the very high profitability recorded by commercially-oriented non-bank microlenders.

Taking a broad view, both camps seem to be reacting to peculiar realities and both will continue to flourish side by side unless there is a broad-based backlash against the high rates charged by commercial microfinance lenders. Microfinance cum social entrepreneurship seems to work best in soft states where the government has not been able to deliver basic services, so a vacuum exists for entrepreneurs to fill it. In countries with stronger states and more developed financial markets, the race is on to see who will reach the large bottom of the pyramid market of the financially underserved in a sustainable manner without the need for public subsidies. The clientele, however, for the commercial microfinance outfits will be less poor than the clientele for the other camp. Several significant advances are being made in commercial microfinance. New products are appearing — savings, microinsurance (life, credit, property, health, agricultural), remittances linked to housing loans, remittances linked to life insurance, agricultural insurance bundled with loans. A slew of alternative delivery platforms are being explored — cellphone banking, partner-agent models wherein a formal bank makes an alliance with an agent non-governmental organization (NGO), agent merchant, or agent cooperative; and smart cards and point of sale (POS) devices. Both camps are aggressively pursuing the application of information communication technology (ICT) to drastically reduce transaction costs and leapfrog classic infrastructural problems, i.e., expensive landlines and bad roads.

The areas where more work is needed are term finance, small-medium enterprise (SME) finance (defined as loans greater than USD5,000 but less than USD200,000), agricultural lending, and health and crop insurance. Credit in larger amounts for fixed investment purposes and with a longer repayment term is the single most critical need. Only with these types of loans will productive structures be modernized and transformed. At present, most microcredit loans range from $50–$3,000 and have terms up to 18 months, but the most common term is one year or less. Without the ability to purchase new equipment, build new plants, and acquire "higher priced green technology", economic growth will be constrained. In a globalized economy, the demand for cost-efficient modern business and production equipment to comply with ever increasing market demands for consumer safety, traceability, and environmental protection is high. For example, biotechnology in Africa will be out of the reach of many interested parties without innovations in term finance. New structures and funds will be needed.

Similarly, SME credit evaluation technologies are not sufficiently developed to permit quick scaling up. SME lending in developed countries has increased rapidly in the last few decades due to wider use of credit scoring and the use of asset-backing lending technologies and structured finance, i.e., securitization of accounts receivables and back-to-back letters of credit. These types of developments are not widespread in developing countries and as a result, with the ever widening subprime mortgage crisis in US financial markets, derivative instruments have gotten a "black eye" now and more regulation, more scrutiny, and more caution is likely to be forthcoming in both developed and developing country financial markets.

In the area of agricultural lending, a new model that links the credit with complementary services such as extension services, marketing information, and post-harvest handling is needed. Value chain finance is emerging as a promising trend because if a farmer is inserted in a supply chain and has a signed marketing contract, marketing risks are essentially removed and incentives exist in the chain for him to receive the latest consumer preferences and to receive know-how on how to meet the order by well-informed market operators who have money at risk as well.

In the area of risk management, term life is emerging as a very easy-to-deliver product for the working poor, but other highly demanded forms of insurance — health, disaster, and agricultural yield insurance — are much harder to design and deliver in a sustainable manner. These three types of insurance are fraught with serious information, pricing, regulatory, and reinsurance issues. However, group delivery models for health insurance or individual health insurance linked to a smart card as well as parametric crop insurance are working well in a few places.

1.5   Foreign Direct Investment[3]

The combinations of opening economies, incentives, and firms seeking international markets have contributed to the dramatic increase in foreign direct investment in emerging markets. This increase can be explained partially by the higher average returns in emerging markets relative to industrialized countries, estimated at 15.3% for emerging markets versus 12.5% for all countries (UNCTAD, 1998). Within developing countries, regional rates of return also differ significantly, ranging from 36.9% for Africa, 19.3% for Asia-Pacific, to 12.8% for Latin America and the Caribbean. But FDI flows have not been uniform to all developing regions, and in fact, flows have been lowest to the region offering the highest returns — Africa. As a result, the revolutionary advances in biotechnology, with strong implications for poverty and malnutrition, have not been equally accessible for the different regions. Making effective use of those technologies requires governments' initiative to invest in infrastructure and other public goods necessary to leverage the FDI. Public policy is a key factor in effectively reducing poverty through investments.

Modernization and dependency theories suggest that initially, FDI increases income inequality within emerging countries (Tsai, 1995). The

---

[3] For greater detail, see Chapter 2, "Linking Globalization, Economic Growth and Poverty" in R. Christy, ed., 2004, *Achieving Sustainable Communities in a Global Economy*; and N. Mhlanga and R. Christy, 2006, "Capital Flows to Africa: An Analysis of the Structure of Official and Private Capital Flows", Cornell University Working Paper.

path of the income effect of capital investment, regardless of the source, can be characterized by Kuznets' inverted-U curve. Whereas modernization theorists would argue that sufficient output must first be produced before it can be redistributed, hence the presence of investment is more important than its origin; dependency theorists are of the view that FDI is utilized by the local labor elites in emerging markets to create an inter-country coalition to maximize their own interests. In this scenario, persistent income inequality is possible through this alliance of the state, labor elite, and foreign capitalists. These observations emphasize the need for a national strategy to leverage FDI to ensure positive results.

The spectrum of entry strategies into a country's market can yield both positive and negative distributional effects. A major positive effect of FDI is that consumers have greater access to consistent quality and capital-intensive products, at a lower price. The country benefits from the infusion of permanent physical capital, which is not always the case for JVs or contracts. FDI can also have an industry crowding-in effect, where local complementary and related industries grow from greater access to loans, a shift in demand, or from positive externalities of capital and technology flows (spillovers).

On the other hand, firms that acquire or directly invest in emerging markets may negatively influence domestic competition and smallholders. This crowding-out effect occurs in many ways, but the most common result is that foreign firms introduce higher market standards such as grades and safety standards, making it difficult for resource-poor farmers and small local firms to compete. Global firms could also source very little domestic talent for their foreign operations, minimizing the multiplier effect (Tsai, 1995). The question therefore becomes how best to engage rural firms and producers in exploiting opportunities presented by increased FDI.

The benefits of FDI can be maximized and costs minimized depending on government policy and the overall investment environment. Positive results are possible if the government has a strategic plan to leverage foreign investment and domestic resources, including human resources, to maximize economic growth and reduce income inequality. A country without a strategic plan is in essence relying on foreign capital to create an enabling environment for all players in the economy, a clearly inadequate policy response. The next section will examine various strategies for governments and private firms to consider when promoting economic growth and development through foreign investment.

1.5.1 *Pre-Conditions and Strategies*

Although no definitive consensus exists on the relationship between FDI and growth at the macro level, a positive association has been shown in cases where receiving countries have reached a certain threshold level in local investment conditions. For instance, several studies point to sufficiently developed financial markets as a prerequisite for growth (Alfaro *et al.*, 2004; Hermes and Lensink, 2003). Loayza and Rancière (2004) find that a positive long-run relationship between financial intermediation and output growth is possible even in the presence of a negative short-run relationship. They conclude that over the long run, financial development supports and promotes economic growth. The process of financial development entails a deepening of markets and services that channel savings to productive investment and allow risk diversification. Those positive aspects of financial development lead to higher economic growth in the long run. However, the path to development is far from smooth; and along the way, economic growth can suffer from the financial fragility that characterizes maturing systems. As economies mature, the same processes can present weaknesses evidenced by systemic banking crises, cycles of booms and busts, and overall financial volatility. Whether intrinsic to the process of development or induced by policy mistakes, those elements of financial fragility can hurt economic growth and will do so until maturity is reached.

Recognizing the possibility of a dual effect of financial intermediation on economic growth, Loayza and Rancière (2004) estimate an empirical model of long- and short-run effects using a sample of cross-country and time-series observations. They find that financially fragile countries, namely those that experience banking crises or suffer high financial volatility, tend to present significantly negative short-run effects of intermediation on growth. For more stable countries, the effect is on average nil.

Similarly, Alfaro *et al.* (2004) find that FDI alone plays an ambiguous role in its contribution to growth, but that when financial markets are well-developed, the relationship is positive and significant. The rationale is that when economies lack development of local financial markets, that limits their ability to take advantage of potential FDI spillovers and linkages. Well-functioning financial markets, by lowering transaction costs, ensure that capital is allocated to the projects that yield the highest returns. To exploit FDI spillovers, local firms need the financial markets to provide loans. The ability of foreign investments to create the backward linkages necessary to achieve scale economies and to encourage creation of new firms also depends on the level of financial market development.

In addition to financial market intermediation, several economists have highlighted the importance of local absorptive capabilities. The absorptive capabilities of the host nation, namely the presence of sufficient human capital to apply the new, more advanced technologies, and the presence of physical infrastructure and distribution channels to support inward investments, is thought to be a deciding factor on how well the economy will benefit from foreign investments. According to Borensztein *et al.* (1998), a strong and robust complementary effect exists between FDI and human capital, implying that the positive growth effect of FDI is enhanced by its interaction with the level of human capital in the host country. Important to note is the converse relationship revealed by the same study, confirming a *negative* correlation between FDI inflows and growth for those countries with insufficient absorptive capacity. From a policy perspective, improving the quality of local infrastructure, increasing the supply of skilled labor and improving technological capacities of local firms are seen as important ways of attracting, driving and benefiting from foreign capital and technology flows.

Sound macroeconomic management, especially monitoring exchange rates, inflation and interest rate volatility, as well as trade openness, also influence FDI flows and effectiveness. Balasubramanyam *et al.* (1996) emphasize trade openness as being crucial for acquiring the potential growth impact of FDI. Economies with more open trade policies are thought to do better in attracting foreign investments and benefiting from them. Bhagwati (1985), for example, argues that an export-promoting strategy is likely to both attract a higher volume of FDI and promote more efficient utilization of those investments than an import-substitution strategy, mainly because economies following export-oriented growth are less distorted. For those countries, trade-related investment measures, such as local content requirements, can be used to encourage spillovers and enable the host nation to extract or re-capture some of the investment rents (Saggi, 2002).

Essentially, the list of pre-conditions for FDI effectiveness could be quite long, including also institutional quality, governance issues and the initial level of income/economic development, but there is a striking lack of consensus on how or *if* each of these are of importance. With regards to the impact of FDI on growth, Alfaro *et al.* (2004) conclude that "whereas on theoretic grounds there is a strong case for expecting FDI to have a positive role on growth, the empirical evidence is fragile, to say the least". Carkovic and Levine (2002) also conclude that FDI inflows do not exert an independent influence on economic growth. On FDI and technology diffusion, Görg and Greenaway (2002) note also that although theory can identify a range of possible channels through which capital/technology spillovers from FDI can be attained, for numerous logical reasons, robust empirical support is hard to find. With regards to the pre-conditions, Saggi (2002) makes the related observation that not enough is known about the relative importance of the pre-conditions on improving capital accumulation, technology transfer and ultimately, growth, making it difficult to craft appropriate policy responses. The literature also still lacks a precise measure of the prerequisite minimum requirements, or how those can be determined for each region or country. Evidence of successful interventions tends to be anecdotal and generally case-specific.

Bibliography

Aitken, B. and A. E. Harrison (1999). "Do Domestic Firms Benefit from Direct Foreign Investment?" *American Economic Review* 89 (3): 605–618.

Alfaro, L., A. Chanda, S. Kalemli-Ozcan, and S. Sayek (2004). "FDI and Economic Growth: The Role of Local Financial Markets." *Journal of International Economics* 64: 89–112.

Balasubramanyam, V. N., M. A. Salisu, and D. Sapsford (1996). "Foreign Direct Investment and Growth in EP and IS Countries." *Economic Journal* 106: 92–105.

Barton, J. H. (2004). "Issues Posed by a World Patent System." *Journal of International Economic Law* 7 (2): 341–357.

Bhagwati, J. N. (1985). "Investing Abroad." Esmee Fairbairn Lecture, Lancaster University.

Blalock, G. and P. Gertler (2001). "Foreign Direct Investments and Technology Transfers Along the Supply Chain." Manuscript.

Blomström, M. and F. Sjoholm (1999). "Technology Transfer and Spillovers: Does Local Participation with Multinationals Matter?" *European Economic Review* 43: 915–923.

Blomström, M., R. E. Lipsey, and K. Kulchycky (1988). "U.S. and Swedish Direct Investment and Exports," in R.E. Baldwin (ed.), *Trade Policy and Empirical Analysis*. Chicago: University of Chicago Press.

Blomström, N., A. Kokko, and M. Zejan (1994). "Host Country Competition and Technology Transfer by Multinationals." *WeltwirschaftlichesArchive* 130: 521–533.

Borensztein, E., J. De Gregorio, and J.-W. Lee (1998). "How Does Foreign Direct Investment Affect Economic Growth?" *Journal of International Economics* 45: 115–135.

Brennan, M., C. Prey, and D. E. Schimmelpfennig (2001). "The Impact of Seed Industry Concentration on Innovation: A Study of U.S. Biotech Leaders." Working Paper, Rutgers University.

Byerlee, D. and K. Fischer (2001). "Accessing Modern Science: Policy and Institutional Options for Agricultural Biotechnology in Developing Countries." *IP Strategy Today*, No. 1.

Carkovic, M. and R. Levine (2002). "Does Foreign Direct Investment Accelerate Economic Growth?" University of Minnesota, Working Paper.

Falconi, C. (1999). "Agricultural Biotechnology Research Indicators and Managerial Considerations for Four Developing Countries," in J. I. Cohen (ed.), *Managing Agricultural Biotechnology — Addressing Research Program Needs and Policy Implications*. CAB International.

Haddad, M. and A. Harrison (1993). "Are There Positive Spillovers from Direct Foreign Investment? Evidence from Panel Data for Morocco." *Journal of Development Economics* 42: 51–74.

Hermes, N. and R. Lensink (2003). "Foreign Bank Presence, Domestic Bank Performance and Financial Development." Paper for SUERF colloquium.

Khush, E. S. (2002). "The Promise of Biotechnology in Addressing Current Nutritional Problems in Developing Countries." *Food and Nutrition Bulletin* 23: 354–357.

Khush, G. (2004). "Biotechnology: Public Private Partnerships and IPR for Developing Countries." International Rice Research Institute, Working Paper.

Krattiger, A. (2002). "Public-Private Partnerships for Efficient Proprietary Biotech Management and Transfer, and Increased Private Sector Investments." *IP Strategy Today*, No. 4.

Kuznets, S. (1966). *Modern Economic Growth*. New Haven: Yale University Press.

Landers, D. (1969). *The Unbound Prometheus*. Cambridge University Press.

Levine, R. (1997). "Financial Development and Economic Growth: Views and Agenda." *Journal of Economic Literature* 33: 688–726.

Levine, R. (2001). "International Financial Liberalization and Economic Growth." *Review of International Economics* 9 (4): 688–702.

Levine, R. and S. Zervos (1998). "Stock Markets, Banks, and Economic Growth." *American Economic Review* 88: 537–558.

Loayza, N. and R. Rancière (2004). "Financial Development, Financial Fragility, and Growth." Online access.

McKinnon, R. I. (1973). *Money and Capital in Economic Development.* Washington, DC: Brookings Institution.

Mokyr, J. (1990). *The Lever of Riches.* New York: Oxford University Press.

Muliokela, S. W. (1999). "Technology Transfer in Rural Communities of Sub-Saharan Africa: Seeds as a Bridging Tool." FAO Plant Production and Protection Papers.

Nuffield Council on Bioethics (2004). "The Use of Genetically Modified Crops in Developing Countries." Follow-up Discussion Paper.

Pigato, M. (2001). "The Foreign Direct Investment Environment in Africa." Africa Region Working Paper Series 15, World Bank, April.

Pray, C. E. and D. Umali-Deininger (1998). "The Private Sector in Agricultural Research Systems: Will It Fill the Gap?" *World Development* 26 (6): 1127–1148.

Rosenberg, N. (1982). *Inside the Black Box.* Cambridge University Press.

Saggi, K. (2002). "Trade, Foreign Direct Investment, and International Technology Transfer: A Survey." *World Bank Research Observer* 17 (2): 191–235.

Sithole-Niang, I., J. Cohen, and P. Zambrano (2004). "Putting GMO Technologies to Work: Public Research Pipelines in Selected African Countries." *African Journal of Biotechnology* 3 (11): 564–571.

Solow, R. (1956). "A Contribution to the Theory of Economic Growth." *Quarterly Journal of Economics* 70 (1): 65–94.

Sommer, A. (1990). "Vitamin A Deficiency and Xerophthalmia." *Archives of Ophthalmology* 108: 343–344.

Stiglitz, J. (2000). "Capital Market Liberalization, Economic Growth and Instability." *World Development* 28 (6): 1075–1086.

Tripp, R. (2003). "How to Cultivate a Commercial Seed Sector." Paper prepared for the symposium Sustainable Agriculture in the Sahel, Bamako, Mali, 1–5 December 2003.

Tsai, P. L. (1995). "Foreign Direct Investment and Income Inequality: Further Evidence." *World Development* 23: 469–483.

UN Conference on Trade and Development (UNCTAD) (2007). *World Investment Report 2007: Transnational Corporations, Extractive Industries and Development.* Geneva, Switzerland: United Nations Publications.

UNCTAD (2000). *World Investment Report: FDI and the Challenge of Development.* Geneva, Switzerland: United Nations Publications.

UNCTAD (1998). *World Investment Report: Trends and Determinants.* Geneva, Switzerland: United Nations Publications.

Wenner, M. D. *et al.* (2007). *Managing Credit Risk in Rural Financial Institutions in Latin America.* Inter-American Development Bank.

PART I

FINANCIAL MARKETS AND THE POOR

Chapter Two

Financial Development and Growth: What Role Can Foreign Capital Play?

Eswar Prasad, Ayhan Kose, Kenneth Rogoff and Shang-Jin Wei*

2.1 Introduction

Financial globalization — the phenomenon of rising cross-border financial flows — is often blamed for the string of damaging economic crises that rocked a number of emerging markets in the late 1980s in Latin America and in the 1990s in Mexico and a handful of Asian countries. The market turmoil and resulting bankruptcies prompted a rash of finger-pointing by those who suggested that developing countries had dismantled capital controls too hastily, leaving themselves vulnerable to the harsh dictates of rapid capital movements and market herd effects. Some were openly critical of international institutions they saw as promoting capital account

*Eswar Prasad is Nandlal P. Tolani Senior Professor of Trade Policy at Cornell University. M. Ayhan Kose is an Economist and Shang-Jin Wei is a Division Chief in the IMF's Research Department. Kenneth Rogoff is the Thomas D. Cabot Professor of Public Policy and Professor of Economics at Harvard University. This article is based on IMF Working Paper No. 06/189, "Financial Globalization: A Reappraisal." See that paper for a detailed list of references to the literature on this topic and for the primary sources from which some of the material in this article is drawn.

liberalization without stressing the necessity of building up the strong institutions needed to steer markets through bad times.

In contrast to the growing consensus among academic economists that trade liberalization is, by and large, beneficial for both industrial and developing economies, debate rages amongst academics and practitioners about the costs and benefits of financial globalization. Some economists (for example, Dani Rodrik, Jagdish Bhagwati, and Joseph Stiglitz) view unfettered capital flows as disruptive to global financial stability, leading to calls for capital controls and other curbs on international asset trade. Others (including Stanley Fischer and Lawrence Summers) argue that increased openness to capital flows has, in general, proved essential for countries seeking to rise from lower- to middle-income status and that it has strengthened stability among industrial countries. This debate clearly has considerable relevance for economic policy, especially given that major economies like China and India have recently taken steps to open up their capital accounts.

To get beyond the polemics, we put together a framework for analyzing the vast and growing body of studies about the costs and benefits of financial globalization. Our framework offers a fresh perspective on the macroeconomic effects of global financial flows, in terms of both growth and volatility. We systematically sift through various pieces of evidence on whether developing countries can benefit from financial globalization and whether financial globalization, in itself, leads to economic crises. Our findings suggest that financial globalization appears to be neither a magic bullet to spur growth, as some proponents would claim, nor an unmanageable risk, as others have sought to portray it.

2.2 Unanswered Questions

The recent wave of financial globalization began in earnest in the mid-1980s, spurred by the liberalization of capital controls in many countries in anticipation of the better growth outcomes and increased stability of consumption that cross-border flows would bring. It was presumed that these benefits would be large, especially for developing countries, which tend to be more capital-poor and have more volatile income growth than other countries.

Despite crises in some emerging market countries, this group has outperformed other groups over the past three decades.
(per capita GDP, weighted by purchasing power parity; 1970=100)

Figure 2.1: Against the odds — Emerging market countries have outperformed other groups over the past three decades, despite crises in some countries
Sources: IMF, *World Economic Outlook*; World Bank, *World Development Indicators.*

Emerging market economies, the group of developing countries that have actively participated in financial globalization, have clearly registered better growth outcomes, on average, than those countries that have not participated (see Figure 2.1). Yet the majority of studies using cross-country growth regressions to analyze the relationship between growth and financial openness have been unable to show that capital account liberalization produces measurable growth benefits. One reason may be traced to the difficulty of measuring financial openness. For example, widely used measures of capital controls (restrictions on capital account transactions) fail to capture how effectively countries enforce those controls and do not always reflect the actual degree of an economy's integration with international capital markets. In recent years, considerable progress has been made on developing better measures of capital controls and better data on flows and stocks of international assets and liabilities. Studies that are based on these improved measures of financial integration are beginning to find evidence of positive growth effects of financial integration. The evidence, however, is still far from conclusive.

Nor is there systematic evidence that financial integration is the proximate determinant of financial crises. Authors who have looked at different manifestations of such crises — including sudden stops of capital inflows, current account reversals, and banking crises — have found no evidence that countries that are more open to financial flows tend to have a higher incidence of crises than those that are less open. Although crisis episodes receive most of the attention, they are just particularly sharp manifestations of the more general phenomenon of macroeconomic volatility. On that score, the results are less favorable: financial globalization has not delivered on the promised benefit of improved international risk sharing and reduced volatility of consumption for developing countries.

In sum, the effects of financial globalization have not been conclusively determined. Although there is little formal empirical evidence to support the oft-cited claims that financial globalization has *caused* the financial crises that the world has seen over the past three decades, the existence of robust macroeconomic evidence of the benefits of financial globalization is elusive, too. Given the shortcomings of cross-country growth regressions, is there another approach that can shed light on the effects of financial globalization?

2.3   Not Created Equal

An alternative perspective on the growth and volatility effects of financial globalization is based on differentiating among various types of capital flows. This is particularly relevant because the composition of international financial flows has changed markedly over time.

Foreign direct investment (FDI) has now become the dominant source of private capital flows to emerging market economies (see Figure 2.2); *equity flows* have also risen in importance, whereas *debt flows* have declined. FDI and portfolio equity flows are presumed to be more stable and less prone to reversals and are believed to bring with them many of the indirect benefits of financial globalization, such as transfers of managerial and technological expertise. Debt flows, by contrast, are widely accepted as being riskier; in particular, the fact that they are procyclical and highly volatile can magnify the adverse impact of negative shocks on economic growth.

The increasing importance of portfolio equity flows to emerging markets has motivated a number of studies examining the growth effects of equity market liberalizations. These papers uniformly suggest that these liberalizations have a significant, positive impact on output growth. Whether the estimated growth effects could be picking up the effects of other factors — especially other reforms that tend to accompany these

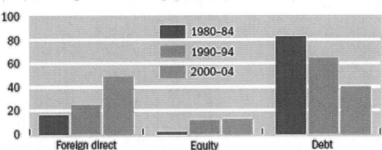

Figure 2.2:   On the rise — Emerging markets now attract more FDI than other types of flows
Source: External Wealth of Nations database from Philip R. Lane and Gian Maria Milesi-Ferretti, "The External Wealth of Nations Mark II: Revised and Extended Estimates of Foreign Assets and Liabilities, 1970–2004," IMF Working Paper No. 06/69 (Washington: International Monetary Fund, 2006).

liberalizations — remains, in our view, an open question. On the other hand, the body of microeconomic evidence (using industry- and firm-level data) supporting the macro evidence of the benefits of equity liberalizations is growing. Some of these papers also document the empirical relevance of various theoretical channels that link equity market liberalization to economic growth, including through increases in investment and total factor productivity growth.

Interestingly, despite the general consensus that FDI is most likely to spin off positive growth benefits, these benefits are harder to detect in aggregate data than those associated with equity flows. Fortunately, recent research using micro data is starting to confirm that FDI flows do have significant spillover effects on output and productivity growth.

From the evidence we have reviewed thus far, a key theme emerges: many of the benefits of financial openness seem to be masked in cross-country analysis using macroeconomic data but are more apparent in disaggregated analyses using micro data. An approach based on micro data also has a better chance of disentangling causal effects and capturing the relative importance of different channels through which financial integration affects growth.

Some economists have used micro data to estimate the costs of capital controls. Such controls seem to cause distortions in the behavior of firms (and individuals), which adjust their behavior to evade capital controls. By insulating an economy from competitive forces, capital controls may also reduce market discipline. Thus, their existence appears to result in significant efficiency costs at the level of individual firms or sectors.

2.4 Making Sense of the Evidence

We now introduce a conceptual framework that assembles these disparate strands of evidence in order to shed some light on why empirical evidence at different levels of disaggregation reaches different conclusions.

A basic building block of our framework is the notion that successful financial globalization does not simply enhance access to financing for domestic investment but that its benefits are catalytic and indirect. Far more important than the direct growth effects of access to more capital is how capital flows generate what we label financial integration's potential *collateral benefits* (so called because they may not be countries' primary motivations for undertaking financial integration). A growing number of studies are showing that financial openness can promote development of the domestic financial sector, impose discipline on macroeconomic policies, generate efficiency gains among domestic firms by exposing them to competition from foreign entrants, and unleash forces that result in better government and corporate governance. These collateral benefits could enhance efficiency and, by extension, total factor productivity growth.

The notion that financial globalization influences growth mainly through indirect channels has powerful implications for an empirical analysis of its benefits. Building institutions, enhancing market discipline, and deepening the financial sector take time, as does the realization of growth benefits from such channels. This may explain why, over relatively short periods, it seems much easier to detect the costs but not the benefits of financial globalization. More fundamentally, even over long horizons, it may be difficult to detect the productivity-enhancing benefits of financial globalization in empirical work if one includes structural, institutional, and macroeconomic policy variables in cross-country regressions that attempt

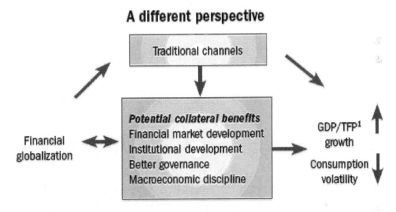

Figure 2.3: Financial globalization yields collateral benefits . . .

to explain growth. After all, it is through these very channels that financial integration generates growth (see Figure 2.3).

One should not, of course, overstate the case that financial integration generates collateral benefits. It is equally plausible that, all else being equal, more foreign capital tends to flow to countries with better-developed financial markets and institutions. We also do not dismiss the importance of traditional channels — that financial integration can increase investment by relaxing the constraints imposed by low levels of domestic saving and reducing the cost of capital. But our view is that these traditional channels may have been overemphasized in previous research.

Is there empirical merit to our conceptual framework? We now turn our attention to marshalling the evidence for a key piece of our argument — that financial globalization has significant collateral benefits.

2.5 Financial Integration's Indirect Benefits

The potential indirect benefits of financial globalization are likely to be important in three key areas: financial sector development, institutional quality, and macroeconomic policies.

A good deal of research suggests that international financial flows serve as an important catalyst for domestic *financial market development*, as reflected both in straightforward measures of the size of the banking sector and equity markets and in broader concepts of financial market development, including supervision and regulation.

Research based on a variety of techniques, including country case studies, supports the notion that the larger the presence of foreign banks in a country, the better the quality of its financial services and the greater the efficiency of financial intermediation. As for equity markets, the overwhelming theoretical presumption is that foreign entry increases efficiency, and the evidence seems to support this. Stock markets do, in fact, tend to become larger and more liquid after equity market liberalizations.

The empirical evidence suggests that financial globalization has induced a number of countries to adjust their corporate governance structures in response to foreign competition and demands from international investors. Moreover, financial sector FDI from well-regulated and well-supervised source countries tends to support *institutional development and governance* in emerging market economies.

Capital account liberalization, by increasing the potential costs associated with weak policies and enhancing the benefits associated with good ones, should also impose discipline on macroeconomic policies. Precisely because capital account liberalization makes a country more vulnerable to sudden shifts in global investor sentiment, it can signal the country's commitment to *better macroeconomic policies* as a way of mitigating the likelihood of such shifts and their adverse effects. Although the empirical evidence on this point is suggestive, it is sparse. Countries with higher levels of financial openness appear more likely to generate better monetary policy outcomes in terms of lower inflation, but there is no evidence of a systematic relationship between financial openness and better fiscal policies.

The evidence that we have surveyed in this section is hardly decisive, but it does consistently point to international financial integration as a catalyst for a variety of productivity-enhancing benefits. Given the difficulties that we have identified in interpreting the cross-country growth evidence, it is encouraging to see that financial market integration seems to be operating through some of the indirect channels.

2.6   A Complication: Thresholds

Some related studies have tackled the question of what initial conditions are necessary if financial openness is to generate good growth benefits for a country whilst lowering the risks of a crisis. What are these conditions?

Financial sector development, in particular, is a key determinant of the extent of the growth and stability benefits financial globalization can bring. The more developed a country's financial sector, the greater the growth benefits of capital inflows and the lower the country's vulnerability to crises, through both direct and indirect channels.

Another benefit of greater financial sector development is that it has a positive effect on macroeconomic stability, which, in turn, has implications for the volume and composition of capital flows. In developing countries that lack deep financial sectors, sudden changes in the direction of capital flows tend to induce or exacerbate boom-bust cycles. Furthermore, inadequate or mismanaged domestic financial sector liberalizations have contributed to many crises that may be associated with financial integration.

Institutional quality appears to play an important role in determining not just the outcomes of financial integration but the actual level of integration. It also appears to strongly influence the composition of inflows into developing economies, which is another way it affects macroeconomic outcomes. Better institutional quality helps tilt a country's capital structure toward FDI and portfolio equity flows, which tend to bring more of the collateral benefits of financial integration.

The *quality of domestic macroeconomic policies* also appears to influence the level and composition of inflows, as well as a country's vulnerability to crises. Sound fiscal and monetary policies increase the growth benefits of capital account liberalization and help avert crises in countries with open capital accounts. Moreover, for economies with weak financial systems, an open capital account and a fixed exchange rate regime are not an auspicious combination. A compelling case can be made that rigid exchange rate regimes can make a country more vulnerable to crises when it opens its capital markets.

Trade integration improves the cost-benefit trade-off associated with financial integration. It also reduces the probability of crises associated with financial openness and mitigates the costs of such crises if they do occur. Thus, recent studies strengthen the case made by the old sequencing literature that argued in favor of putting trade liberalization ahead of capital account liberalization.

This discussion suggests that there are some basic supporting conditions, or thresholds, that determine where on the continuum of potential costs and benefits a country ends up. It is the interaction between financial globalization and this set of initial conditions that determines growth and volatility outcomes (see Figure 2.4).

A comparison of Figures 2.3 and 2.4 highlights a fundamental tension between the costs and benefits of financial globalization. Many of the threshold conditions are similar to the collateral benefits. In other words, financial globalization is a catalyst for a number of important collateral benefits but can greatly elevate the risk-to-benefit ratio if the initial conditions in these dimensions are inadequate.

A different threshold is related to the level of integration itself. Industrial economies, which are far more integrated with global financial markets, clearly do a better job than emerging markets of using international capital flows to allocate capital efficiently, thereby accruing productivity gains and sharing income risk. Does this mean that, to realize the collateral benefits, developing countries' only hope is to attain a level of financial integration similar to that of industrial economies and that the risks they encounter along the way are unavoidable? After all, if the short-term costs

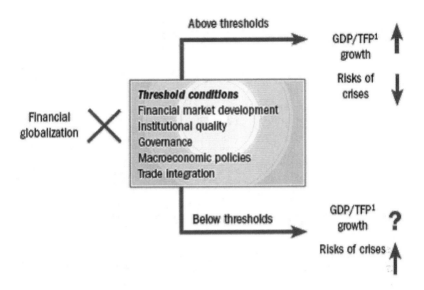

Financial globalization leads to better macroeconomic outcomes when certain threshold conditions are met. This generates tension because many of the threshold conditions are similar to the collateral benefits.

[1]Total factor productivity.

Figure 2.4:   … but initial, or threshold, conditions are a complication

take the form of crises, they could have persistent negative effects that detract from the long-term growth benefits. Furthermore, the distributional effects associated with these short-term consequences can be particularly painful for low-income countries.

2.7 Risk-Benefit Calculus

Our synthesis of the literature on financial globalization, while guardedly positive about its overall benefit, suggests that as countries make the transition from being less integrated to being more integrated with global financial markets, they are likely to encounter major complications. For developing countries, financial globalization appears to have the potential to generate an array of collateral benefits that may help boost long-run growth and welfare. At the same time, if a country opens its capital account without having some basic supporting conditions in place, the benefits can be delayed and the country can be more vulnerable to sudden stops of capital flows. This is a fundamental tension between the costs and benefits of financial globalization that may be difficult to avoid.

Does this imply that a country that wants the collateral benefits of financial globalization has no alternative but to expose itself to substantial risks of crises? Or, alternatively, would developing countries do best to shield themselves from external influences while trying to improve the quality of their domestic policies and institutions to some acceptable level? Our view is that, although the risks can never be totally avoided, there are ways to improve the benefit-risk calculus of financial globalization. There is, however, unlikely to be a uniform approach to opening the capital account that will work well for all countries.

The collateral benefits perspective may provide a way for moving forward on capital account liberalization that takes into account individual country circumstances (initial conditions), as well as the relative priorities of different collateral benefits for that country. Depending on a country's internal distortions — particularly those related to the domestic financial sector — one can, in principle, design an approach to capital account liberalization that could generate specific benefits while minimizing the associated risks. Although we have laid out a framework for thinking about these issues, further research is clearly needed in a number of areas before one can derive strong policy conclusions about the specifics of such an approach.

Meanwhile, we should recognize that some of the more extreme polemic claims made about the effects of financial globalization on developing countries, both pro and con, are far less easy to substantiate than either side generally cares to admit.

Chapter Three

The Securitization of Microloans

Vicki L. Bogan*

3.1 Introduction

Microfinance Institutions (MFIs) provide financial services to low-income households in developing countries around the world. To many, microfinance and micro-credit are synonymous. However, microfinance refers to an array of financial services that include credit, savings, and insurance, while micro-credit is the provision of credit which is usually used as capital for small business development. MFIs can operate as Non-Governmental Organizations (NGOs), credit unions, non-bank financial intermediaries or commercial banks. To protect themselves from perceived risks due to the target client's lack of collateral as a guarantee against default, MFIs are known to charge very high nominal interest rates.[1] The loans are short-term, the average loan size is very small, and only a few programs require borrowers to put up collateral. Globally, there are more than 67 million

---

*Vicki Bogan is an Assistant Professor in the Charles H. Dyson School of Applied Economics and Management at Cornell University. She teaches courses in finance. Her research interests are in the areas of financial economics and applied microeconomics centering on issues involving financial markets, market structure, and investment decision-making behavior. Contacts: 454 Warren Hall, Cornell University; 607.254.7219; vlb23@cornell.edu

[1] Interest rates which are still generally less than the cost of scarce capital in these markets.

households served by microfinance programs (Armendáriz de Aghion and Morduch, 2005). Through MFIs, many would-be entrepreneurs with few assets have been able to escape positions as poorly paid wage laborers or farmers. MFIs have expanded the frontiers of institutional finance and have brought the poor, especially poor women, into the formal financial system by enabling them to access credit in order to fight poverty.

Through initiatives like the United Nations' "International Year of Microcredit 2005," microfinance has become increasingly visible on the world stage. Though significant strides have been made to expand microfinance, further scaling up is necessary and remains a formidable challenge facing the microfinance industry. There are billions of people in developing countries who still lack access to formal financial services. Microfinance organizations have had various degrees of sustainability, and asymmetric growth across the developing world has led to diverse rates of interest being charged. Furthermore, high operating costs and capital constraints for MFIs prohibit them from meeting the enormous demand. Dehejia *et al.* (2005) also show that the demand for credit by the poor is **not** inelastic. This paper recognizes the potential of microfinance in the development process and explores the applicability of securitization[2] to microloans to facilitate future growth and improve the sustainability of MFIs. Whereas much of the existing literature focuses on ways to "intervene in credit markets" to enable the poor to have access to capital,[3] this paper examines a way to harness the capital markets for the mutual benefit of MFIs and

---

[2] Securitization is the process of consolidating loans into a single group and issuing an asset-backed security having a face amount equal to the cumulative outstanding principal balance of the loans. The loans that have been pooled together serve as the collateral for the security. An investor owning the security is entitled to the principal and interest cash flows received from the loans in the pool. Appropriate credit enhancement can insure that interest and principal will be paid when due, even if some of the borrowers fail to make their timely payments.

[3] Generally, when financial markets are discussed with respect to economic development, it is done in the context of "pro-poor markets". However, embedded in the literature around pro-poor markets is the idea that market outcomes will disproportionately benefit the poor. As Gabre-Madhin and Nagarajan (2004) and others have pointed out, this concept is problematic since market processes do not *necessarily* accrue gains in a disproportionate manner to a relatively less-endowed segment of the population.

investors with the main goal of facilitating increased access to capital for poor borrowers.

3.2 Securitization Overview

As we explore the potential of securitization for MFIs, it is useful to look to examples of successful securitization in other industries. There are significant parallels between the current microfinance industry and the pre-1968 US mortgage market (see Table 3.1). As late as the 1950s and 1960s, the housing finance market was a fragmented, inefficient, and illiquid market, with mortgage rates varying considerably from region to region, and some locations having practically no funds available at all. This was a direct consequence of the near impossibility of selling individual mortgages on the secondary market. Lending institutions would issue a mortgage, collect payments, and file the mortgage away until the principal was paid off. The problem: a lack of available, consistently priced capital put a ceiling on the number of new mortgages that could be issued.

In 1968, the US government created the Government National Mortgage Association, commonly known as Ginnie Mae. Ginnie Mae helped to revolutionize the American housing industry by pioneering the issuance of mortgage-backed securities. Today, Ginnie Mae buys and pools packages

Table 3.1: US mortgage market versus microfinance programs

Pre-1968 US Mortgage market	Microfinance programs
• Individual lenders' lack of capital put a ceiling on the number of new mortgages that could be issued	• Minimal savings by constituents leads to lack of loanable funds
• Dearth of funds available for lending	• As grant and subsidy money runs out, even operational sustainability becomes an issue
• Illiquid and inefficient market	
• US government belief that home ownership was good for its citizens and its economy in general	• Governments and developmental economists alike believe that microloans have dramatic social and economic impacts

of qualifying mortgages[4] and converts them into securities. Ginnie Mae guarantees investors the timely payment of principal and interest on these securities and consequently these MBSs have an implied AAA rating since Ginnie Mae issues carry the full faith and credit of the US government. In a single step, the issuance of Ginnie Mae mortgage-backed securities converts individual mortgages into safe liquid securities for investors around the world. Like Ginnie Mae, the Federal National Mortgage Association (Fannie Mae) and the Federal Home Loan Mortgage Corporation (Freddie Mac) also issue mortgage-backed securities. There are also non-agency mortgage-backed securities, created from non-conforming mortgages, which consist of AA down to B rated bonds.[5] By channeling global capital into the American housing market, securitization facilitated the development of a multi-trillion dollar market. Thus, the securitization of mortgages revolutionized the American housing industry. We also saw a similar type of transformation in the US student loan market.

3.3 MFI Funding Market

Today, MFIs rely on deposits, loans, and/or grants as sources of capital. While most MFIs are *operationally* sustainable, almost all have failed to achieve *financial* sustainability,[6] despite receiving large amounts of funding in the form of subsidies. In the late 1990s, experts had estimated that no more than 1% of the NGO programs worldwide were financially sustainable (Morduch, 1999). More recently, the July 2003 *Microbanking Bulletin* reported that of 124 microlenders surveyed, just over one-half were financially sustainable (Armendáriz de Aghion and Morduch, 2005). Additionally, many growth-oriented MFIs find themselves constrained by lack of

---

[4] Mortgages that meet the US government established underwriting standards.

[5] Non-agency mortgage-backed securities are created from mortgages that do not necessarily meet the US government established underwriting standards. The "Subprime Mortgage Crisis" which began in the latter half of 2007 was precipitated by non-agency mortgage-backed securities and other non-agency mortgage-related securities, not the Ginnie Mae securities mentioned above.

[6] Operational sustainability is the ability of institutions to generate enough revenue to cover operating costs. Financial sustainability refers to whether or not the institution requires subsidized inputs in order to operate.

funding (Jansson, 2003). As the grant money begins to dwindle, a better structure is needed; a structure that will enable operational sustainability, financial sustainability, and even growth.[7] Furthermore, it has been shown (see Bogan, 2008) that both operational and financial sustainability are negatively related to MFI grants as a percent of assets.

Currently, there are three commonly employed types of financing models for microfinance (Ananth, 2005):

- *Model 1: The Self-Help Group (SHG) Bank Linkage Model*
  This model is dominant in the Indian Microfinance and accounts for nearly 20 million clients. Since the SHGs borrow directly from the bank, the bank bears the entire credit risk.
- *Model 2: Financial Intermediation by the Microfinance Institution*
  The MFI utilizes deposits, donor funds, and/or borrows from commercial sources in order to lend to clients. The incentives of the MFI to maintain supervision levels are high in this case as it bears all of the credit risk of the portfolios.
- *Model 3: The Partnership Model — MFI as the Servicer*
  This model, which is a hybrid of the two models above, was pioneered by ICICI Bank to address the following issues: (i) to separate the risk of the MFI from the risk inherent in the microfinance portfolio, (ii) to provide incentives for partner MFIs to continuously maintain high supervision levels, and (iii) to deal with the limited ability of the MFI to bear risk. The loan contact is directly between the bank and borrower as in the SHG Bank Linkage Model, thus separating the risk of the MFI from the risk of the underlying portfolio. To address incentive issues, the structure requires the MFI to provide a guarantee through which it shares with the bank, the risk of the portfolio to a certain specified limit. The partnership model is viewed as a precursor to securitization, as the microfinance assets originated under the partnership model facilitate participation of a wider investor base.

---

[7] Financial institutions with large deposits have been less inclined to seek other funding sources through mechanisms like securitization. The debate as to whether savings should be the primary and most important source of MFI funding continues (e.g., see Harper and Vogel, 2005). Nonetheless, all MFIs could potentially benefit and grow if given access to more capital and/or "cheaper" capital.

Ananth (2005) contends that a model of financing that starts with the partnership model of financing and culminates in securitization would significantly relax the capital constraints faced by many MFIs. As the MFI funding market evolves, securitization could prove to be an invaluable financial tool for MFIs.

Generally, the nature and magnitude of the benefits of securitization will vary according to the type of assets being securitized. Beshouri and Nigro (1995) have demonstrated the limited potential for the securitization of small business loans in the US as a primary funding mechanism. However, a preliminary look reveals that, conditional on having appropriate credit enhancement, microfinance portfolios do have the desired attributes that make them good candidates for securitization. For instance, microfinance assets represent weekly steady cash flows from clearly identifiable borrowers, while portfolio details reveal self-reported losses of less than 5% among top MFIs. Ideally for securitization, receivables that are being securitized must be periodic. With most MFIs following weekly repayment schedules, this criterion is easily satisfied. In addition, most MFIs advance loans that are fairly similar in terms of maturity, interest rates and risk profiles.

3.4   Microfinance Institution Benefits

The benefits of securitization to the MFIs are compelling. MFIs have higher cost structures due to the small loan size, borrower-intensive lending, significant monitoring and operating costs, and wide dispersion of borrowers. Through securitization, MFIs could sell the originated loans, book profits, and originate more loans with the proceeds from securitization. Thus, MFIs could manage their capital better and free their loan origination process from the constraints of their balance sheet capacity. By broadening their borrowing sources, reducing the cost of borrowing, imparting pricing flexibility on the lending side, and enhancing return on assets deployed, securitization could help MFIs satisfy their higher capital needs.[8] Additionally,

---

[8] MFIs typically incur significantly higher operating costs than other retail non-banking finance companies (NBFCs). For instance, while the overheads/average funds deployed ratio for NBFCs is around 2.0%–2.5% per annum, it is in the range of 6% to 14% per annum for MFIs.

given the relationships with borrowers, MFIs could assume the role of the servicer in a securitization transaction to earn servicing fees.

Due to a large demand-supply gap for microloans, a significant percentage of the poor borrowers who currently are taking loans at exorbitantly high rates from the unorganized sector are potential customers of MFIs. Also, since MFIs charge financially-weak borrowers high interest rates, the high interest rates could be suppressing the current demand. Hence, a reduction in lending rates could actually spur the demand for microfinance loans. With securitization, MFIs could originate and service a larger number of loans, which would enable them to optimize their existing distribution network and correspondingly reduce their operating costs.[9] If MFIs pass on their operating efficiency gains to end borrowers, the ultimate long-run beneficiary would be the poor.

3.5   Investor Benefits

While one of the primary objectives in economic development has been to identify "investors" with *at least partially philanthropic motives*, the use of securitization could provide a method to facilitate economic development without the limitation of concentrating on such a specific type of investor. With a larger pool of investors, there would be a larger available supply of capital for MFIs.

There are economic gains from trade in securitization that would benefit even a purely self-interested investor. Specifically, securitization can:

(1) create new classes of securities that appeal to investors with different appetites for risk;

(2) create non-redundant securities that enable investors to improve portfolio efficiency;

(3) enable investors to take on only those components of a particular asset's cash flows that accord with their preferences and portfolio needs.

---

[9] The Crisil Study — "Securitization of Microfinance Assets: A Winning Proposition" (December 12, 2004).

By structuring microloan-backed transactions into tranches with varying degrees of seniority, credit enhancement, and informational complexity, securitization provides investors with relatively low levels of expertise with less risky, senior claims, whilst leaving the more risky and complex tranches for specialists who can exploit informational economies of scale and recover investments in information. There are also a host of other benefits of microfinance as an asset class (i.e., securitized instruments backed by microfinance receivables):

- High-yielding assets: Microloans typically have yields of between 20% and 36% per annum. Thus, highly-rated securitized paper backed by microfinance receivables would provide attractive returns as compared to similarly rated "plain vanilla" debt instruments. In the short term, investors could earn even higher returns than other asset classes.[10]

- Short-term investment opportunity: Since microfinance receivables have a short tenor (typically less than a year), securities created from microloans offer investors an additional short-term investment opportunity. Additionally, given the lesser uncertainty associated with shorter-tenor loans, the stress levels applied to the assessed pool are lower in absolute terms, resulting in smaller levels of required credit enhancement.

- Ability to diversify portfolio across asset classes: Investors would have another asset class with unique risk characteristics in which to invest.

- Very high granularity of loans: Microfinance loans have a very small ticket size.

- Microfinance lending model has experienced superior credit quality: The credit quality of the assets originated in this sector has been very good with minimal credit losses of around 1.5% to 2.5%.[11]

---

[10] The Crisil Study (December 2004) estimates that investors in securitized paper backed by microfinance receivables can expect to earn around 150 basis points over and above a P1+ paper of one-year duration. The returns would be around 40–50 basis points over a P1+ (so) securitization transaction backed by established retail asset classes like commercial vehicle loans.

[11] Several MFIs, adopting the Grameen Bank, self-help group or other forms of lending models, have experienced low delinquencies in the past. This could be attributed to the concept of group cohesion, wherein the group provides a collateral or loan guarantee through a

Collections from current monthly billings are over 95% in several cases. This is far superior to that exhibited by other retail asset classes.[12]

- Low prepayment risk enables premium structures: Microfinance portfolios have lower prepayment levels than several other asset classes like personal and housing loans. Generally, prepayments result in prepayment losses for the investor, which have to be covered through credit enhancements. Since microfinance assets have no/lower prepayments, securitized pools backed by microfinance assets can have lower required credit enhancements.

3.6 Risk Analysis

Generally, securitization allows the isolation, evaluation, and allocation of specific risks to different investors. While some of the investor risks can be mitigated through appropriate credit enhancement structures, pricing the residual risk borne by the originator is very important. With respect to the securitization of microfinance receivables, most of the general asset-backed security risks do apply as well as some additional risks that are specific to the asset class. Thus, understanding the risks involved as they relate to the microfinance business and evaluating the various mitigation measures against these risks is essential.

Asset/Collateral Risk: Since microloans typically do not require collateral, there is no risk associated with the variation in the value of the underlying asset.

---

group repayment pledge. Therefore, if one group member defaults, the other group members make up the payment amount. As the lending model has other group members paying on behalf of the primary borrower should the latter face difficulty in repayment, this mechanism ensures high collection efficiency. The better MFIs have reported extremely high collection efficiencies.

[12] There is considerable debate as to whether the low default rates are underestimated (see Morduch, 1999). However, Chowdhry *et al.* (2005) suggest that securitization can successfully expand the supply of funds to MFIs even assuming higher than reported default rates.

Counterparty Risk: There are risks that one or more of the parties to the transaction (e.g., entity providing credit enhancement) fails to meet their obligations.

Credit Risk: The uncollateralized nature of the microfinance receivables does make them more risky. However, MFIs have used social sanctions and denial of future credit as a substitute for the traditional forms of collateral. Additionally, with their regular repayment schedules, MFIs are viewed as being able to screen out undisciplined borrowers as well as allowing the institution to get hold of cash flows before they are consumed or diverted. Repayment often begins before investments bear fruit, thereby necessitating that the client has an additional income source on which to rely (Morduch, 1999).

With most securitized assets, a credit rating agency is involved. In microfinance, the lack of a long credit history makes it difficult for the rating agencies to evaluate the risk of default on the securities. Furthermore, the present rating and assessment agencies use different grading systems.[13] However, the reported low loan default rates and even lower loan loss rates for most leading MFIs show them to be creditworthy.[14] Since most microfinance lending takes place with groups of borrowers that are from the same geographic area and that are engaged in the same types of businesses, correlation of borrower credit risks is another issue of concern for microfinance receivables. Yet, correlation between individual borrowers could be mitigated to the extent that the entire loan pool is geographically and sectorally diversified as when the pools of receivables from different MFIs are combined.

Exchange Rate/Currency Risk: Microfinance activity takes place in developing countries with weak currencies that are susceptible to inflation fluctuations. The short duration nature of the loans does mitigate much of this risk as changes in exchange rates usually take place over several months or years. From a capital markets perspective, five primary methods can be used to mitigate currency risk: (1) forward contracts, (2) future contracts,

---

[13] See the Microfinance Rating and Assessment Fund website.
[14] For example, the Grameen Bank default rate has been quoted to be as low as 2%. However, these rates are self-reported and thus should be taken with caution.

(3) currency options, (4) currency swaps, and (5) back-to-back loans[15] (Bhatia, 2004). However, underdeveloped local capital markets may make these risk management techniques more difficult to employ.

Interest Rate Risk: There are risks arising out of variation in interest rates. Generally, swaps and options are used to hedge interest, price and exchange rate risks. A few countries do have the potential to tap these derivative markets. However, the use of some of these derivative instruments is not possible in some countries due to the lack of financial market development.

Legal/Regulatory Risk: There is a risk that, in the event of bankruptcy of the originator, the judicial courts would attach the microloan receivables such that the cash flows would be lost.

Liquidity Risk: There is a risk involving the ability to liquidate the underlying assets and generate liquidity to service the investors in a timely manner.

Political/Country Risk: In terms of political risk, it has been noted that MFIs tend to be established in countries that are somewhat stable. Expropriation is the most extreme form of political risk but is less relevant in the discussion of securitization of microfinance receivables as there is no foreign property to seize. There is transfer risk which is the risk that a government will not allow foreign currency to leave the country regardless of its source. Convertibility risk is also an issue in that a country's government may decide not to sell foreign currency to borrowers with obligations denominated in hard currency.

Prepayment Risk: Prepayment risk is a significant factor when dealing with mortgage-backed securities and other longer-tenor types of loans. However, due to the short-term nature of the loans and the characteristics of the end borrower, the risks associated with loan obligations being repaid ahead of schedule are small.

---

[15] Back-to-back loans have been frequently used by MFIs but tend to expose the MFI to the local bank's credit risk. In general they are not widespread today, but were common when stiff exchange controls made it very expensive to take an investor's home currency and convert it into the needed currency.

Reinvestment Risk: If the securitization structure is such that the special purpose vehicle (SPV)[16] reinvests the funds received from the end borrowers and makes payments to investors only on pre-specified dates, the variability in the returns earned represents reinvestment risk.

Servicing Risk: There is a risk that the MFI (servicing agent) is not capable of collecting payments despite the borrowers' ability and willingness to pay.

Commingling Risk: Since the funds collected are retained by the servicer for a short period of time, there could be potential for loss of funds due to a credit event or bankruptcy of the servicer.

3.7 Keys for Successful Securitization

The potential benefits to MFIs, investors and most importantly the poor suggest that, with appropriate credit enhancement, securitization could be a viable and desirable option for this asset class. However, countries must have the requisite legal framework and infrastructure to support the use of such sophisticated financial instruments. Adequate governance, contract enforcement, accounting standards, and regulation are necessary.

Presently, securitization in emerging markets is in its early stages and has involved mostly cross-border deals. Schneider and Huttenrauch (2005) discuss the criteria for domestic securitization ranging from country-specific issues to loan characteristics and data requirements, focusing on whether MFIs can meet such criteria. Further, they discuss the country-specific issues related to securitization and articulate that any legal and regulatory framework for securitization markets to develop and flourish should ensure the following:

- The regulation must permit transfer of assets legally from the original lender to a third party.
- The legislation must provide for the establishment of an insolvency-remote entity, whose purpose can be strictly limited.

---

[16] An entity formed as a trust which has no other activities besides holding transferred loans in a securitization deal. This entity ensures that these loans are serviced in accordance with the terms of the deal and issues the securities that are collateralized by the loans.

3.7.1 *Credit Enhancement*

The number of true securitization deals involving microloan receivables is small but increasing.[17] However, an essential element to securitization deals will be the type of credit enhancement. As with any asset-backed security, the form of credit enhancement or guarantee is crucial. In the US, the securitization market started with home mortgage loans and spread to other asset classes such as auto loans, student loans, and hospital receivables. Whereas the aforementioned asset classes are characterized by large markets, large loan sizes, long maturities, and proven loan performances, microfinance receivables are highly granular, uncollateralized,[18] and short term. However, the successful securitization of credit card receivables (see Calomiris, 2004) implies that this is not an insurmountable obstacle. With the proper credit enhancement, many of the investor risks previously identified could be ameliorated or even eliminated.

There are numerous forms of both internal and external credit enhancement that can be used for asset-backed securities. External forms of credit enhancement include corporate guarantees and letters of credit. The most common internal forms of credit enhancement are reserve funds, over-collateralization, and a senior/subordinated structure. With respect to microloan-backed securities, any of these forms could be utilized effectively for an individual issuance. However, the creation of an efficient, liquid, secondary market would be more easily achievable if a sound guarantor was used. In the US mortgage market, a large guarantor with adequate capital was vital. Ginnie Mae, Fannie Mae, and Freddie Mac facilitated the creation of a huge secondary market. While no one developing country government would be in the position to guarantee microloan-backed

---

[17] In 2006 there were two true securitization deals. ProCredit Bulgaria securitized €47.8 million of its Euro-denominated microloans with credit enhancement provided by the European Investment Fund and Germany's KfW. The securities received a BBB credit rating from a global credit rating agency. Bangladesh Rural Advancement Committee (BRAC) securitized US$180 million equivalent of local currency microloans. The issuance received a AAA credit rating from a local credit rating agency.

[18] Many traditional MFIs do not require collateral from their clients. In cases that they do, it is often collateral with a negligible salvage value (crops, utensils, jewelry, etc.) that has only a notional value which serves to deter borrowers from behaving imprudently.

securities, a large donor organization like the International Finance Corporation, the World Bank, or some other international organization could commit to providing the necessary credit enhancement. Additionally, this centralized organization could facilitate the creation of a secondary market for microloans by establishing underwriting standards, servicing requirements, and monitoring.

Although securitization has most often been identified as a replacement for subsidies, as Morduch (2005) suggests, this does not necessarily have to be the case. Securitization and subsidization could be complementary. "Smart subsidies" and donor funds could be used to provide the necessary credit enhancement and/or guarantees.

3.8 Challenges

While there are many powerful arguments in favor of securitization, there are also some arguments against it. Jansson (2003) discusses the securitization challenges in the context of the Latin American microfinance industry. He notes that past research efforts have focused on developing and strengthening the asset side of microfinance institutions; their product delivery mechanisms, information systems and human resources. However, with the rapid growth of the industry in terms of both portfolio sizes and number of institutions, he stresses that more attention needs to be paid to the funding side of these institutions. In addition, Jansson (2003) identifies and examines the issues facing MFIs such as access to capital markets and the search for additional equity. He suggests that a cursory analysis of securitization as a financing instrument reveals it may not be an attractive or even feasible option for the majority of MFIs. Several reasons are given:

- For it to be cost effective, the amount in question needs to exceed about $25 million, which is more than most MFIs have in their loan portfolios.
- Legal frameworks do not enable filing of a security interest in accounts receivables, making securitization difficult and costly.
- Due to limitations of certain local capital markets, domestic securitization of individual portfolios may be out of reach for certain MFIs. Thus, global securitization may be the only feasible option. While

global securitization would engage commercial investors and provide fresh funds to MFIs whilst avoiding the legal obstacles inherent in local legislations, the disadvantage is that it does not do much to improve the local capital markets, as the investors are all located in industrialized countries.

3.9 Conclusion

MFIs need access to more capital. Even donor organizations such as the International Finance Corporation realize that only by weaning off donor dependency and adopting a commercial orientation can MFIs truly attract the capital and savings base they need to scale up their microloan portfolios and start meeting the demand. Securitization, with appropriate credit enhancement, could ameliorate the capital constraint and financial sustainability issues plaguing most MFIs. Due to the myriad of benefits to investors, microloan receivables could be developed into an attractive, viable, mainstream, asset class. As with the securitization of life insurance assets and other types of assets, microloan securitization would require a substantial volume of transactions to reach public markets before it could even approach the level of success of mortgage-backed or other asset-backed securities. However, given the billions of people in developing countries who still lack access to formal financial services, there is a great amount of potential volume. If a suitable, sizeable guarantor is identified, microloan receivables could be pooled on a large scale to create an efficient, liquid market that provides ample capital flows to MFIs.

Bibliography

Ananth, B. (2005). "Financing Microfinance: The ICICI Bank Partnership Model." *Small Enterprise Development* 16 (1): 57–65.

Armendáriz de Aghion, B. and Morduch, J. (2005). *The Economics of Microfinance*. Cambridge, MA: The MIT Press.

Beshouri, C. P. and Nigro, P. J. (1995). "Securitization of Small Business Loans." *The Journal of Small Business Finance* 4 (1): 1–29.

Bhatia, R. (2004). "Mitigating Currency Risk for Investing in Microfinance Institutions in Developing Countries." *Social Enterprise Associates* (Working Paper No. 3).

Bogan, V. (2008). "Microfinance Institutions: Does Capital Structure Matter?" (Cornell University, Dept. of Applied Economics and Management, WP 2008-09).

Calomiris, C. W. (2004). "Credit Card Securitization and Regulatory Arbitrage." *Journal of Financial Services Research* 26 (1): 5–27.

Chowdhry, B., Cassell, D., Gamett, J. B., Milkwick, G. J., Nielsen, C. D. and Sederstrom, J. D. (2005). "Pricing Microfinance Loans and Loan Guarantees Using Biased Loan Write-Off Data." (Mimeo, UCLA Anderson School).

Dehejia, R., Montgomery, H. and Morduch, J. (2005). "Do Interest Rates Matter? Credit Demand in the Dhaka Slums." (Mimeo, New York University Working Paper).

"Developing Markets BlueOrchard Finance SA Transaction Overview." (2005). *The Federal Reserve System and the Aspen Institute Conference Papers.*

Gabre-Madhin, E. and Nagarajan, N. (2004). "Making Markets Work for the Poor." In *Achieving Sustainable Communities in a Global Economy* (pp. 45–83). Singapore: World Scientific.

Harper, M. and Vogel, R. (2005). "The Role of Savings as a Form of MFI Funding." *Micro Banking Bulletin: The Scope of Funding Microfinance* (11): 5–8.

Jansson, T. (2003). "Financing Microfinance." (Mimeo, Inter-American Development Bank).

Meehan, J. (2004). "Tapping the Financial Markets for Microfinance: Grameen Foundations USA's Promotion of this Emerging Trend." (Mimeo, GFUSA Working Paper Series).

Morduch, J. (1999). "The Microfinance Promise." *Journal of Economic Literature* 37 (4): 1569–1614.

Morduch, J. (2005). "Smart Subsidy for Sustainable Microfinance." *Asian Development Bank — Quarterly Newsletter of the Focal Point for Microfinance* 6 (4).

Schneider, C. and Huttenrauch, H. (2005). "Securitization: A Funding Alternative for Microfinance Institutions." (Presented at the Financial Sector Development Conference 2005).

Chapter Four

$\mathscr{A}$ Vision for Scaling Microfinance: More than Dollars and Smarts

*Deborah Burand, Esq.**

4.1 Introduction

When Warren Buffet announced the largest charitable gift in history, namely the contribution of 5/6th of his shareholdings in Berkshire Hathaway to the Bill & Melinda Gates Foundation, he explained his decision in a pithy soundbite. According to Buffet, "philanthropy is a tougher game" than business: "In philanthropy, the most important problems are those which have already resisted both intellect and money."

When it comes to scaling microfinance, Buffet has it exactly right. Dollars and smarts are not enough to solve the problem of helping microfinance to reach scale. Not even mega-philanthropists like Bill Gates, who

*Ms. Burand wrote this paper in 2007 while serving as the Executive Vice President, Strategic Services, Grameen Foundation. She now is the Vice President and General Counsel of the Overseas Private Investment Corporation. This paper borrows heavily from the work of others, like Lee C. Buchheit, Esq., whose eloquent writings on the design of a new international financial architecture inspired this paper. While acknowledging these grand thinkers, all opinions in this article are her personal views and should not be attributed to current or past employers, or, for that matter, to anyone else.

Deborah Burand, Overseas Private Investment Corporation, 1100 New York Avenue, NW, 12th Floor, Washington, DC 20527.

has recently determined to invest, through the Bill & Melinda Gates Foundation, $750 million over the next several years to deepen and expand the reach of financial services to the world's poor, can provide sufficient capital to ensure that microfinance reaches its promise, unless this new breed of philanthropists also invests in building a new international financial architecture that values financial access as highly as financial stability. Simply put, to scale microfinance requires dollars, smarts, and, importantly, a vision for a new financial order, an order that aims at tapping the power of commercial sources of capital to finance the growing funding needs of microfinance providers.[1]

Over a decade ago, on the heels of yet another round of financial crises in the world, starting with the Mexico peso crisis in December 1994, and then followed by crises in Thailand, Indonesia, South Korea, Russia, Brazil and Argentina, policymakers worldwide attempted to build a new "international financial architecture" that could not only prevent future financial crises, but also ease the destructive power of those crises that inevitably occur. The goal of this new international financial architecture was simple: make international capital flows to emerging markets more efficient, stable and transparent. Actually building such a new international financial architecture, however, was anything but simple.

As described by Lee C. Buchheit, Esq. in his 1999 article, "A Lawyer's Perspective on the New International Financial Architecture," this architecture stood on four legs. It aimed to:

(1) Moderate private sector financial flows to emerging markets to avoid a boom/bust pattern of lending;
(2) Ensure that investors in emerging markets had the information and economic incentives to make prudent investment decisions;
(3) Reinforce the ability of debtor countries to endure temporary economic or financial shocks or disruptions; and

---

[1] Some have estimated that today's microfinance providers are in need of $10–$20 billion in capital over the next five years.

(4) Facilitate prompt, orderly, non-contagious workouts of debtor countries when crises do occur, with attendant losses falling on those who made the investment decision.

So what does this discussion that so dominated G-7 and G-8 discussions in the 1990s have to do with microfinance reaching scale today? The short answer is — a lot. The longer answer is that many of the tools that were developed in the late 1990s to address macroeconomic challenges in lending to emerging markets are readily transferable to the challenge of bringing microfinance to scale through access to appropriate and sustainable commercial sources of finance. In short, to scale microfinance, we also need to foster capital flows into this sector that are efficient, stable and transparent.

Here is a similarly simple to articulate, but hard to build, vision for scaling microfinance. Take the four legs of the international financial architecture described above, and substitute the words "microfinance providers" for "emerging markets" and "debtor countries," and you have got a concrete vision for scaling microfinance that sounds like this:

> "A new international financial architecture is needed to make capital flows to *microfinance providers* more efficient, stable, and transparent. To this end, a new international financial architecture is needed that will:
>
> (1) Moderate private sector financial flows to *microfinance providers* to avoid a boom/bust pattern of lending;
>
> (2) Ensure that investors in *microfinance providers* have the information and economic incentives to make prudent investment decisions;
>
> (3) Reinforce the ability of *microfinance providers* to endure temporary economic or financial disruptions; and
>
> (4) Facilitate prompt, orderly, non-contagious workouts of *microfinance providers* when crises do occur, with attendant losses falling on those who made the investment decision."

Visions are as important for articulating not only what one hopes to achieve in the world, but, by inference, also highlighting what one wants to avoid. The above vision statement does both. Moreover, like the four pillars of the international financial architecture described by Buchheit, the above microfinance-oriented pillars are equally split between prevention and cure — the first two principles aim at preventing crises, and the second two principles aim at responding to (and possibly curing) crises if and when they arise.

The following is a stock-taking of some of the key initiatives that have taken place to date in the world of microfinance at building an international financial architecture that attracts and retains flows of commercial capital to microfinance. It also is a call to those of us in the microfinance world to do much, much more.

4.2 Building an International Financial Architecture

4.2.1 *Moderate Private Sector Financial Flows to Microfinance Providers to Avoid a Boom/Bust Pattern of Lending*

In a series of scenario-building exercises, CGAP (the Consultative Group to Assist the Poor) recently gathered microfinance professionals together to ponder where microfinance may find itself in 2015 and to identify the key drivers of that crystal ball gazing.[2] One driving factor identified by those of us at the table was the growing enthusiasm by investors for investing in microfinance, an enthusiasm that also has been noted in a recent study undertaken by MicroRate of the mushrooming number of specialized microfinance investment vehicles (called by MicroRate, "MIVs"). According to some estimates, there are now over 80 MIVs in the world, and that number continues to grow. CGAP research suggests that the amount invested in MIVs doubled in the last year, from $987 in 2005 to $2 billion in 2006. Much of the MIV investment in microfinance providers to date has been in the form of debt (as opposed to equity); and of that debt, most has been denominated in hard currency.[3] Yet most microfinance

---

[2] See CGAP Focus Note No. 39, "Financial Inclusion 2015: Four Scenarios for the Future of Microfinance" (October 2006).

[3] A CGAP-MicroRate survey from 2005 finds that 74% of MIV investment has been provided in the form of debt; and of that debt, 70% has been denominated in hard currency.

institutions (MFIs) are still underleveraged relative to commercial banks.[4]

This growing interest in investing in microfinance is a blessing for the industry; but, like all blessings when taken in too strong a dose, it may also be a curse. While neither CGAP nor MicroRate have described these new sources of funding as a lending "boom" or "bubble," the risk is there as most serious observers of microfinance will admit, albeit quietly.

Several observers have suggested that some of the recent investments in microfinance may have been attracted more by the underlying subsidies supporting those transactions (such as credit enhancements provided in the form of a donor-funded or otherwise highly subsidized guarantee) than by the actual cash flow of the underlying microfinance business activity being financed. Put differently, does it matter to an investor in search of investment grade paper if the business she is financing is microfinance, or is she solely in search of investments that enjoy highly rated, credit support? Whether this is an accurate perception of investors' motivations, the risk is that today's chatter about the glories of investing in microfinance may eventually wane, as financial enthusiasm often does, and then investors' enthusiasm will swing to the next new thing.

In the meantime, however, some MFIs are enjoying their moment in the sun.[5] With no spoilsport like former Federal Reserve Board Chairman Alan Greenspan in sight who threatens to take away this punch bowl of bubbling capital, some MFIs are borrowing at record levels — often with little understanding of the true costs and structural or documentation risks of their borrowings (as evidenced by a growing number of covenant defaults quietly taking place among microfinance borrowers).[6] They are borrowing in dollars and euros to fund assets denominated in local

---

[4] The median MFI debt:equity ratio of MFIs reporting to the MIX (Microfinance Information eXchange) is around 2:1, compared to commercial banks that are leveraged at a rate that is closer to 9–12:1.

[5] The above referenced CGAP survey from 2005 finds that ten microfinance institutions attracted 26% of the aggregate amount of MIV investment.

[6] CGAP and Grameen Foundation recently surveyed the management teams of 16 MFIs in 14 countries around the world, half of which mobilize and intermediate deposits. A key finding of that survey is that many of the surveyed MFIs are underestimating the true costs and risks of their funding sources — debt and equity.

currencies, with little to no hedges or other risk mitigation strategies to guard against foreign exchange risks.[7] They are borrowing in short-term or demand funds to finance medium-term assets. They are borrowing at floating interest rates to finance assets earning fixed returns. They are signing loan documentation without understanding (or, as at least one MFI has confessed, even reading) the terms. They are "pledging" microcredit portfolios to secure borrowings in countries where such pledges of intangible assets are legally unenforceable, and some are even "over-pledging" by giving multiple lenders claims on the same asset. All of which suggests that moderating financial flows while stepping up investment readiness training for MFIs might be an increasingly desirable goal.

When the international financial architects of the 1990s attempted to come up with measures that would moderate financial flows to emerging markets, they looked to tools and practices that would discourage excessive borrowing as well as flows of "hot money" (meaning short-term, hard currency-denominated, financing). This caution is something that could and should take hold in the microfinance world too.

While some investors in microfinance have complained recently that there is more funding than suitable microfinance investments, one needs to ask whether the funding being pushed at microfinance providers is itself "suitable." What kind of commercial sources of funding do we want to see invested in microfinance? Can a sustainable microfinance industry be built on the back of short-term loans, denominated in hard currency? Would it be a good thing for the overall health of the microfinance industry if it were to come to rely on large capital flows from internet-based platforms that intermediate the extension of six-month, dollar-denominated loans from, say, college students in Ithaca, New York to poor basketmakers in Benin City, Nigeria — even if such loans are made at zero percent interest rates? Do we think it is appropriate for MFIs to execute complex loan agreements containing covenants that they have not read, do not understand, or, if having read and understood, have little likelihood of meeting? If the answer to any of these questions is no, then

---

[7] See CGAP Focus Note No. 31, "Foreign Exchange Rate Risk in Microfinance: What is it and how can it be managed?" (January 2005).

much work needs to be done on both the demand and supply side of the equation — work that would encourage responsible borrowing by micro-finance providers and discourage irresponsible lending to microfinance providers by investors.

Developing standard forms of loan documentation for the microfinance industry that fairly represents the interests of both the borrower and lender is one important step that could be taken in this direction. Not only could this standardization offer valuable time savings to both lenders and MFIs as it would cut substantially time spent in negotiations, but standardized loan documentation could lead to a more liquid market in the trading of microfinance loans (or even securitization of such loans), which in turn should lower MFIs' cost of funds so that they can serve their poor clients more efficiently and cheaply.

Training microfinance providers to learn how to negotiate and under-stand better those contractual obligations that they are assuming when tapping commercial sources of financing is another important step. MFIs also need more tools to help them evaluate the costs and risks of vary-ing commercial funding sources. Happily, donors like Rockdale Foun-dation and other industry stakeholders, like CGAP, are now investing in the creation of a growing array of technical guides and tools to help MFIs better understand the structure and documentation of various forms of financings.[8] Additionally, regional and global microfinance networks increasingly are running investment-readiness trainings for MFIs and some, like Grameen Foundation's Capital Management and Advisory Center (CMAC), now offer advisory services directly to individual MFIs to support the evaluation, negotiation and structuring of their commercial financings.

Building tools to help microfinance institutions better hedge against currency and interest rate risks is yet another step. Given the recent

---

[8] See, for example, "Commercial Loan Agreements: A Technical Guide for Microfinance Institutions" (prepared for CGAP by Cleary, Gottlieb, Steen & Hamilton (2006)), and "Foreign Exchange Risk Mitigation Techniques: Structure and Documentation, A Tech-nical Guide for Microfinance Institutions" (also prepared for CGAP by Cleary, Gottlieb, Steen & Hamilton (2006)). Both of these technical guides have been translated into several languages and are downloadable from the CGAP website (www.cgap.org).

increase in international lenders' interest in microfinance, the need for instruments to mitigate cross-border lending risks, including foreign exchange and interest rate risks, has grown. Because of the relatively small size of MFI borrowings, perceived counterparty risk of MFIs, and often exotic currencies used in MFIs' operations, standard hedging tools, like foreign exchange forwards, futures, swaps or options, often are not available or are too expensive for microfinance providers to access. One breakthrough under discussion is the possible launch of a foreign exchange hedging fund, supported in part by the Dutch, and aimed at small and medium enterprises, including microfinance providers.

Finally, other stakeholders — ranging from bank regulators to rating agencies to existing investors in microfinance — should voice dismay when they observe excessive or inappropriately structured borrowings by MFIs or flows of "hot money" coming into the microfinance industry. In this regard, welcome steps are being taken by some of the specialized microfinance rating agencies to draw attention to the amount of MFIs' unhedged foreign currency exposure.

4.2.2   Ensure that Investors in Microfinance Providers Have the Information and Economic Incentives to Make Prudent Investment Decisions

Transparency is a watchword in the microfinance industry, just as it was in the 1990s for would-be international financial architects. According to a common dictionary definition found in Merriam Webster's Collegiate Dictionary, "transparency" means to be free from pretense or deceit, to be easily detected or seen through, and, finally, to be readily understood.

There is now near universal recognition that transparency in the marketplace is a good thing. The more transparency, the better. Even microfinance has become enamored with transparency, as evidenced by CGAP's award each year to the world's most transparent microfinance provider. But transparency for transparency's sake somehow misses the point. The world of microfinance, just as the world of international capital markets, needs transparency in order "to be readily understood." And that is a challenge for microfinance, particularly with the growing number of investors who are intent on making cross-border investments into microfinance.

In October of 1933, John Foster Dulles, writing in *Foreign Affairs*, concluded his article on "The Securities Act and Foreign Lending" with the following admonition about the need for understanding risk when investing across borders:

> The remedy…is not to be found in legislative restraints …. Rather it calls for our education in financial matters, to the end that foreign risks will be recognized and appraised and assumed deliberately only by those who can afford them.

That advice rings true today. The risks of spikes in repayment defaults by borrowing microfinance providers, or of the proliferation of loan agreements being signed by MFIs that contain overly broad cross-default clauses that are certain to tumble one distressed loan after another in a domino-effect, can be addressed only if the microfinance industry takes it upon itself to understand better the fruits of our transparency campaign.

An analogy can be made to the shaky start of eco-tourism in Latin America in the mid-to-late 1980s. Adventuresome tourists, fresh from camera-popping safaris across African savannahs, came to the rainforests of Bolivia and Brazil in search of equally riveting photo-opportunities and communes with nature. At first they often were disappointed. For those of us working on international environment issues and who hoped to captivate this new breed of eco-tourists (and their wallets), we soon learned that it was not enough to bring them to one of the most diverse ecosystems on earth, we also needed to help our fellow wanderers understand the beauty and complexity of what they were seeing. That is, we needed to make the wonders of the rainforest more "transparent."

Some may argue that the goal of building an "international financial architecture" is too rigid and static to encompass the fluidity of the fast-changing world of microfinance. And they may be right. Perhaps, again borrowing from the world of eco-tourism, the better analogy is to build a transparent "ecosystem" for investors in microfinance. But for the ecosystem of microfinance to be truly transparent engenders a responsibility on all of us in the microfinance world not simply to push for a dump of economic, financial, and social performance data on current and would-be investors in microfinance. Rather, we have a responsibility to develop and refine microfinance institutions' capacity to present those numbers and statistics in ways that lead investors from seeing to understanding.

An important step being taken in this direction is the development of microfinance benchmarks, which allow the financial and operational performance of microfinance providers to be compared against each other. Just a decade ago, data about microfinance performance was largely anecdotal, and, where there was quantitative data, it was focused largely on the performance of MFIs working in Latin America. Today, by contrast, there is standardized quantitative financial and operational data available to the public for nearly 1,000 microfinance providers located in all regions of the world, of different legal forms (ranging from regulated banks to unregulated non-profits), and at different stages of institutional development (commercializing, transforming, deposit-taking, etc.).[9] This has allowed benchmarking by geographic region, by legal form, and by stage of institutional development that can be used by investors, policymakers and MFI management to inform decisionmaking.

Steps to supplement these financial and operational benchmarks with social performance benchmarks, such as the growing adoption by poverty-focused MFIs of the Grameen Foundation's Progress out of Poverty Index (also called PPI) that provides statistically robust data on the likely poverty levels of MFI clients, will be an important leap forward to educate socially-minded investors as they seek to invest in double bottomline providers of microfinance.

Similarly, the expected launch of an association for retail microfinance investors is a needed addition to the evolving microfinance "ecosystem." Such an association should take a leadership role in conducting meaningful research about the risks and rewards of investing in microfinance, and in disseminating that research to a broad commercial, retail investor base.

---

[9] This information can be accessed through the Microfinance Information eXchange (MIX) at www.themix.org.

4.2.3 Reinforce the Ability of Microfinance Providers to Endure Temporary Economic or Financial Disruptions

As net private capital flows to emerging markets now run at an annual rate of $500 billion (a more than fourfold increase from 2002), the microfinance industry has also enjoyed a wave of new investors and access to new (at least to microfinance) financial products, such as CLOs (collateralized loan obligations), syndicated loans, securitization of microcredit portfolios, IPOs, private placements, and bond offerings, to name a few. If, or as some suggest *when*, the tide turns, and the recent years' rush of capital into emerging markets starts to rush back out again, the funding of microfinance may also take a downward turn.

In the past, there was evidence that microfinance providers (and their clients) were not particularly affected by financial shocks to the formal economies where they operated. Whether the commercialization and integration of microfinance providers into the more formal economies where they work changes this risk calculation is deserving of more research.[10] As microfinance becomes increasingly integrated into financial markets and the formal sector, one can no longer assume that microfinance providers will continue to enjoy a counter-cyclical position within their respective financial sectors. Rather, we may find that the risks of investing in microfinance are more correlated to broader macroeconomic indicators than in the past. If this is the case, then the fates of commercially-funded microfinance providers will likely rise or fall in step with the financial fortunes of both the countries where they work and the countries where their investors raise capital.

---

[10] Some are starting to attempt this research although the data samples often are small and findings are untested given the dearth of recent financial or economic crises in the developing world. See, for example, a recent working paper from the Stern School of Business of New York University, which suggests that the performance of microfinance providers is less correlated to domestic macroeconomic conditions than is the performance of comparable commercial banks. See *Financial Times*, "Microfinance: Not as risky as you think," by Kathryn Tully (May 25, 2007).

Protecting microfinance providers, and, equally important, their clients — the microentrepreneurs — from unexpected, temporary economic or financial disruptions is an area of growing concern among microfinance stakeholders. Moreover, since MFIs often work in disaster-prone or conflict-ridden areas, these economic or financial disruptions may be based on a natural disaster such as a flood or earthquake, or a manmade disaster such as war or civil strife. The challenges facing microfinance providers that choose to serve poor clients living in "risky areas" may have everything to do with *where* microfinance providers work and very little to do with *how well* they work. Not surprisingly, many microfinance providers share in common with their target clientele, the poor of the world, a high degree of vulnerability to risks outside of their control. Yet microfinance providers have more resources at their disposal than do their poor clients to manage these risks. Unfortunately, not enough microfinance managers are acting proactively to mitigate or spread these risks to those in the financial world that are better equipped to handle such disruptions.

One step that some have taken is to set up contingent credit lines or emergency liquidity funds that are aimed at giving microfinance providers breathing room should traditional sources of funding suddenly dry up or disasters strike causing their clients to default on loan repayments. Another step that is being explored is the development of insurance products aimed at mitigating or insuring against catastrophic risks. Weather-indexed insurance, credit insurance, and catastrophic loss of business insurance are just a few of the products now being designed specifically with the needs of MFIs and their clients in mind. Over time, one can imagine even the re-engineering of catastrophic bonds (so-called "CAT" bonds) to meet the needs and particularized risks of the microfinance market, perhaps to be called micro-CATs.

Laudable as these risk-sharing financial instruments may be in helping MFIs manage risk without overly limiting their outreach to the poor, this is an area that is still new to much of the microfinance industry and where much more attention is needed. Insurance and re-insurance companies have much to contribute to this area. Similarly, just as investment readiness training is an important pre-condition to attracting sustainable flows of commercial capital to microfinance, so too is risk-mitigation training a pre-condition to helping MFI managers anticipate and plan for temporary economic or financial disruptions when those capital flows are interrupted by events outside of their control.

Enhancing the risk management capacity of MFI managers and spreading of catastrophic risks to other financial actors that are better equipped to manage those risks should be welcome by local regulators as well as investors. In the absence of these risk-sharing or off-loading arrangements, some bank regulators are pondering the introduction of front-loaded, preventive measures into their specialized microfinance laws and regulations so as to limit the chance of seeing deposit-taking MFIs encounter a liquidity crisis or insolvency. These regulators are beefing up their specialized microfinance laws and regulations aimed at loan concentration limitations, capital adequacy ratios, asset classification, provisioning, liquidity reserve requirements, management information systems, and governance. It is not unusual, for example, for regulators to subject deposit-taking MFIs to capital adequacy ratios that are more onerous than those applied to local commercial banks. Instead of the more typical 8% capital requirements imposed under Basel I to assets that are risk-weighted at 100%, some regulated microfinance institutions are being required to hold capital in amounts of 15% or more against 100% of their outstanding microcredits. In essence, to address regulators' concerns about the ability of deposit-taking MFIs to find adequate sources of capital in the face of a weakening loan portfolio, they are requiring these MFIs to build relatively larger equity cushions than that required of commercial banks. Finding alternative ways to manage this risk should lower regulatory-imposed transaction costs to the benefit of both MFIs and the clients of MFIs.

4.2.4 *Facilitate Prompt, Orderly, Non-Contagious Workouts of Microfinance Providers When Crises Do Occur, with Attendant Losses Falling on Those Who Made the Investment Decision*

This is the area where the least work has been done in the microfinance sector, perhaps understandably so as there are few examples to date of repayment defaults by microfinance providers. Yet lack of workout experience in the microfinance sector should not excuse a lack of planning for this eventuality. The time is now, before a crisis occurs, to train microfinance providers in sound debt management policies, to help them understand the role that 3rd party credit enhancements can (and cannot) play when crises occur, to ensure that only meaningful pledges of assets are offered by MFIs to lenders, and to instill a healthy respect in borrowing MFIs for the complications of managing loan obligations that enjoy sweeping cross-default clauses, to name a few.

Finally, there is a regulatory and legal enabling role to be played here too. Investors need to understand better where they stand *vis-à-vis* other claimants with respect to MFIs' assets should a workout become necessary. For example, does an unsecured lender to a deposit-taking MFI stand in front of or behind depositors when it comes to claiming the MFI's assets in the case of a bankruptcy? Ask one of today's lenders to a regulated microfinance provider and see if he or she knows the answer to this question. Still more troubling, ask a local bank regulator and see if he or she knows.

Moreover, in countries where the application of bankruptcy laws to MFIs is uncertain, policymakers have an opportunity to clarify, before the fact, the various priority positions of various classes of investors in MFIs so that these investors understand their legal rights and the priority of claims. This also avoids the making of politicized decisions about claimants' rights in the heat of a workout. As a general rule, all MFIs, even non-profit MFIs that are organized under charitable institution laws rather than corporate laws, should enjoy bankruptcy protections that customarily are made available to corporate borrowers, such as the protection against set-off.

Similarly, the applicability and appropriateness of the corrective action tools available to bank regulators need to be reassessed before such tools are applied to regulated MFIs. For example, a "stop lending" order imposed by a bank regulator on a weakening MFI is likely to push that MFI to quickly fail given the often vital importance of ongoing lending operations to the health of its existing microcredit portfolio. Additionally, while the world has seen "borrower runs" on MFIs, there is still much to be learned about how to manage "depositor runs" on regulated MFIs. This can be complicated by the unique nature of those depositors — a possibly physically remote, widely spread, illiterate group of poor individuals who likely will be unimpressed by the publication of financial statements in newspapers or financial ratings posted in MFI offices. All of which points to the need for more work to be done in the area of building deposit insurance schemes and other measures that are aimed at protecting this unusual group of depositors and assuaging their fears before a crisis occurs or before the failure of one deposit-taking MFI sparks a contagious depositor run on other microfinance providers.

In conclusion, the day that Warren Buffet made the decision to contribute the lion's share of his wealth to the Bill & Melinda Gates Foundation was a good day for all of us who champion the cause of poverty alleviation and increased financial access in the world. Yet microfinance holds a promise that does not wholly depend on future billionaires' generosity. That is because microfinance can reach scale *without* depending on the largesse of the rich, so long as the microfinance sector can tap the power of commercial sources of capital for the sector's needs. But such capital flows to microfinance need to be efficient, stable, and transparent, otherwise the gains in scale achieved by tapping the power of commercial capital will be unsustainable, and much needless damage will occur when money rushes out of the microfinance sector just as quickly as it is now rushing in.

Here is one important way to spend at least a small portion of Warren Buffet's bequest to the Bill & Melinda Gates Foundation — namely, to invest in the building of an international financial architecture for the microfinance sector. But as Mr. Buffet also has acknowledged, it takes more than dollars and smarts to tackle the world's most important problems. As argued in this paper, it also takes vision. It is time for a vision of a new financial order to take root in the world, a vision that is intent on scaling microfinance by tapping the power of the capital markets and that prizes financial access as well as stability.

$\mathcal{I}$nnovations in Index Insurance for the Poor in Low-Income Countries

Jerry Skees*

5.1 Introduction

This chapter examines an innovation in risk mitigation — index insurance for weather risk. To establish the context and justification for insurance interventions, the paper first explores the nature of risk and, specifically,

*Jerry R. Skees is The H.B. Price Professor of Policy and Risk in the Department of Agricultural Economics, University of Kentucky, and President of GlobalAgRisk, Inc.; jskees@uky.edu

This paper is a revision of a significantly longer document that was produced by GlobalAgRisk, Inc., under USAID/DAI Prime Contract LAG-I-00-98-0026-00 BASIS Task Order 8, Rural Finance Market Development. The involvement of GlobalAgRisk, Inc., with World Bank projects on agricultural risk management has also contributed to the conceptual development needed to produce this document. GlobalAgRisk, Inc., professionals Jerry Skees, Anne Goes, and Celeste Sullivan developed the original document with assistance from Richard Carpenter, Mario Miranda, and Barry Barnett. These contributions and the support of USAID and, in particular, Lena Heron of USAID, who provided guidance and editorial assistance when developing the original primer, are gratefully acknowledged. Assistance from Lauren Mitten, John Jepsen, and Mary Miller of DAI is also acknowledged. The reader is referred to the original document for details on how to determine if these ideas will work in their country and how to design a pilot project to test these innovations. Microlinks has posted the original primer: http://www.microlinks.org/ev_en.php?ID=14239_201&ID2=DO_TOPIC

the impact of weather risk on agricultural enterprises and rural households. Agriculture remains a dominant economic activity for the poor in many lower income countries, comprising more than 40 percent of the workforce on average. Furthermore, some 60 countries had more than 20 percent of their Gross Domestic Product tied to agriculture in 2004 (World Bank data set). In the economic development literature, there is increasing recognition that the lack of rural financial markets for the poor is one reason so many poor are locked into poverty (Anderson; Barnett, Barrett, and Skees; Barrett and McPeak; and Carter *et al.*).

First, this chapter examines the effects of weather on income, behavior, and economic activity, and why weather-based agricultural insurance is needed in lower income countries. To provide background to the need for innovation in agricultural insurance, the chapter also provides a brief review of traditional agricultural insurance mechanisms used in higher and middle income countries, and the limitations to using those mechanisms in lower income countries. Next the chapter explores how index insurance works; the advantages, constraints, and preconditions to developing these products; and the role of government and donors in supporting development of index insurance. The chapter closes with a discussion of the applications for index insurance and a look to the future.

For simplicity, the products discussed in this paper are referred to as index "insurance." Nevertheless, as explained later, national regulatory agencies differ in how they define the term "insurance." Thus, these products may not be considered insurance products under every system (Hazell and Skees).

5.2 Effects of Weather Risk in Lower Income Countries

In agriculturally dependent economies, weather is a significant factor for economic well-being. Particularly in areas of rain-fed agriculture, variations in the weather are a major determinant of agricultural production. While variations are expected, natural disasters such as torrential rain, flooding, and prolonged drought can devastate a rural economy by damaging the major source of household, regional, or national income. Where there are no mechanisms in place to protect against large losses from extreme weather events, income and economic activities are likely to be depressed. Unmanaged weather risk can contribute to poverty and inhibit development. Beyond the immediate effects of a disaster, the chance or risk that a disastrous event will occur influences behavior and economic activity:

- Agricultural households can experience loss of income and assets;
- Agricultural households will choose low-risk, low-return activities and will not risk investing in technology;
- Financial institutions may restrict lending to farm households; and
- Overall investment in the rural sector may be deterred.

Weather-related disasters can quickly destroy sources of current income such as growing crops. Even more devastating, they can also destroy household assets — often accumulated over years of savings and productive investments — that are needed to generate future income. In lower income countries, an extreme weather event can push rural and small-holder farm households, often with few resources, into a cycle of poverty, as illustrated in Figure 5.1.

Figure 5.1 shows the asset positions for two hypothetical households A and B. Initially, both households experience upward growth in their

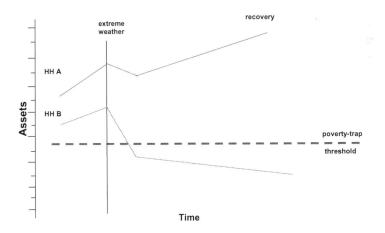

Figure 5.1: Economic impact of a natural disaster on households with different asset positions

Source: Carter *et al.*

asset level and income, though B is still close to the poverty line. If a catastrophic weather event takes place, both households may experience an immediate decline in their assets and income due to loss or damage to productive assets, or due to the cost of recovery. Household A retains more productive assets and is therefore able to recover more quickly. For a poorer household, such as B, the depletion of assets may push the household below the poverty line. Once the asset position of a household falls below the poverty line, its recovery may be slow or it may be unable to generate sufficient new income to rise above the poverty level and regain its previous economic position. This situation is referred to as a poverty trap because once households on the margin slip into poverty, they often lack the assets needed to improve their economic well-being. Weather insurance that targets poorer rural and farm households could help households avoid the poverty trap by compensating for weather-induced losses, thus enabling lost productive assets to be replaced and stimulating faster recovery.

Recognizing the potential for losses from weather events beyond their control, households that are highly vulnerable to shocks often manage risk by engaging in activities characterized by low risk but also low expected return. This decision reduces the financial risk but also prevents the household from pursuing activities that would generate more income. While low-risk strategies such as crop diversification and supplemental off-farm employment may have less income variability, the prospects for economic growth are also much lower than would be the case if the household were investing in more profitable activities (Anderson; Dercon, 2004; Carter et al.). Livelihood strategies with the prospect of a higher expected return would involve investments in productive assets — such as farm improvements, intensification, new technology, and education — in addition to start-up costs associated with new endeavors. These higher-return strategies are risky because limited resources would be invested in something that has an uncertain return in the presence of a potentially destructive weather risk.

Still, in many cases low-risk, low-return strategies are not entirely effective at reducing exposure to extreme weather risk. For example, in many countries it is common practice to hold livestock as an asset that can be used to smooth income and manage risk. In the event of an illness or a minor economic downturn, some of the livestock can be sold to support the household's basic needs (Dercon, 1996). However, if a loss event is serious and widespread, and affects many households in the same area — like drought — too many livestock enter the market at once, lowering the value of the asset just when it is most needed. In addition, holding livestock as an asset can be an unreliable strategy because livestock are also susceptible to weather risks (drought, floods, and freezes).

Households employ a variety of other mechanisms to reduce their risk or to cope with a financial loss. Informal loans made by relatives, other members of the community, or money lenders are another common way in which households can access cash following a crisis. Though the interest on informal loans is often much higher than a bank rate, informal loans are more accessible to the rural poor. These strategies, while not necessarily economically efficient, do allow rural households to deal with temporary economic hardships resulting from illness, injury, or some other unexpected expenditure. However, when a major weather-related disaster strikes, these informal strategies often break down when correlated catastrophic losses occur. If an entire community experiences disastrous weather effects, the social networks that could be relied upon for assistance may be unable to offer support because all members may be experiencing hardship. It is difficult to help your neighbor when you are also suffering from the same event.

Financial institutions and other enterprises are cautious about extending credit to rural households and agricultural enterprises beset by weather risk. Though there is potential for growth in rural areas and the agricultural sector, the potential for widespread economic loss in these areas is an inhibiting factor. Restricting the amount of investment in the agricultural sector is one way for a bank or other enterprise to reduce exposure to these risks. Underinvestment in the agricultural sector is a rational yet inefficient way to reduce exposure to weather risk.

Without access to more efficient alternatives such as insurance, inefficient strategies may be the only choice for rural households to cope with their risk and for financial institutions and other enterprises to protect their business investments. The strategy of risk avoidance and conservative investment behavior may be effective at reducing risk exposure to some extent; however, the tradeoff, or cost, is that opportunities for growth are hindered. Research from Tanzania suggests that rural households faced with exposure to major shocks may give up 25 percent of their potential income by adopting less risky strategies (Dercon, 1996). Rosenzweig and Binswanger's work in an Indian village suggests this "risk premium" is as high as 50 percent.

Weather risks are unpredictable in terms of both frequency and severity. The uncertainty surrounding when a damaging event could occur and what its effect might be can deter investment and growth. Individuals or enterprises may be unwilling to invest their limited resources in opportunities that promise higher expected returns if there is also a risk of total or partial loss. Insurance is one way to remove some of the uncertainty about future economic status. Individuals will be more willing to invest in economic activities that offer higher expected returns if they can use insurance to protect themselves from potential losses resulting from an extreme weather event. Insurance is a way to reduce operational risk, making it possible to take more financial risk to finance new technologies, education, or infrastructure (Barnett, Barrett, and Skees).

5.3   Why Weather-Based Agricultural Insurance is Needed in Lower Income Countries

There are a number of positive benefits that weather insurance could offer in helping rural households mitigate risk, including improving their access to rural and agricultural finance. In place of these viable formal alternatives, many of the strategies used by rural households in lower income countries to manage weather risk are inefficient and inconsistent with longer-term growth objectives. Various informal strategies for coping with correlated risk, such as mutual aid networks and semi-formal microfinance activity, can suffer from many of the same challenges that make it difficult to develop formal financial markets.

There are also significant benefits in finding mechanisms that will allow lower income countries to transfer weather risk into global markets. Depending on the type of product developed, households, intermediaries such as rural banks or agribusinesses, and even national governments should be able to benefit from weather insurance (Hess et al.; Skees and Barnett, 2006).

5.3.1 *Weather Insurance Can Spur Rural Financial Markets by Transferring Risk*

Formal-sector financial services in higher income countries include a wide array of opportunities for saving, borrowing, and insuring to manage risk and plan for a more secure future. Each of these three complementary components are needed for rural financial markets to be effective. Following a loss event, households may borrow money to smooth consumption or replace lost productive assets. However, many of the poor in lower income countries simply cannot borrow due to a lack of available financial services, credit history, or collateral. Savings and insurance solutions are activities that occur before the onset of a loss event. For some types of insurance, the only requirement is to pay the premium. Thus, in some cases, insurance can be obtainable by the poor who have no ability to borrow. It is also possible that insurance could serve as a substitute for collateral. Financial services provided by the formal sector can prove to be less costly and more efficient than many of the informal risk-coping strategies used by the rural poor as described above.

Access to rural finance is increasingly acknowledged as a means to help alleviate the persistence of poverty traps in lower income countries. The practice of microfinance entities making small loans to the poor is growing. To the extent that these small loans are made to individuals on the margins of poverty, there will be significant repayment problems when their livelihoods are affected by natural disaster. Given that many natural disaster events are widespread and affect many people at the same time, the correlated losses of the individuals have the potential to create a significant default on the portfolio of microloans. For example, in the northern regions of Peru, El Niño events, such as the one that occurred in 1998, can cause major flooding. While not entirely tied to El Niño, following the last such event, default rates on microfinance loans increased from a rate of 8 percent to nearly 18 percent in the Northern department of Piura. It is a common banking practice to both restrict access to credit and charge higher interest rates when these types of risks are present.

In short, correlated risks from weather events can be a major constraint to the development of formal financial services. The banking systems of most countries are not designed to absorb natural disaster risk. Natural disaster risk must be transferred into a global market to be diversified into a global portfolio of insurance risks. Thus, insurance markets can be the missing link for stronger development of rural finance. Financial institutions in lower income countries should be more willing to provide credit to rural and farm households that have weather insurance because these households will be able to utilize insurance indemnity payments to repay their loans. Weather insurance products could also be used by the financial institutions themselves to protect their portfolios against excessive loss due to defaults associated with extreme weather events. This protection should also improve institutions' willingness to provide credit to agricultural enterprises and rural households. Skees (2003), McCord, and Skees and Barnett (2006) address the possibilities for linking index insurance to micro lending.

5.3.2 Weather Insurance Can Support Development and Improve Government and Donor Response to Natural Disaster in Lower Income Countries

Using weather insurance to manage the risk of catastrophic weather events should stimulate economic development by improving stability and opportunities for growth in the agricultural and financial sectors. Weather insurance can also be used to improve government and donor response to natural disaster by providing quick access to resources for disaster relief and recovery needs.

Natural disasters can depress economic output, damage infrastructure, and increase fiscal demands on government and donor organizations. Weather insurance for quick response for emergency assistance can have an immediate impact on reducing vulnerability to weather risk by:

- Protecting rural livelihoods, thereby reducing poverty;
- Protecting the productive capacity of rural enterprises and farm households;
- Protecting financial institutions against weather-related loan defaults; and
- Financing disaster relief and encouraging social safety net policies.

When resources are limited, disaster response may cause financial resources to be diverted from other budget allocations and programs. Over time, other potential benefits can emerge that contribute to development, including:

- Promoting investment in higher-return activities among rural households;
- Expanding rural finance through improved access and better terms of credit for farm households and agricultural enterprises; and
- Providing a mechanism to manage the most costly source of risk, so government funds can be used for other social purposes during a natural disaster.

5.4 Traditional Agricultural Insurance

Traditional crop insurance mechanisms used in higher and middle income countries are not suitable or even feasible for lower income countries. Besides inherent constraints associated with these mechanisms, most of these traditional crop insurance programs are subsidized to lower the cost of the premiums. In addition, farm households make up a small fraction of the population in most of the countries that provide subsidized crop insurance. The same is not true in many lower income countries, which makes it even more unlikely that lower income countries can afford to adopt the practice of subsidized crop insurance.

5.4.1 Constraints to Traditional Weather Insurance

As mentioned, weather risk is often correlated risk and can be a major constraint to the development of the formal rural and agricultural financial markets because a widespread, severe weather event may result in excessive loan defaults across the affected area (Skees and Barnett, 2006).

Since traditional approaches to insurance attempt to assess the risk of the insured individual, this can be an expensive undertaking subject to many administrative problems, especially for farm-level agricultural insurance. Two dominant problems associated with using traditional insurance at the farm-level are adverse selection and moral hazard. Adverse selection occurs when potential insurance purchasers know more about their risks than the insurer does, leading to participation by high-risk individuals and non-participation by low-risk individuals. Moral hazard refers to the careless, irresponsible, and even fraudulent behaviors of the insured after they purchase the insurance.

Insurance is a business that depends upon trust. Insurers deal with adverse selection and moral hazard by incurring more cost to obtain more information, and charging higher premiums, or not insuring at all. The financial goal of any insurance program is to operate on an actuarially sound basis, where indemnities paid out and the cost of operation (including profits), on average, equal total premiums collected.

5.4.2 Two Types of Traditional Crop Insurance: Named Peril and Multiple Peril Crop Insurance

Most agricultural insurance is traditional insurance that makes an indemnity payment when the farm household incurs a loss. To pay indemnities, the insurance provider must make estimates of loss for each farm household that makes a claim. Most of this discussion focuses on forms of crop insurance. Insurance for livestock is of a different class because weather events are not generally the major risk for livestock.

There are two dominant types of traditional crop insurance: (1) named peril, and (2) multiple peril. Named peril insurance involves assessing losses based upon a specific risk or peril. Hail insurance is the most common named peril insurance. For well over 100 years, hail insurance has been available mostly in North America and Europe. Hail damage is easily identifiable and special procedures have been developed to make field assessments of the degree of damage. Because hail losses are typically localized events, hail insurance has been offered in the marketplace without government subsidies. By contrast, multiple peril crop insurance, which covers losses due to any of a large number of risks, has rarely been offered without government subsidies. Implementation of multiple peril crop insurance becomes increasingly complex. If one is insuring for multiple perils, it is nearly impossible to first identify the "set of events" that may have created the losses and then perform a loss assessment that attempts to separate the actual loss by event. If there is crop loss, there is no clear way to tell if the loss is due to a weather event or to management practices. In North America, the "average" yield is estimated using individual farm records. If the yield is below a certain percentage of the "average" yield, a payment is made.

To provide weather insurance such as multiple peril crop insurance based on losses of individuals, an insurer must know a great deal about the individual who is being insured. There is almost always an imbalance of information that creates the twin problems of adverse selection and moral hazard. Monitoring and administrative costs to control adverse selection and moral hazard are costly (Hazell; Skees and Barnett, 1999).

Financing correlated losses is another major challenge for multiple peril crop insurance, as it is for most types of weather insurance. The correlated risk covered by most types of weather insurance can result in large numbers of claims at the same time in the same geographic area. This means that in the event of a severe weather event in the early years of establishing the indemnity fund, premiums may not be adequate to cover losses. Indemnities for a single severe weather event can exceed premiums in a single year by several times. It requires careful planning to ensure that adequate capital is available when major events create claims that exceed premiums. These issues are critical to the financial viability of any insurance company offering insurance against adverse weather events.

5.4.3   *Subsidizing Traditional Agricultural Insurance*

With the exception of hail insurance, most crop insurance has involved heavy subsidies to mitigate the expense of the premiums. For example, both the United States and Canada have three forms of subsidy: (1) a direct premium subsidy, (2) subsidy in the delivery costs, and (3) some form of government sharing for the most catastrophic risk. The world experience with multiple peril crop insurance has been particularly troublesome: the amount paid by the farmer is typically a fraction of the total cost of delivery and underwriting this form of insurance. For example, in the United States, the farmer pays only about 30 percent of the total cost. In middle income countries that have tried multiple peril crop insurance, direct subsidies have typically been lower. However, because of poor actuarial performance — indemnities exceeding premiums — there have been unintended subsidies. Poor actuarial performance will most certainly accompany multiple peril crop insurance programs that do not invest significantly in trying to control adverse selection and moral hazard (Hazell).

Of course, no country can afford to implement a crop insurance program fraught with problems that result in extremely poor actuarial performance. Furthermore, when there are large numbers of households that operate small units as in lower income countries, it is increasingly expensive to control the adverse selection and moral hazard that lead to poor actuarial performance. Clearly, the focus must be on how to make weather insurance more affordable for lower income countries.

5.5 A New Approach — Index Insurance for Weather Risk

Given that lower income countries can ill-afford to follow the path of higher income countries in providing subsidies for weather insurance such as multiple peril crop insurance programs, it is important to develop new approaches that focus on lowering many of the cost items discussed above. As will be more clearly developed below, index insurance is designed for that explicit purpose (Hazell and Skees; Skees, 2003).

The unique characteristic of index insurance that distinguishes it from traditional forms of insurance is that indemnity payments are based on values obtained from an index that serves as a proxy for losses rather than upon the individual losses of each policyholder. The underlying index is based upon an objective measure (for example, rainfall, wind speed, or temperature) that exhibits a strong correlation with the variable of interest (for example, crop yields, or default rates).

Index insurance has a defined threshold and a limit that establish the range of values over which indemnity payments can be made. The threshold marks the point at which payments begin. Once the threshold is reached, the payment increases incrementally as the value of the index approaches the limit. For example, an index insurance contract designed to transfer the risk of drought would begin making indemnity payments if rainfall levels, as measured at an agreed weather station, fall below the threshold over a defined time period, such as a month or a season. Indemnity payments would increase proportionately for each millimeter (mm) of rainfall below the threshold until the agreed limit is reached. The maximum indemnity would be paid when rainfall is less than, or equal to, the limit.

The *payment rate* for an index insurance contract is the same for each policyholder who has the same contract, regardless of the actual losses sustained by the policyholder. The amount of indemnity payment received will depend upon the amount of liability purchased (the value of the insurance).

The following example illustrates the structure of an index insurance contract for drought risk that begins making payments when rainfall is 100 mm or less. The maximum indemnity payment is made when rainfall is at or below 50 mm for the season.

- *Index Variable*: Total accumulated rainfall measured at a local weather station for the cropping season.
- *Threshold*: 100 mm of rainfall.
- *Limit*: 50 mm of rainfall.
- Liability purchased by the policyholder: $50,000.
- *Payment Rate*: Based upon shortfalls in rainfall, the payment rate is calculated as the difference between the threshold value and the actual realized value of the index, divided by the threshold minus the limit:
  = (threshold − actual value)/(threshold − limit)
  = (100 − actual value)/(100 − 50)
- *Indemnity Payment*: The payment rate multiplied by the total liability:
  = (100 − actual)/(100 − 50) × $50,000

Table 5.1 shows indemnity payments due under the contract for different scenarios. The amount of indemnity paid per mm of deficient rainfall is calculated by multiplying the payment rate by the amount of liability purchased ($50,000). If the threshold is 100 mm, the farmer is likely to experience economic losses when rain is less than that amount. Then, payment when rain is, for example, 80 mm (second case in Table 5.1) is

Table 5.1: Payments due under different rainfall level scenarios

Total rainfall	Indemnity payment due
110 mm	None. The threshold has not been reached
80 mm	$20,000
50 mm	$50,000
40 mm	$50,000. The limit of 50 mm has been exceeded

Source: Author.

as follows:

$$(100 - 80)/(100 - 50) \times \$50,000$$
$$= (20)/(50) \times \$50,000$$
$$= (0.40) \times \$50,000$$
$$= \$20,000$$

Regardless of the type of index on which an index insurance contract is based, when the threshold is reached, the amount of the payment made is based not on the actual losses sustained by the person who purchased the policy but on the value of the index relative to the threshold (subject to the limit) and the amount of the liability purchased. The payment could be less than, or more than, the loss sustained by the individual policyholder.

5.5.1 *Advantages of Index Insurance*

When comparing index insurance to traditional farm-level agricultural insurance, it is useful to recall the equation that highlights the various components that influence the price of insurance. The advantage of index insurance for lower income countries is that it can be simpler and less costly to administer relative to traditional forms of insurance. Index insurance can control some of the cost factors associated with weather insurance in the following ways:

Simpler Information Requirements. Because index insurance indemnity payments are not tied to actual losses incurred, there is no need to classify potential policyholders according to their risk exposure. As already discussed, this is a significant informational constraint on traditional agricultural insurance. It is unlikely that the information required for traditional agricultural insurance will be readily available in a lower income country, and it would require a great amount of effort to develop or obtain the information. However, in the case of index insurance based on rainfall, no household-level information is needed. The risk assessment uses historic rainfall data to evaluate the impact and frequency of insufficient rainfall.

No Loss Adjustment. One of the significant challenges for traditional insurance products is the high cost of loss adjustment. As discussed, under a traditional insurance policy, the insurer has to determine whether each individual household has suffered an insured loss and, if so, the extent of the loss. This can be extremely costly, particularly in remote rural areas. In the case of index insurance, there is no need to conduct household-level loss adjustment. Indemnities are based solely on the realization of the underlying index relative to the pre-specified threshold.

Reduction of Moral Hazard. Because the indemnity does not depend on the individual's actual losses, the policyholder cannot change his or her behavior to increase the likelihood of receiving a payment.

Reduction of Adverse Selection. Index insurance is based on widely available information, which reduces the opportunity that informational asymmetries can be exploited or that the most risky individuals will be the primary purchasers of the insurance.

Low Administrative Cost. Indemnity payments are based solely on the realized value of the underlying index as measured by government agencies or other third parties. Without the need for individual risk assessments or loss adjustment, the costs to the insurer can be significantly less, particularly for individuals with very small units.

Standardized and Transparent Structure. Index insurance contracts can have simple and uniform formats. Contracts do not need to be tailored to each policyholder and so, again, administrative costs are lower. Thus, index insurance contracts should be more easily understood by the insured than many forms of traditional insurance.

Reinsurance Function. Since index insurance pays for large correlated losses, it can also be used to protect local insurers against large losses from correlated weather risks. As mentioned previously, the potential for large financial losses from correlated weather risk is an inhibiting factor to the development of insurance markets. Using index insurance as reinsurance — insurance on an insurance portfolio — would make it easier for local insurers to offer traditional farm-level agricultural insurance without the threat of large financial losses that could result from a natural disaster.

5.5.2 *Limitations and Preconditions of Index Insurance*

Index insurance addresses some of the factors that limit the development of traditional insurance in lower income countries. However, it is not without its limitations. This highlights the importance of conducting a thorough feasibility study to determine if index insurance is appropriate. The reader is referred to the original primer for further discussion on how to address these issues. Some of the challenges of index insurance are the following:

Basis Risk. With an index insurance contract, there is basis risk, which is the chance that the indemnity payment a policyholder receives does not match the actual loss. The insured could suffer a loss and not receive any or enough indemnity to compensate for the loss. It is also possible that an insured who has not suffered a loss could receive an indemnity. Too much basis risk will deter interest because individuals will feel that the index will not be representative of their loss experience and will therefore offer them poor protection against risk. While basis risk is an inherent problem with index insurance, basis risk can be minimized through product design and application.

Reliable and Accessible Data. For index insurance to be viable, it is critical that the underlying index is objectively and accurately measured. If data used for the index cannot be trusted or are not accurate, the system will fail. Making the data publicly available to both insurers and policyholders can help build confidence in the accuracy of the numbers. Whether provided by government or other third-party sources, index measurements must be widely disseminated and secure from tampering.

Education. Potential policyholders may have no previous experience with insurance or similar products. Educational initiatives are necessary to convey the concepts of index insurance and help users assess whether or not these instruments can provide them with effective risk management. Local insurers and government regulators are likely to require some education on index insurance.

Financing of Large Losses. In lower income countries, local insurance companies typically do not have the financial resources to offer weather insurance without adequate and affordable reinsurance to protect against financial losses that could occur if many policyholders suffer losses from the same event. Effective financing arrangements must be made to ensure that some type of reinsurance is available for the insurer who offers index insurance, whether it is through international reinsurers, national or provincial governments, or international development organizations.

While index insurance can potentially overcome many of the problems associated with traditional insurance, there are still significant challenges that must be overcome for index insurance to become a viable risk mitigation mechanism in lower income countries. Governments and donors can play an important role in addressing these challenges.

5.6   Role of Governments and Donors

Governments often feel the pressure to act. However, they may not know what to do or what the options are. In many countries, governments do not consider the role that insurance markets can play in coping with exposure to weather risks. Instead, they tend to focus on the provision of government aid following an extreme weather event. The expectation of this aid among citizens reduces the demand for weather insurance.

Donors and development programs should inform governments of their options and encourage government action that does not distort the market or crowd out the private sector. For long-term sustainability of insurance markets, it is best if the role of government is one of facilitator and not direct deliverer of insurance products. This role includes establishing an appropriate enabling environment and providing certain public goods. More specifically, a government or donor can support such things as:

- Improvements in the legal and regulatory environment;
- Improvements in data systems and data collection;
- Educational efforts about the use of weather insurance;
- Product development; and
- Access to global markets.

In some cases, governments or donor agencies may choose to provide financing for catastrophic losses as discussed below. In general, however, governments should not be in the business of providing insurance. In any case, governments should not provide direct premium subsidies, which undermine the incentives to private-sector insurance companies. Also, such subsidies generally favor wealthier farm households and thus erode poverty objectives. Even targeted premium subsidies rarely work as planned.

5.6.1 *Supporting Improvements in the Legal and Regulatory Environment*

Insurance is a highly regulated activity in all countries. Even if the index products are developed as non-insurance products, they will likely be subject to some form of regulatory control. A failure to consider the impact of the regulatory system and to obtain the necessary regulatory authorizations could result in the provision of the index insurance being unlawful and in the providers of the insurance, and possibly intermediaries, committing a criminal offence. Unfortunately, in many lower income countries, laws and regulations are simply not in place to accommodate the development and use of these types of weather insurance products. Without proper contract law and enforcement, the market for these innovations will not develop.

Government and donor support can be quite helpful in getting technical assistance to lower income countries to update their laws and regulations, making them consistent with international law to improve the chances of gaining access to global markets for risk transfer. Human capacity building within financial regulatory agencies is also a critical public investment.

In many lower income countries, the legal and regulatory systems are not sufficiently developed to facilitate and regulate insurance contracts. Financial regulators may not have the capacity to regulate the special nature of weather insurance. Regulators must ensure that insurers' capital reserves are sufficient to meet potential claims, or that insurers have access to capital through reinsurance to handle extreme losses.

Insurance markets may be missing in lower income countries because of a number of weaknesses in the enabling environment. Stable governments and contract enforcement procedures are preconditions for rural financial markets to work properly. It is also important to have an insurance regulatory body that understands the differences between various classes of insurance.

If an effective legal system is not in place, insurance contracts may lose validity. For example, it is not uncommon for insurance companies to refuse to pay valid claims simply because there is no effective oversight. This, however, can undermine public confidence and demand for insurance. On the other hand, insurers may be reluctant to sell policies if there is a possibility that the government could alter the terms of the insurance contract after the insurance is sold. If judges and lawyers do not have a good understanding of insurance law, insurers may be forced to make indemnity payments in excess of their obligations under the policy.

5.6.2   *Supporting Improvements in Data Systems and Data Collection*

In supporting the development of weather insurance markets, governments can have a direct and immediate effect by providing greater access to existing data. Data are critical to the development of weather insurance markets and they must be credible. The equipment involved in developing weather data must be reliable, accurate, and secure from any potential tampering, and professionals who work with the equipment must be trustworthy. Most governments have reasonably good systems for collecting weather data, but they are missing quality systems for archiving and sharing historic weather data. Even more troublesome, some countries do not view the collection of weather data using government resources as a public good. Rather, they view it as a profitable resource and consequently charge for access to the data.

Other types of information are also important in the development of weather insurance: for example, yield data and other information on losses caused by extreme weather events, changes in land use and input use intensity, and records of past disaster management activities or infrastructure changes. Government can play an important role in facilitating index insurance by collecting, maintaining, and archiving data needed to develop index insurance for weather risks for public use and also for use by those with commercial interests wishing to develop innovative weather insurance products.

5.6.3   Supporting Educational Efforts About the Use of Weather Insurance

Potential users must be educated about the advantages and disadvantages of index insurance products. To increase the likelihood that information is presented in a balanced way and that sufficient investments are made in a broader educational effort for an untested product, public funds from governments and/or donors may be required. If insurance is not commonly available in the countryside, general education about insurance and risk management may be necessary. Index insurance policies are typically much simpler and easier to understand than traditional farm-level insurance policies. However, potential users may need help in evaluating how well the index insurance works for their individual risks.

5.6.4   Supporting Product Development

One of the challenges associated with private-sector development of new financial products is the ease with which they can be copied and replicated by others. This "free rider" problem discourages many companies from making initial investments in new product development, especially in underdeveloped markets. Thus, some level of government and/or donor support for product development can be justified. These investments should be targeted at feasibility studies and developing pilot tests of new products with the involvement of local private-sector partners. Every attempt should be made to ensure that the knowledge and technology for new product development will be passed on to local experts as soon as possible.

5.6.5   Supporting Access to Global Markets

Ultimately, access to global insurance and reinsurance markets is important for developing sustainable weather insurance instruments. In most cases, domestic insurance companies in lower income countries lack the financial resources needed to withstand the large losses that accompany the significant adverse weather events that damage crops or assets. This is one reason why insurance for weather risk is not offered by domestic insurance markets. Access to external financing to cover large losses when they occur is critical for a solvent insurance market. Regulatory officials must understand how to establish rules and regulations that both facilitate access to global insurance and reinsurance markets and regulate how domestic insurance companies must protect their positions to enable them to make full payment of indemnities if there are significant losses. By doing so, a regulator can facilitate access to global markets. The regulator can also provide information about global markets to local stakeholders, change regulations to allow local companies to use these markets, and support locally appropriate product development, as discussed above. These tasks are clearly within a government's regulatory and administrative spheres of influence and can aid in facilitating market development for weather insurance with relatively modest budgetary outlays. Governments should refer to international experience and best practice guidance to establish an appropriate enabling environment, provide public goods that support market development, and undertake any other interventions. Governments should be particularly cautious of pressure from narrow special interest groups for rule changes favorable to their causes.

5.6.6 *Supporting Financing for Catastrophic Losses*

Until a sufficient volume of business has been established, extreme losses for the insurance pool may need to be underwritten, perhaps through contingent loans from government and/or donors, until international reinsurers are willing to participate in the risk sharing of a new product. For example, the World Bank has a contingent loan for the Mongolian Index-based Livestock Insurance Pilot (Mahul and Skees). If losses for the insurance companies and the domestic reinsurance fund are fully exhausted, the World Bank loan can be accessed to make indemnity payments.

Another possible role for government or donors is to provide financing for low-probability, high-consequence events. Evidence suggests that those at risk tend to ignore the probability of the most extreme and infrequent loss events, but insurers do not ignore these events and consider the probability of such catastrophic losses when setting premiums. This creates a gap between what buyers are willing to pay and what sellers are willing to accept for protection against very infrequent but catastrophic losses. Governments can provide the financing in a number of ways that still provide incentives to domestic insurers to operate in a proper fashion (Lewis and Murdock; Skees and Barnett, 1999; Skees, 1999).

5.7 Applications of Index Insurance

There are examples of how index insurance is being used to manage weather risk in lower income countries. While index insurance relies upon certain preconditions and principles, each country presents unique challenges that will influence how index insurance is structured and implemented. As the following examples illustrate, index insurance can support several common development objectives, including protecting rural livelihoods and reducing poverty, strengthening rural finance, and improving disaster relief and safety net policies.

5.7.1 Examples of Household-Level Index Insurance

India. Rainfall index insurance has been sold by private companies since 2003 to compensate farmers for agricultural losses due to drought and excess rain. In 2005 the Indian government insurance company also began selling this form of insurance. Thus far, these insurance products are being sold with no subsidies. In 2005 about 250,000 small Indian farm households purchased some form of index insurance for weather risk. The interest has been significant enough that private investments are being made to increase the number of weather stations to reduce basis risk (Bryla and Syroka).

Mongolia. The Mongolian pilot project, supported by the World Bank, offers insurance to herders to protect against high livestock losses due to severe winters (Mahul and Skees). Private insurance companies sold index insurance for livestock to 2,400 herders in 2006, the first pilot year. The participation rate exceeded expectations for the first year — around 9 percent of the herders who were eligible purchased the insurance in the first year. The index is based upon county-level livestock mortality rates that are collected by the national statistics office. Though the index is based on livestock mortality and not on a specific weather event, the major underlying cause of large livestock losses is summer drought followed by severe winter weather. Importantly, the Mongolian project explicitly separates the commercial and the social side of the insurance. Commercial insurers sell the Base Insurance Product, which indemnifies for losses when livestock mortality for the county is between 7 and 30 percent. When losses exceed 30 percent mortality, the government pays for them with a Disaster Response Product. Herders who do not purchase the Base Insurance Product can pay a small administrative fee to register for the Disaster Response Product. Three of the primary rural lenders that are making micro loans to herders have already discounted interest rates for herders purchasing the Base Insurance Product.

Malawi. The World Bank helped to develop a rainfall index insurance pilot in 2005 for groundnut farmers in Malawi to protect against drought losses (Hess and Syroka). Nearly 900 farmers purchased the insurance in the first year (Bryla and Syroka). The intended outcome is to improve access to credit for smallholder farmers. Two rural financial institutions agreed to extend credit to farmers who purchase the index insurance, enabling the farmers to obtain loans for purchasing higher-quality certified seed.

5.7.2   *Example of Intermediate-Level Index Insurance*

Peru. Developed under a USAID project, an El Niño Southern Oscillation Index Insurance pilot has received preliminary approval by the banking and insurance regulators. The ENSO Insurance is based on an index of sea surface temperatures off the coast of Peru and would pay when there are anomalies in these temperatures. When the Pacific Ocean warms significantly, there is extreme rainfall and flooding in the northern regions of Peru. These periods of extreme rainfall have caused significant crop failures and damage to infrastructure and the rural economy. These conditions also result in a large increase in the number of loans that are not paid back to rural lenders. The ENSO Insurance is designed to protect the portfolio risk of the intermediaries — the microfinance institutions and other rural lenders. When the catastrophe occurs, the rural lenders incur added costs because they must add more provisions or reserves as their loan problems increase. This occurs at the same time that depositors, due to the disaster, begin withdrawing their money and the poor are requesting more loans to help them face the crisis.

5.7.3 Examples of National- and International-Level Index Insurance

Mexico. The Mexican government is using index insurance to reinsure two disaster relief funds: FONDEN and FAPACC. FONDEN (Fondo de Desastres Naturales) — the Mexican National Fund for Natural Disasters — was created in 1995 to provide disaster relief funds for the repair of uninsured infrastructure and relief for low-income victims of disasters. FAPACC (Fondo para Atender a la Población Afectada por Contingencias Climatológicas) is a specialized natural disaster fund established to provide immediate assistance to restore the productivity of subsistence farmers by protecting the productive assets of vulnerable populations without access to formal insurance markets (ISMEA). The program offers contingent payments for damage to productive assets caused by drought, frost, hail, excess rainfall and flood, and windstorm. By using index insurance to reinsure the government emergency response, the government is able to maintain the sustainability and solvency of the disaster relief programs.

Ethiopia. The World Bank and the United Nations World Food Program (WFP) have developed a rainfall index insurance contract to pre-finance some share of the WFP emergency operations in Ethiopia (Syroka and Wilcox). The index insurance, purchased through a global reinsurer, AxaRe, is designed to provide the WFP with rapid and predictable funding and is expected to improve the timing of its response to a drought crisis by four months. The amount of the protection purchased was a fraction of the total food needs, demonstrating that blending emergency food reserves with financial solutions that use index insurance may be a better way to deal with these problems than simply depending on deploying food aid after an event. While an international donor purchased this food security index insurance, it should be possible to structure similar indexes that could be sold to a wide range of donors, NGOs, or local entities that need quick response when events clearly suggest that a food security problem is emerging.

5.8 A Look to the Future

Index insurance for weather risk has many potential applications. For example, feasibility work funded by the Inter-American Development Bank focused on using measurements of the inflow of water into an irrigation reservoir in Mexico to pay when the storage of water is well below normal and results in large cutbacks in released water. This type of risk mitigation could be used to facilitate water markets and, given the importance of irrigation in many lower income countries, could be a highly important innovation. There are also reported examples of private-sector transactions in lower income countries whereby agribusiness intermediaries such as input suppliers and processors are using index insurance to protect against business losses that are correlated with adverse weather events. This type of use has been extended to other industries. In India, for example, rainfall index insurance is being offered to salt and brick manufacturers whose production can be disrupted by excessive rainfall. Exporters, importers, and processors of agricultural products may also find value in using index insurance that pays when there are certain adverse weather events.

Advances in technology are increasing the availability of data that could be used to support index insurance. Satellite technology is quickly evolving to provide more and better quality information on flood events as well as crop and pasture conditions. The cost of these data has declined considerably in recent years. The government of Vietnam is considering the use of radar satellite technology that penetrates cloud cover to support flood index insurance for rice production in the Mekong Delta. Satellite information is reliable and can provide up-to-the-minute data. It could be used by the private sector, non-governmental organizations, governments, or international organizations to provide index insurance for agricultural production or disaster relief.

Indeed, the potential applications of index insurance are noteworthy. Still, these innovations and applications will not come without careful consideration of where index insurance for weather can work and where it cannot. As emphasized throughout this paper, development of index insurance products requires careful dialogue with government policy makers and regulators. Though weather risk can be a major constraint in economic development, it is by no means the only constraint. Managing weather risk may not be the highest priority or the most beneficial endeavor for a country. Developing effective and sustainable insurance programs requires time and a commitment from stakeholders. Discussions with stakeholders will reveal their needs and priorities. A thorough feasibility study should determine if index insurance would be appropriate, beneficial, and economical. While this dialogue may not result in the development of index insurance products, a careful feasibility study that examines weather risks and how society is currently paying for these large weather risks is an important activity. Finally, index insurance products can also serve as the first step in developing more advanced weather insurance products and improving access to broader rural financial services in lower income countries. It is hoped that this paper has provided the needed information to encourage consideration of this important innovation.

Bibliography

Anderson, J. R. (2002). "Risk Management in Rural Development: A Review." Agriculture and Rural Development (ARD) Department Strategy Background Paper 7, The World Bank, February.

Barnett, B. J., C. B. Barrett, and J. R. Skees (2006). "Poverty Traps and Index-based Risk Transfer Products." Unpublished Working Paper, July.

Barrett, C. B. and J. G. McPeak (2005). "Poverty Traps and Safety Net." *Poverty, Inequality, and Development: Essays in Honor of Erik Thorbecke*. A. de Janvry and R. Kanbur, eds. Norwell, MA: Kluwer Academic Publishers.

Binswanger, H. P. and M. R. Rosenzweig (1986). "Behavioral and Material Determinants of Production Relations in Agriculture." *Journal of Development Studies* 22: 503–539.

Bryla, E. and J. Syroka (2007). "Developing Index-based Insurance for Agriculture in Developing Countries." United Nations Sustainable Development Innovation Briefs, Issue 2, March.

Carter, M. R., P. D. Little, T. Mogues, and W. Negatu (2005). "The Long-Term Impacts of Short-Term Shocks: Poverty Traps and Environmental Disasters in Ethiopia and Honduras." University of Wisconsin-Madison, Department of Agricultural and Applied Economics, BASIS Collaborative Research Support Program (CRSP) Brief No. 28, May.

Dercon, S. (2004). "Growth and Shocks: Evidence from Rural Ethiopia." *Journal of Development Economics* 74: 309–329.

Dercon, S. (1996). "Risk, Crop Choice, and Savings: Evidence from Tanzania." *Economic Development and Cultural Change* 44: 485–513.

Hazell, P. B. R. (1992). "The Appropriate Role of Agricultural Insurance in Developing Countries." *Journal of International Development* 4: 567–581.

Hazell, P. B. R. and J. R. Skees (2006). "Insuring against Bad Weather: Recent Thinking." *India in a Globalising World: Some Aspects of Macroeconomy, Agriculture, and Poverty.* R. Radhakrishna, S. K. Rao, S. Mahendra Dev, and K. Subbarao, eds. New Delhi: Academic Foundation and Hyderabad: Centre for Economic and Social Studies (CESS).

Hess, U., J. R. Skees, A. Stoppa, B. J. Barnett, and J. Nash (2005). "Managing Agricultural Production Risk: Innovations in Developing Countries." Agriculture and Rural Development (ARD) Department Report No. 32727-GLB, The World Bank, June.

Hess, U. and J. Syroka (2005). "Weather-based Insurance in Southern Africa: The Case of Malawi." Agriculture and Rural Development (ARD) Department Working Paper 13, The World Bank, January.

ISMEA (Istituto di servizi per il mercato agricolo alimentare) (2006). *Risk Management in Agriculture for Natural Hazards.* Rome, December.

Lewis, C. M. and K. C. Murdock (1996). "The Role of Government Contracts in Discretionary Reinsurance Markets for Natural Disasters." *Journal of Risk and Insurance* 63: 567–597.

Mahul, O. and J. R. Skees (2006). "Piloting Index-based Livestock Insurance in Mongolia." Access Finance: A Newsletter Published by the Financial Sector Vice Presidency of the World Bank, Issue 10, The World Bank, March.

McCord, M. J. (2003). "The Lure of Microinsurance: Why MFIs Should Work with Insurers." Briefing Note 1, MicroInsurance Centre, January.

Rosenzweig, M. R. and H. P. Binswanger (1993). "Wealth, Weather Risk and Composition and Profitability of Agricultural Investments." *Economic Journal* 103: 56–78.

Skees, J. R. (2003). "Risk Management Challenges in Rural Financial Markets: Blending Risk Management Innovations with Rural Finance." The thematic papers presented at the USAID Conference: Paving the Way Forward for Rural Finance: An International Conference on Best Practices, Washington, DC, June 2–4.

Skees, J. R. (1999). "Opportunities for Improved Efficiency in Risk Sharing Using Capital Markets." *American Journal of Agricultural Economics* 81: 1228–1233.

Skees, J. R. and B. J. Barnett (2006). "Enhancing Micro Finance Using Index-based Risk Transfer Products." *Agricultural Finance Review* 66: 235–250.

Skees, J. R. and B. J. Barnett (1999). "Conceptual and Practical Considerations for Sharing Catastrophic/Systemic Risks." *Review of Agricultural Economics* 21: 424–441.

Skees, J. R., D. Varangis, D. Larson, and P. Siegel (2005). "Can Financial Markets Be Tapped to Help Poor People Cope with Weather Risks?" *Insurance against Poverty*. S. Dercon, ed. Oxford: Oxford University Press, WIDER Studies in Development Economics.

Syroka, J. and R. Wilcox (2006). "Rethinking International Disaster and Finance." *Journal of International Affairs* 59: 197–214.

PART II

BIOTECHNOLOGY AND THE POOR

Chapter Six

Overcoming Poverty Through Improved Agricultural Technology

Robert W. Herdt*

Given the experience of the past 50 years, how should technology be designed to contribute positively to the lives of poor rural people? Many are skeptical that technology has or will contribute positively to the lives of the poor.[1] They see agricultural technology as one of the forces keeping people poor. For them, technology is part of a system reinforcing the power structure that controls wealth and income and concentrates it in the hands of the already wealthy. To be explicit about my own position: I am convinced that agricultural technological change has been, on balance,

---

*Robert W. Herdt is the International Professor of Applied Economics and Management (Adjunct) at Cornell University. He is also Advisor to the Director of International Programs of the College of Agriculture and Life Sciences, and a member of the Advisory Council to the Cornell Institute for International Food and Agriculture, and The Essential Electronic Agricultural Library. Before coming to Cornell, Herdt was Director of Agricultural program, and then Vice President, of the Rockefeller Foundation; Agricultural Economist at IRRI; was on the faculty of the Department of Agricultural Economics at the University of Illinois; and on the staff of the Secretariat of the CGIAR at the World Bank in Washington, DC (http://www.people.cornell.edu/pages/rwh13/).

[1] Much of the literature about the "Green Revolution" is in this tradition. In some ways the term has become a rallying cry for those who oppose technological change. See the review by Freebairn, 1995; Holt-Gimenez, Altieri and Rosset, 2006.

a positive force for improving the lives of poor people in the developing world.[2] In this paper I examine research that speaks to the issue and argue that while we can learn from looking at past experience, we must go beyond that experience. Future technology should be designed in the light of reasonable expectations about the future economic, social, institutional and ecological environments in which poor rural people will live, and what we know about how technology makes its impact.

I began with the predisposition that the best way to understand the central question is to examine empirical studies that show the situation before and after, or with and without, technological change. A vast literature related to the "Green Revolution" exists and surely, I thought, there must be many empirical, data-rich studies that leave little doubt about the answer to the question. This paper summarizes a selected few of the available empirical studies about the impact of agricultural technical change. Such studies cover a range across a continuum best characterized by its extremes — at one extreme are studies that carefully follow changes in a small group of households in one place over a long period of time of dynamic technology; at the other extreme are complex, data-based models that can be used to simulate the results of introducing almost any conceivable technology, policy or institutional change on dozens of groups in many countries. This paper may be seen as a journey from one end of this spectrum (micro-level observations before-and-after change) to the other (macro-level models capable of posing and answering complex "what-if" questions). Insights are gained from studies across the spectrum, but one extreme is of limited value without the other. Global models grounded in rigorous understanding of local situations are more satisfactory than straightforward before-and-after or with-and-without comparisons. The

---

[2] Indeed, I have spent my professional career promoting technological innovation in developing country agriculture, having become favorably disposed toward the proposition early on (see: Herdt and Mellor, 1964) and reinforced in it along the way (Herdt and Capule, 1983; Barker and Herdt, 1985). Throughout, I have been even more convinced it was more important to do something I *thought* was positive than to spend my career seeking to become *absolutely* sure of this or another proposition. Reviewing the arguments does not contradict that position, although I wonder if it will change the minds of those convinced to the contrary.

agricultural technology of most value to poor people can build on the latest scientific breakthroughs across the spectrum, but must be tailored to the bio-physical agricultural realities and the social, economic, political and institutional realities of the local places in which those poor people find themselves.

To anticipate the conclusion of this paper: Many empirical studies report significant improvements in the lives of poor rural people after the introduction of new technologies; other studies report no change and some report negative effects. One count of the number of papers with positive and negative results shows there are about as many that reach one conclusion as the other, although studies in Asia tend to show positive results and those in Latin America tend to show negative results. I conclude those differences have much more to do with the pre-existing distribution of land, the institutional environment that determines power relationships and the functioning of economic markets in different societies than about agricultural technology *per se*. I conclude therefore, that the lack of technological improvements to drive food supply ahead of food demand can lead to food scarcity and misery; however, technology alone cannot offset an oppressive political system or overcome entrenched monopolistic market power. Dynamic agricultural technology is a necessary but not a sufficient condition for overcoming poverty in early stages of development.

6.1   Poverty, Technology and Their Relationship

Figure 6.1 intuitively illustrates the way technology and poverty often seem to be posed. Technology is improving (increasing) moving from left to right; poverty is improving (lessening) moving up. The upper right quadrant with the X's shows situations where technology improved and poverty improved; the lower right quadrant with the Z's depicts situations where technology improved and poverty worsened. The other two quadrants complete the possibilities. Within the quadrants one may distinguish situations like X_1, X_2, and X_3, where poverty is improving faster than technology, as contrasted with X_4 where poverty was reduced by a smaller proportion than technology was improved. One might compare before-and-after or with-and-without studies to determine where the preponderance of experience has fallen.

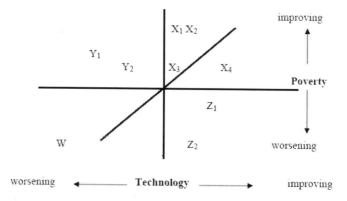

Figure 6.1: Relationship between poverty and technology

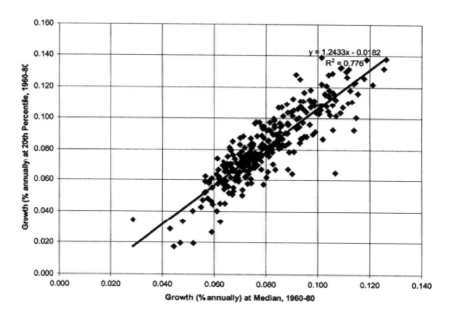

Figure 6.2: Growth of US farm income at median and 20th percentile
Source: Gardner, 2000.

Figure 6.2 shows how in the United States the farm income of the poorest 20% of farmers in over 300 counties changed compared to average farm income in the same counties from 1960 to 1980, a period of significant technological change. The fitted regression equation shows that *"agricultural incomes at the lower levels increased more than proportionally with average incomes."*[3] A similar analysis using data from 69 countries during 1960–2000 gave similar results (Gallup, Radelet *et al.*, 1999).

Those studies relate income growth to poverty, however, not agricultural technology change and poverty. Research on that relationship poses challenges because of the difficulty inherent in measuring both poverty and technology and the relative scarcity of data on income distribution in developing countries. Even when data are available, they have limitations.

Relative measures of poverty are simplest. Individuals (or groups of people with a given income) are arrayed from poorest to wealthiest and the lowest income fraction, say 10 or 20 percent, is defined as "the poor." While useful for illustrations like Figure 6.2, this approach has limited value for tracking movement out of poverty because some fraction will always be at the bottom of the distribution. Another limitation is that the lowest 10% in one place may have consumption patterns similar to middle or high income in another place, raising questions about the appropriateness of grouping them.

References to poverty by international agencies and the media often refer to the number of people living on less than $1.00 a day. Few would disagree that such persons are poor, even if the price of food is extremely low,[4] although people living on less than $2 a day are also poor and it is arbitrary to say that moving above $1 or even $2 a day is really moving out of poverty. Still, the number of people below the $1 and $2 a day poverty lines gives some indication of poverty, and if the number declines poverty has fallen. A considerable improvement on the number of poor is provided by indicators that take into account both the number of people below the line and the distance each person or sub-group is below that standard (Foster, Greer *et al.*, 1984).[5] When the focus is on the poor in rural areas,

---

[3] Gardner, 2000, p. 1066.

[4] Many studies make use of the purchasing power parity (PPP) concept to compare income across countries and over time. It uses a careful economic approach to correct local income data for exchange rates and inflation and is probably the best widely available international measure of income.

[5] A huge literature exists, an example of which is: Maxwell, 1999.

data availability becomes even more challenging — there simply are not many developing country data sets that reflect rural income distribution, and few of those are suitable for cross-country comparisons.

Measuring technology as implied by Figure 6.1 is challenging also. Technology is "the way things are done" and is not amenable to being measured like length or weight. It can be characterized as improving or worsening only for well-defined circumstances. An agricultural technology may be characterized as a particular combination of labor, machinery, seed, fertilizer, and pesticide.[6] Different types of agricultural technologies are each better-or-more poorly suited for specific soil and climate conditions that may vary within fairly short distances. Agriculturalists call areas of suitability "agro-ecological zones" or "recommendation domains," recognizing this reality. Technology "improves" when the ratio of output to input increases, but that ratio depends on the "suitability" of the technology to immutable factors like soil and climate. Because outputs and inputs are purchased and sold, the suitability of technology is also affected by the costs of inputs and prices, a factor that may be most obvious in case labor and machinery are important inputs in a technology.

Measures often used to reflect the level of technology, such as fertilizer application rates, percent of land irrigated or percent of a crop planted to a variety, are really indicators of input use.[7] They may be useful reflections of the "level of technology" within homogenous agro-ecological zones, but are less useful for indicating levels across such conditions. The greater the range of conditions, the less suitable such an approach, and it is quite limited for cross-country work. As in the case of poverty, a relative level of technology may be a lot easier to measure than an absolute level of technology. Despite the difficulty in measuring the relationship between changes in poverty and technology, many researchers have sought to understand it. In what follows, I briefly summarize several such studies.

---

[6] In parallel and perhaps of interest to those at this conference, a financial technology may be characterized as a particular combination of finance literacy, credit terms, information flow, risk management and enforcement mechanisms, but that concept is not pursued here.

[7] See analyses of agricultural productivity like: Griliches, 1963; Antle, 1983; Hayami and Ruttan, 1985; Norton, Ortiz and Pardey, 1992; Evenson, Pray and Rosegrant, 1999.

6.1.1   *Palanpur Village, India*[8]

Palanpur Village was first the subject of research in 1957–1958 when it was identified as a potential site for a government-sponsored credit cooperative. Located in the state of Uttar Pradesh about 8 hours' travel from Delhi, the village was the subject of continued research over the next 40 years, with surveys in 1962–1963, 1974–1975, 1983–1984, and 1993 (the final study was less detailed than the earlier ones and some information is not available for that year). Those most recently involved in the research regard its choice as fortunate for, "*whilst no village in a country with more than a half-million villages can be regarded as representative, it was more important that the village should not have some major peculiar feature.*"[9] In the 1950s it was a village of some 500 people, dominated by agriculture using technology hundreds of years old. Water was lifted by animal power using a "Persian Wheel," wheat varieties grew five to six feet tall, wheat and rice yields were low, fields were planted to several crop mixtures, most production was for home consumption and over 50 percent of the population was in poverty.

Three driving forces dominated events over the next 40 years: demographic growth, resulting in a doubling of population; agricultural technical change including the rapid spread of irrigation using new machinery, changing crop varieties and chemical fertilizer; and growing employment opportunities in nearby towns. By 1974 nearly half the wheat was planted to semi-dwarf wheat varieties 2.5 to 3 feet tall rather than 5 to 6 feet, "normal" wheat yields had more than doubled, real income per capita had nearly doubled, and the population had increased to 750 people. Changes continued, and by 1983 about 60 percent of wheat fields were planted to semi-dwarf wheat varieties, normal wheat yields had increased another 50 percent, population had increased to 960 and real agricultural wages were double their 1957 level. By the 1990s many villagers commuted to those towns for regular paid work.[10] The authors seem predisposed to the

---

[8] The material in this section is taken from Lanjouw and Stern, 1998. Any incorrect interpretations of the material in that book are the responsibilities of the author of this paper.

[9] *Ibid.*, p. vi.

[10] *Ibid.*, p. vii.

Table 6.1:   Agricultural indicators in Palanpur Village, India

	1957–1958	1962–1963	1974–1975	1983–1984
% semi-dwarf wheat	0	0	45	60
Yield of wheat	41	41	114	101
"Normal" yield of wheat	45	50	100	155
Real agricultural wages	2.5	2.3	3.1	5.0
Real income/capita	161	152	275	194
Population	528	585	757	960
% in poverty	47	54	11	34

Source: Taken from various tables in (Dreze, Lanjouw et al., 1998).

"common argument that the 'Green Revolution' technology usually leads to a sharp increase in income inequality ... and it may come as a surprise that income inequality was lower after than before the event ... the available evidence would be hard to reconcile with the notion that the Green Revolution is typically associated with a marked increase in local income inequality."[11]

Table 6.1 shows that change over the period was not linear, thus it is difficult to separate short-term fluctuations from longer-term trends. The authors point out the difficulty of assessing income changes because of the differences from one survey to the next, the potential sensitivity to "the choice of price index to use to deflate nominal income figures in different years ... and, this is the chief difficulty, private incomes fluctuate a great deal from year to year, mainly due to the varying quality of the harvest."[12] This leads the authors to introduce the concept of "normal" yields as a way of abstracting from weather-related influence in particular years. The proportion of irrigated land increased from 50 percent in 1957–1958 to nearly 100 percent in 1974–1975, the new wheat varieties were rapidly adopted after 1962–1963 and other changes continued.[13] Wheat yields doubled, real agricultural wages increased by 50 percent and the proportion of the village below the poverty line fell sharply, even while the total population

---

[11] Ibid., p. 164.
[12] Dreze, Lanjouw and Sharma, 1998, p. 161.
[13] Ibid., p. 135.

was growing. But fluctuations in economic conditions meant that poverty continued to be a threat.

The authors conclude: "For this village we submit that the relationship between technological change and economic inequality is, for practical purposes, a minor issue ... The point is that whatever change has taken place in the distribution of income or wealth has negligible social significance compared to the **persistent** inequalities relating to ownership, caste, gender, and education."[14] The degree of income inequality in the village was not much different in 1983–1984 than before the new technology had been introduced. It is possible that agricultural technology might have had the effect of worsening income inequality while other forces offset that effect. However, it seems just the opposite was the case, because between 1974–1975 and 1983–1984: "the strongest component in the rise in inequality was associated with the continued growth of outside jobs which had now become distributed more strongly toward the richer households ... Inequality was further increased by the effects of a poor agricultural year."[15] Therefore, despite their predisposition to the opposite, the authors reached a relatively robust conclusion — that new agricultural technology improved the distribution of income and reduced poverty in Palanpur.

6.1.2   *East Laguna Village, Philippines*[16]

East Laguna Village was selected in 1976 as "a typical rice village" to serve as the site for an intensive observation of rural economic dynamics. From then through 1997, it was the subject of 10 household surveys on various aspects of agricultural technology and rural life and an intensive, year-long record-keeping project (Hayami, Kikuchi *et al.*, 1978). Unknown at the time of its selection, the same village had been the subject of a reconnaissance survey on agrarian structure and rural life in 1966. At that time this small village, isolated in the midst of rice fields, took more than four hours of hard travel to reach from Manila. A decade earlier, in the mid-1950s the national

---

[14] *Ibid.*, p. 227.

[15] Lanjouw and Stern, 1998, p. 407.

[16] This section draws on the quarter-century of research in the village by Yujiro Hayami, reported in Hayami and Kikuchi, 2000.

government had constructed an irrigation system that enabled farmers to change from producing one crop of rainfed rice to growing two crops of rice in a year, effectively doubling production. In 1962 an elementary school was opened in the village and in 1965 a country road connecting it to the nearest town was completed. Over 40% of farmers were using small two-wheel tractors for land preparation in the middle 1960s, before the modern varieties were introduced. Located close to the International Rice Research Institute (IRRI), farmers in the village adopted new IRRI varieties in the middle 1960s, as soon as they were available. By 1976 the semi-dwarf rice varieties were being planted on over 95% of the rice land in the village. Land reform over a 20-year period encouraged the larger landlords to sell land and strengthened the rights of tenants and raised their share of profits from rice production. Those events, together with the construction of a major highway from Manila south toward the village, had eliminated its seeming isolation by the mid-1970s.

But change had already become well-established. In the 1990s the researchers recorded: "East Laguna Village appears to be as dormant under the shade of coconut trees today as it was when we first visited it in the 1970s. Under the surface, however, its economy and social organization have experienced dramatic changes. Besides the dramatic diffusion of modern rice technology, major forces that caused economic and social changes were (i) continued population pressure on limited land resources; (ii) implementation of land reform programs; (iii) public investments in infrastructure, such as irrigation systems, roads and schools; and (iv) growing urban influences accelerated by improvements in transportation and communications systems."[17]

Table 6.2 gives estimates of several important indicators of agricultural technology and income for the village. The uneven adoption pattern of the several elements of agricultural technology is evident. Tractors preceded varieties and fertilizer. Once farmers were using tractors, new seeds and fertilizer, they continued increasing the intensity of use of those three inputs over time. But the pattern for insecticide was different. As with the other three, its use increased dramatically from 1966 to 1976, but then

---

[17] *Ibid.*, p. 13.

Table 6.2:   Agricultural indicators in East Laguna Village, Philippines

	1956	1966	1975[a]	1987	1996
% modern varieties	0	0	95	100	100
Rice yield t/ha	1.9	1.9	3.2	4.3	4.5
Village rice output t/yr	136	401	676	761	958
Fertilizer kg/ha/crop	n.a.	15	67	103	111
Insecticide kg/ha	n.a.	0.1	2.6	1.9	1.1
% tractor use	n.a.	39	100	98	98
Population	n.a.	399	639	871	1200
Real income/capita[b]	n.a.	3.7	6.2	10.3	12.2
Real income/capita[c]	n.a.	10.4	10.0	9.3	12.2
% in poverty	n.a.	n.a.	69	69	56

Source: Taken from various tables in (Hayami and Kikuchi, 2000).
[a] 1975 or 1976, as available in the original.
[b] '000 Pesos "deflated" by the price of rice.
[c] '000 Pesos "deflated" by the consumer price index.

declined over the next two decades.[18] Rice yield showed a steady increase over the period and total annual rice production of the village more than doubled between 1966 and 1996 with no increase in area.

Village population increased threefold in 30 years with migration of agricultural laborers from surrounding non-rice growing villages comprising much of the growth in the 1960s and 1970s. *"Despite the sharply increased population of agricultural laborers, they were able to subsist because of the expansion in wage employment opportunities. First, employment increased in the early phases of the Green Revolution because of the labor-absorptive nature of the new rice technology. Later as tenant farmers became affluent and their children were educated for urban occupations, hired labor was substituted for family labor. In this way the benefits of new rice technology and land reform that accrued*

---

[18] This area was not subject to an intensified campaign against pesticide use; rather, it seems that farmers came to recognize that *either* it did not make economic sense to apply such high rates of pesticides to the newer more pest-resistant IRRI varieties (Herdt, Castillo and Jayasuriya, 1984) *or* they should reduce pesticide rates because of the detrimental health effects of pesticides (Antle and Capalbo, 1994).

disproportionately to farmers have spilled over to agricultural laborers. More importantly, non-farm employment opportunities for villagers have expanded, especially since the late 1970s when major improvements in the highway system were accomplished ... As the village became closely integrated with the urban economy, a new class of 'non-farm workers' was created in East Laguna Village. Typically, they commute from their homes within the village to permanent salaried jobs in nearby towns and by the mid-1990s comprised nearly 20 percent of all village households."[19]

As in the case of Palanpur, measuring changes in real income, in particular choosing an appropriate deflator, was a challenge. Early in the study period, the price of rice was an appropriate deflator because it was the primary product that villagers bought and sold, and using it showed that real income more than tripled. Toward the end of the period villagers were much more integrated with the outside economy, which argues for using some other index. When deflated by the consumer price index, per capita incomes were essentially unchanged over the four periods. However, the authors believe the consumer price index may also be inappropriate for rural villagers. In any case, despite the dramatic increase in rice yields, rice production, and employment outside the village, per capita incomes increased only modestly and the extent of poverty in the village declined only modestly. The authors credit the positive economic effects on the ability of villagers to take advantage of opportunities generated by the market and conclude that *"the experience of East Laguna Village since the early 1960s suggests strongly that the misery of the poor would have been magnified further by rapid population growth with the closed land frontiers, if the village had continued to rely on traditional agriculture in isolation from urban market activities."*[20]

6.1.3 High-Yielding Rice Varieties in Tamil Nadu, India

A third village study that sheds light on our central question was conducted between 1973–1974 and 1985 in 11 villages of Tamil Nadu state

---

[19] Hayami and Kikuchi, 2000, p. 227.
[20] *Ibid.*, p. 243.

in South India.[21] The area shares many features in common with East Laguna Village and Palanpur: rice is the predominant crop, the villages are largely comprised of small farmers, and the villages are not isolated from urban influences of relatively nearby towns.

The study is based on a firm foundation — one year of monthly household survey data "covering detailed aspects of farm management, employment, sources of income, household assets, food consumption, and expenditure patterns. The household survey also included farm and non-farm households in the rural areas."[22] The motivation for the original study was the desire of researchers from Cambridge and Madras Universities to understand the impact of rapid agricultural change in the region (Farmer, 1977). The work was undertaken in 11 villages originally selected as a representative sample of the study region and follow-up research was undertaken in the same villages. The motivation for the follow-up research was "to understand more fully both the short- and long-term impacts of technological change on rural welfare, and in order to assist in the design of appropriate technologies, policies and institutional change to enhance the poverty-reducing role of technological change."[23]

A follow-up study was undertaken in 1982–1983 with careful preparation and sufficient financing to include a comprehensive sample of household heads in the same 11 villages. Unfortunately, the weather did not cooperate — a significant drought affected the area with the result that many farmers did not plant rice and it was decided to continue the research in 1983–1984 in the hope that weather would be closer to normal. It was, but researchers were unable to obtain enough additional funding to implement as comprehensive a study, so the sample in the second period is not exactly comparable to the first period. The authors focused their analysis around comparisons of small and large farms, using one hectare as the dividing line. Some of the changes that occurred during the period are shown in Table 6.3. Relative to the large

---

[21] This section draws on the well-known study of high-yielding rice in South India: Hazell, Ramasamy, Rajagopalan, Aiyasamy and Bliven, 1991.

[22] Ibid., p. 4.

[23] Ibid.

Table 6.3:   Farming indicators, 11 villages in Tamil Nadu, India

	1973–1974	1983–1984	% change
Small farm rice yield	1773	2777	57
Large farm rice yield	2524	2176	−14
Small farm crop output value	1426	2013	41
Large farm crop output value	3854	6280	63
Small farm cultivation costs	700	908	30
Large farm cultivation costs	1534	3396	121
Small farm net income	726	1105	54
Large farm net income	2320	2884	24
Small farm net income from farming[a]	1115	1845	65
Large farm net income from farming	2548	2931	15
Landless laborers' net income from farming	827	1681	103

Source: Hazell, Ramasamy et al., 1991.
[a] Farm income + agricultural wages.

farms, small farms increased rice yields more, increased value of all crops less, increased cultivation costs less, increased farm net income more and increased income from farming more. Over this period, change favored small farms. In addition, the earnings of landless laborers increased even more than those of small farmers. Both landless and small farmers benefited from increases in earnings from agricultural labor and, although not shown in Table 6.3, from gains in non-farm income also, contrary to expectations of some.

The authors concluded: "The landless laborers gained the largest proportional increase in family income (125 percent) followed by small paddy farmers, who almost doubled their incomes (90 percent). Large paddy farmers gained relatively little (18 percent) because of sharp increases in their farm costs, especially the costs of fertilizers and hired labor. The non-paddy farms — which do not have access to irrigated land — and the nonagricultural households increased their incomes by 17 and 55 percent, respectively ... These gains in absolute welfare have also been accompanied by an improvement in equity. Whether measured by income or by consumption expenditure, the relative welfare of the large paddy farms has declined, while that of the landless laborers and the small paddy farms has improved."[24]

Others who have looked at the effects of agricultural technical change over time in India have also found a more dynamic pattern of change than they anticipated when undertaking the research. Authors of one study in North India found that "*while regional disparities widened in the initial phase — from the mid-1960s to the mid-1970s — subsequent years have witnessed a narrowing of differences as technology has diffused into some of the hitherto bypassed regions in the wake of improved infrastructure. Moreover, the second-generation effects of the Green Revolution have begun to be reflected in the variety of new economic opportunities created as a result of agricultural growth. Increased participation of the rural poor in these noncrop activities has led to an improvement in their income level and to a reduction in poverty.*"[25]

6.1.4 *Generalizations from Village Studies*

Although the above studies suggest that agricultural technical change has increased incomes and reduced poverty, they are but a few of many studies that might be examined. One researcher sought to examine all the studies he could find that examined income distributional impact of the Green Revolution and that were published between 1970 and 1989. Of approximately 300 reviewed, about 40% "*concluded that farmers' income disparities had increased, for studies based on community or local farming-region case approaches, but only 20% of studies reported negative effects of technology on income distribution in India or the Philippines (the two most favored locations for the new technology).*"[26] The burden of evidence seemed related to the approach used in the papers reviewed. "*In case studies (community and farm), less than one-third showed that disparities increased and almost 37% concluded that farmers' income distributions were either unchanged or became more equal. In the analytical studies (including theoretical) too, a low proportion (28%) concluded that income disparities were increasing; the interpretative essay, by*

---

[24] Hazell, Ramasamy, Rajagopalan, Aiyasamy and Bliven, 1991, p. 55.
[25] Sharma and Poleman, 1993, p. 3.
[26] Freebairn, 1995, p. 270.

contrast, had the highest proportion of conclusions that farmer income disparities had increased (50%) and only 4% showed no change or greater equality.[27] While it may be some comfort to "technology boosters" that analytical studies, presumably based on data like those in the village studies reviewed above, showed a low proportion of cases with increasing income disparities, "technology bashers" will likely focus more on the "interpretative essays." On balance, the Freebairn examination of the "Green Revolution" literature does not lead to a strong conclusion about the effect of technical change on rural poverty.

Four reasons for the inability to draw strong conclusions are identified by the authors of the studies. First, technological change had often started prior to the initial year of the study, or the sample of households in the first or second period represents different sub-sets of the population, so the results do not really show comparable before-and-after situations. Second, weather was often quite different among the various study years, so some "correction" for the impact of the weather was made to get a judgment about technology effects.[28] Third, there is considerable variation among the villages included in multi-village studies and the apparent impact of technology varies across villages. There is no way to know whether technology had differential impact or whether it was more appropriate for the agro-ecological zones of some villages than others, invalidating the impact comparisons. Fourth, in every case study, authors express reservations about their ability to correct for the effects of inflation and believe their results do not completely separate technology effects from price effects. Hence, even if all the field data are completely accurate, the validity of conclusions drawn by comparing the later years with the earlier years is questioned, even by the authors of each study.

The studies reviewed in the earlier sections of this paper, among the best of the before-and-after type, all have serious limitations for

---

[27] *Ibid.*, p. 272.

[28] For example, one study notes that the task of evaluating some of the economic and social changes was greatly complicated "by the severe drought of 1982/83 and by the incomplete village coverage of the 1983/84 resurvey. Clearly comparisons between 1973/74 and 1982/83 must grossly underestimate the impact of the intervening changes" (Hazell, Ramasamy, Rajagopalan, Aiyasamy and Bliven, 1991, p. 55).

understanding the effects of technological change. They are useful for describing household- and village-level effects, such as patterns of consumption, the amount of labor hired for agricultural operations or the change in quantity of output. But they have limited value for understanding the aggregate effects of such changes in many villages that are open to broader economic forces that affect labor demand and product prices.

The direct effect of technological change is on the quantity of inputs used to produce a unit of output. If widespread, the relative use and price of inputs (including land and labor) change; that induces farmers to change their production and as a result output price will change; the income obtained from production changes; and as a result, consumption changes. A technological change is an improvement if the cost of inputs used per unit of output produced is reduced, generating a savings. If the input saved is family-supplied labor, the value of the labor saved depends on its next best alternative use. In the case of the East Laguna Village, the new technology allowed increased numbers of farmers' children to continue in school while laborers were hired, thereby increasing the income of hired labor and reducing the imputed returns to family labor. The less direct impact of a technological improvement is to increase output. Depending on the speed and spread of technological change, the output increase may put downward pressure on the product's price. Those who consume large quantities of the product are benefited by having to pay less for their food. To summarize, technological change may affect the following variables:

• labor input per unit of output
• other input use (e.g., seed and fertilizer) per unit of output
• wage rates, other input costs
• quantity of output.

Finally, the preferences of farmers, laborers and others generate demand for the output and hence determine its price together with above production conditions.

6.1.5 *Technology's Impact in Madagascar*

A recent study from Madagascar is valuable for its focus on the link between poverty and agricultural technology. Madagascar, while part of Africa, has a farming system and food consumption pattern much more like Southeast Asia than like the rest of Africa. Rice dominates, with 70% of the rural population growing rice and that single grain providing 45% of the total food calorie consumption (Minten and Barrett, 2006). The analysis is built around the impact of agricultural productivity differences on three sub-groups in the population: rice farmers who are net sellers of rice; farmers who are net buyers of rice; and wage laborers, most of whom work in rice farming. While virtually everyone in Madagascar is poor, the farmers who do not produce enough rice to meet their own consumption requirements and hence are net buyers are much poorer than the net sellers. Agricultural laborers are as poor or poorer. The study covered virtually the whole country with data obtained from interviews with focus groups in 1,381 of the 1,392 "communes" in Madagascar (the commune is the lowest level to which the central government reaches).

The analysis identified the factors associated with communes whose farmers are relatively more or less well-off. Then the authors built a multi-equation model examining the three ways technological change may affect income and poverty: *"(1) lower real food prices, thereby benefiting net food consumers; (2) output response that outpaces price declines, thereby benefiting net food suppliers; and (3) increased real wages, thereby benefiting unskilled workers."*

Applying appropriate analytical techniques, the authors estimated that communes with rice yields twice the average had 38% fewer food insecure people and a seasonal "lean period" 1.7 months shorter than the average. Those same communes had 31%–44% lower rice prices during the April–September harvest months and 18%–26% lower rice prices in the lean season compared to the average commune. They estimated that while net food buyers capture much of the benefit of lower prices, farmers were nonetheless able to capture 10%–60% of the gains from improved rice productivity. Finally, the communes with twice the rice yield had agricultural wages 65%–89% higher than average.[29] In other words, those communes that had higher rice yields also had conditions that favored the rural poor — net rice buyers and laborers.

---

[29] Minten and Barrett, 2006, pp. 15, 19 and 20.

Using the relationships estimated in the first part of the analysis, the authors conducted a series of simulations of the effects of alternative changes in technology and transportation infrastructure. They conclude that, controlling for geographic and physical characteristics, areas that *"have higher rates of adoption of improved agricultural technologies, broader access to irrigation and, consequently, higher crop yields enjoy lower real food prices, higher real wages for unskilled workers, greater profitability for farmers, and better welfare indicators, in particular fewer people in extreme poverty."*[30]

6.2 Trade and Technology — Macroeconomic Effects

The Madagascar analysis suggested that an increase in rice production had a relatively large impact on prices locally, in the communes with higher yields. In many other countries, however, food prices are more strongly influenced by national or world market forces, so local technologically-induced production has much smaller effects on local food prices. Understanding the effect of agricultural technical change in such situations may require a model that reflects national or global markets. In recent years there have been advances in large, computable models that can analyze international as well as national implications of a broad range of issues like those we are considering. The Global Trade Analysis Project (GTAP) is one such effort. GTAP *"is a global network of researchers and policy makers conducting quantitative analysis of international policy issues. GTAP's goal is to improve the quality of quantitative analysis of global economic issues within an economy-wide framework."*[31] Although it has a focus on understanding the trade effects of various policies, GTAP has immense versatility and can be adapted and expanded to ask a broad range of questions including whether defined patterns of technological change will reduce or increase poverty. One recent study evaluated the effect on poverty of annual productivity growth in agriculture over the 1991–2001 period in 11 developing countries and then compared that with estimates of what would have happened

---

[30] *Ibid.*, p. 29.
[31] https://www.gtap.agecon.purdue.edu/about/project.asp

to poverty with different patterns of technological change (Valenzuela, Ivanic et al., 2005).

The researchers estimated a "poverty function" that maps changes in prices to changes in poverty based on detailed data about the income households earned for the land, unskilled labor, skilled labor and capital they committed to producing grains, livestock, other food, durables, non-durables and services.[32] The demand for each of the six products, together with output resulting from the committed inputs, and the exposure of each economy to international trade generated a set of internal prices that were fed into a household model to calculate poverty changes. The implied prices were used to estimate a consumer price index used to deflate incomes. Technological change modifies the quantity of inputs required to generate a unit of output; different kinds of technical change reduces or increases inputs at different rates with a baseline established from the observed historical configuration of technical change represented as an annual rate of change in productivity.

As reported by the authors and summarized in Table 6.4, "annual productivity growth in agriculture has a positive effect in reducing poverty across all the developing countries used in the study. This is in line with previous empirical studies which associate agricultural productivity improvements with a reduction in poverty. The results varied, for instance, Bangladesh shows that agricultural growth can lift a sizable amount of people out of poverty. On the other hand, Chile shows that there is no appreciable gain in poverty reduction by expanding agricultural activities."[33] The technological change that occurred over the period had different effects depending on: what changes in factor use it generated, the pattern of factor ownership among households, the pattern of demand, the extent to which a country is open to international trade, and so forth. The benefits depend on the extent to which households are self-employed in agriculture or non-agriculture, wage dependent, or dependent on income from various diverse sources. The analysts then ask what the effect of different patterns

---

[32] The sources of household data and their reconciliation with the GTAP model structure are discussed in Ivanic, 2004.

[33] Valenzuela, Ivanic, Ludena and Hertel, 2005, p. 9.

Table 6.4:   Effect of 1991–2001 agricultural productivity growth on poverty

Country	Percent change in poverty rates	Change in poverty headcount '000	Country	Percent change in poverty rates	Change in poverty headcount '000
Bangladesh	−4.52	−1,737	Peru	−0.17	−29
Brazil	−1.65	−145	Chile	−0.59	−4
Philippines	−1.35	−134	Mexico	−0.58	−93
Thailand	−1.13	−14	Zambia	−0.41	−30
Venezuela	−1.07	−61	Indonesia	−0.15	−48
Colombia	−0.72	−61			

Source: Valenzuela, Ivanic *et al.*, 2005, p. 15.

of technical change in agriculture would have had on poverty and con-clude that the historic pattern was quite good in some countries but that "much more poverty reduction may be achieved in Mexico, Philippines, and Venezuela by redirecting productivity growth in different sectors."[34]

6.3   Conclusions

Poverty is the result of many interacting forces in an economy. It is a condition wherein the poor earn too little to consume above the poverty level, both because of the cost of the goods and services they consume and because of the earnings they receive for their labor, land and other assets.

Micro-economic village studies were undertaken, in part, assuming that a line could be drawn around an area and all economic activities within that area monitored in order to understand the effects of technical change. Technological change that increases the productivity of land and labor under competitive market conditions raises the returns to those factors but also reduces product prices, offsetting those gains and providing benefits to consumers. The effects are complex and interact, depending on the extent of competition in the market and other characteristics of the economy.

---

[34] *Ibid.*, p. 10.

Direct observation of such effects is affected by the drawn-out nature of technical change, which can take years, and because weather effects are different each growing season.

The research in Palanpur found that the relationship between techno-logical change and economic inequality was minor, with other *persistent* inequalities relating to asset ownership or power relationships dominating. Some villages are quite isolated like those in Madagascar, while others are well-linked to larger markets, like those in East Laguna. The differences affect how powerfully agricultural technical change can affect prices, wages and hence poverty; as well as how powerfully forces outside the village, like increasing availability of off-farm jobs, changes in prices of non-farm prod-ucts, and population growth, affect people in the village.

The village study approach generates many valuable and interesting insights, but alone it is not powerful enough to answer the central question of this paper. The authors of the Tamil Nadu study recognized this and developed a regional macro-economic model to simulate the impact of technological change under normal weather conditions. They believe that because "*the model can correct for weather conditions as well as simulate with-and without- Green Revolution situations, it enables us to overcome the major limitations of our survey data analysis.*"[35]

In addition, macro-economic models help us understand the impact of forces beyond the villages studied. International markets are important for most agricultural products, even though most governments seek to insu-late their domestic food markets. It is virtually impossible for governments to prevent domestic prices from following international prices — all are affected by the long-term downward trend in real prices of food grains of the past century (FAO, 2002). That trend can be attributed to pervasive technical change in agriculture globally, in developed as well as developing countries. Any effort to understand local or national change will be lim-ited if it does not recognize that international markets can have local price effects. Using models that incorporate international effects, it has been demonstrated that the technical change many developing countries expe-rienced between 1990 and 2001, under prevailing policy and institutional

---

[35] Hazell, Ramasamy, Rajagopalan, Aiyasamy and Bliven, 1991, p. 31.

regimes, has reduced poverty, but also that in many cases a different kind of technical change could be designed that would have reduced poverty by an even greater amount (Valenzuela, Ivanic *et al.*, 2005).

A given technological change will have different effects on income and poverty depending on economic conditions within a village, how that village is connected to the rest of the country, how the poor make their living and what the poor consume. The effect of technological change can be predicted if "all other things are assumed to remain unchanged." A technology that "saves" labor will reduce the income of laborers. A technology that "saves" land (i.e., increases yield/hectare) will reduce the income to land and increase the returns to other factors. In both cases, however, "all other things" do not remain unchanged. The changes in all other things depend on the nature of the economy including such factors as the pattern of consumer demand, the percent of the economy dependent on agriculture, the percent of labor force in agriculture, and the openness to outside markets.

I conclude that only by combining insights from micro-economic studies of places experiencing technical change and macro-economic models that incorporate larger forces can we understand the impact of technical change. Empirically, the institutional environment that determines power relationships, the pre-existing distribution of land, and the functioning of economic markets in different societies are more important for income distributional changes than agricultural technology. However, the lack of technological improvements to ensure food supply stays ahead of food demand can lead to food scarcity and misery. That is, the lack of technological change can lead to poverty, but its presence alone cannot offset an oppressive political system or overcome entrenched monopolistic market power. Dynamic agricultural technology is a necessary but not a sufficient condition for overcoming poverty in economies at early stages of development.

Bibliography

Antle, J. (1983). "Infrastructure and aggregate agricultural productivity: International evidence." *Economic Development and Cultural Change* 31 (April): 609–619.

Antle, J. M. and S. M. Capalbo (1994). "Pesticides, productivity, and farmer health: Implications for regulatory policy and agricultural research." *American Journal of Agricultural Economics* 76: 598–602.

Barker, R. and R. W. Herdt (1985). *The Rice Economy of Asia*. (Resources for the Future, Washington, DC).

Dreze, J., P. Lanjouw, *et al.* (1998). Economic development in Palanpur, 1957–1993. *Economic Development in Palanpur Over Five Decades*. P. Lanjouw and N. Stern. (Oxford University Press, Calcutta, Chennai, Mumbai). 114–238.

Evenson, R., C. Pray, *et al.* (1999). Agricultural research and productivity growth in India. Research report 109, International Food Policy Research Institute, Washington, DC.

FAO (2002). World agriculture: Toward 2015/2030. Food and Agriculture Organization of the UN, Rome, Italy.

Farmer, B. H. (1977). *Green Revolution? Technology and Change in Rice Growing Areas of Tamil Nadu and Sri Lanka*. (Macmillan, London).

Foster, J., J. Greer, *et al.* (1984). "A Class of Decomposable Poverty Measures." *Econometrica* 52: 761–766.

Freebairn, D. K. (1995). "Did the Green Revolution concentrate incomes? A quantitative study of research reports." *World Development* 23 (2): 265–279.

Gallup, J. L., S. Radelet, *et al.* (1999). Economic growth and the income of the poor. CAER II Discussion Paper 36, Harvard Institute for International Development, Cambridge.

Gardner, B. L. (2000). "Economic growth and low incomes in agriculture." *American Journal of Agricultural Economics* 82 (5): 1059–1074.

Griliches, Z. (1963). "The sources of measured productivity growth: U.S. agriculture, 1940–1960." *Journal of Political Economy* 71 (August): 331–346.

Hayami, Y. and M. Kikuchi (2000). *A Rice Village Saga: Three Decades of Green Revolution in the Philippines*. (Barnes & Noble and International Rice Research Institute, New York).

Hayami, Y., M. Kikuchi, *et al.* (1978). *Anatomy of a Peasant Economy*. (International Rice Research Institue, Los Banos, Philippines).

Hayami, Y. and V. Ruttan (1985). *Agricultural Development: An International Perspective*. (The Johns Hopkins University Press, Baltimore and London).

Hazell, P. B. R., C. Ramasamy, *et al.* (1991). Economic changes among village households. *The Green Revolution Reconsidered: The Impact of High-Yielding Rice Varieties in South India*. P. B. R. Hazell and C. Ramasamy. (The Johns Hopkins University Press, Baltimore).

Herdt, R. W. and C. Capule (1983). Adoption, spread and production impact of modern rice varieties in Asia. International Rice Research Institute, Los Baños, The Philippines.

Herdt, R. W., L. L. Castillo, *et al.* (1984). The economics of insect control on rice in the Philippines. *Judicious and Efficient Use of Insecticides on Rice*. (International Rice Research Institute, Los Banos, Philippines).

Herdt, R. W. and J. W. Mellor (1964). "The Contrasting Response of Rice to Nitrogen: India and the United States." *Journal of Farm Economics* 46 (1).

Holt-Gimenez, E., M. A. Altieri, *et al.* (2006). Ten Reasons Why the Rockefeller and the Bill and Melinda Gates Foundations' Alliance for Another Green Revolution Will Not Solve the Problems of Poverty and Hunger in Sub-Saharan Africa. Food First Policy Brief 12, Institute for Food and Development Policy, http://www.foodfirst.org/pubs/policy/pb12.html.

Ivanic, M. (2004). Reconciliation of the GTAP and Household Survey Data. GTAP Research Memorandum 5, Global Trade Analysis Project, West Lafayette, Indiana.

Lanjouw, P. and N. Stern, Eds. (1998). *Economic Development in Palanpur Over Five Decades*. (Clarendon Press, Oxford).

Maxwell, S. (1999). The Meaning and Measurement of Poverty. ODI Poverty Briefing 3, Overseas Development Institute, London.

Minten, B. and C. Barrett (2006). "Agricultural Technology, Productivity, and Poverty in Madagascar." 2006.

Norton, G. W., J. Ortiz, *et al.* (1992). "The impact of foreign assistance on agricultural growth." *Economic Development and Cultural Change* 40 (December): 775–786.

Sharma, R. and T. T. Poleman (1993). *The New Economics of India's Green Revolution*. (Cornell University Press, Ithaca).

Valenzuela, E., M. Ivanic, *et al.* (2005). Agricultural productivity growth: Is the current trend on the track to poverty reduction? Global Trade Analysis Project, West Lafayette, Indiana.

Chapter Seven

Agricultural Biotechnology in Latin America: Economic Benefits, Regional Capacity, and Policy Options

Greg Traxler*

7.1 Introduction

The global pace of scientific discovery in biotechnology research has been impressive, but the application of the new science has lagged in most developing countries, including those of Latin America and the Caribbean (LAC) (Trigo *et al.*, 2002). The vast potential for biotechnology to contribute to agriculture in the region stands in stark contrast to the modest impact that it has had to date. The crops deployed to date have been temperate crop events developed in the US that have been adapted for use in the region. It is clear that the region is far from taking full advantage of the potential benefits from biotechnology, but a strategy for overcoming the obstacles has yet to be elaborated.

Across many dimensions, the region is a study in contrasts. The use of cellular biology techniques such as plant propagation, tissue culture, genetic markers, marker-assisted and gene-assisted selection, and molecular diagnosis of pests and diseases have diffused widely and without

---

*Greg Traxler, Senior Program Officer of Agricultural Development at Bill & Melinda Gates Foundation.

controversy, but the use of genetically modified organisms (GMOs) remains controversial. The region includes two of the world's top three GMO-growing countries (Argentina and Brazil), and accounts for 78% of the transgenic crop area in the developing world (James, 2006). The rate of area expansion of GMO technology has been rapid when compared to nearly any previous agricultural innovation, but this exists alongside disappointment with the limited geographic reach and product line scope of transgenic technology (Traxler, 2005). Support for research in the use of biotechnology for animal agriculture has been even more modest than for crops.

This study discusses the past experience, present status, and near-term potential to access biotechnology science of countries in the LAC region. A simple conceptual model of a complete scientific system is presented and discussed. Empirical indicators of research capacity will be presented for each country in the region. Issues of financing the spread of improved plant varieties and GMO technology in the region will then be discussed.

7.2   The Use and Impact of Transgenic Technologies in Latin America

This section reviews the evidence on economic benefits and rates of return to GMOs in Latin America. Other recent papers have reviewed the literature on farm-level benefits in all developing countries (Brookes and Barfoot, 2005; Qaim and Matuschke, 2005; Raney, 2006). Here we present evidence on the size of economic benefits in LAC and on how the benefits have been shared amongst industry, farmers, and consumers. Some data on the effect of GMO adoption on pesticide use will also be presented.

GMOs have been legally grown in seven LAC countries since 1996 (Table 7.1). Latin America has 78% of the total DC area, largely due to the spread of herbicide tolerant (HT) soybeans in Argentina, Brazil and Paraguay. All GMO area is planted to HT, Bt, or stacked (both HT and Bt genes) varieties of soybean, yellow maize or cotton. This review has uncovered published benefit estimates of impact for eight developing country cases, four of which occur in Latin America: cotton, maize and soybeans in Argentina, and cotton in Mexico.

Table 7.1: GMO cropped area in LAC, by country, 2006

Country	2006 GMO area (000 ha)	Crops planted commercially
Argentina	18,000	Cotton, soy, maize
Brazil	11,500	Soy, cotton
Paraguay	2,000	Soy
Uruguay	400	Soy, maize
Mexico	60	Cotton, soy
Colombia	30	Cotton, maize, carnation
Honduras	2	Maize

Source: James, 2006.

7.2.1 *Herbicide-Tolerant Soybeans*

RoundupReady (RR) soybeans were commercially released in Argentina and the United States in 1996. The sale and use of RR technology is protected in the US through patents and sales contracts with farmers, but neither form of intellectual property protection is used in Argentina. Argentine farmers are also legally allowed to use farm-saved seeds. Thus, in Argentina, RR soybeans are widely available from black market sources at little or no premium over conventional varieties. By 2003, about 98 percent of the Argentine soybean area was cultivated with RR varieties (Chudnovsky, 2005).

Yields of RR soybeans are not significantly different from yields of conventional soybeans in either the United States or Argentina. It is the reduced herbicide and tillage expenses that generate the farm-level benefits of RR soybeans. Many farmers switched to low-till or even no-till cultivation practices after adoption of RR soybeans, and machinery and labor costs are also lower due to the reduced time needed for harvesting (Qaim and Traxler, 2005). In Argentina, total variable cost of production is about eight percent ($21 per hectare) lower for RR soybeans than for a conventional crop.

The global welfare effects of the spread of RR soybeans have been analyzed in several studies (Falck-Zepeda *et al.*, 2000; Price *et al.*, 2003; Sobolevsky *et al.*, 2005), but only Qaim and Traxler (2005) and

Trigo and Cap (2003) explicitly model the diffusion of the technology in Argentina.

Qaim and Traxler (2005) estimate that in 2001, RR soybeans created surplus of more than $1.2 billion, or about 4 percent of the value of the world soybean crop at the global level. The largest share of these overall benefits went to soybean consumers, who gained $652 million (53 percent of total benefits) due to lower prices. Soybean producers received net benefits of $158 million (13 percent), and biotechnology and seed firms received $421 million (34 percent) as technology revenue.[1] Soybean producers in countries where RR technology was not available faced losses of $291 million in 2001 due to the induced decline of about 2 percent ($4.06/mt) in world market prices.[2] This underlines that national restrictions to GM technology access can bring about considerable taxation of the domestic farm sector. A case in point is Brazil, the second largest soybean producer in the world. Farm-level benefits in Brazil could be similar to those in Argentina (Paarlberg, 2003), yet, due to a protracted biosafety process and uncertainty with respect to legal responsibilities, RR soybeans were not officially approved for commercialization until 2005.

Trigo and Cap (2003) estimate that accumulated RR soybean benefits in Argentina from 1996 until the year 2001 were approximately $5.2 billion, with nearly $2 billion occurring in 2001. A number of reasons explain the much higher benefit estimate when compared to Qaim and Traxler. Trigo and Cap attribute a $1.95 billion increase in farm profit due to soybean area expansion to RR soybean adoption.[3] They also include $365 in increased profit accruing to firms selling glyphosate. Overall, Trigo and Cap estimate

---

[1] Gross technology revenues are used as a measure of monopoly rent. No research, marketing, or administration costs are deducted. If we assume, for example, that these costs amount to 33% of technology fee revenues, the monopoly rent would fall to around $280 million (26% of total surplus).

[2] Sobolevsky et al. (2005) show comparatively small producer surplus effects for South America in 2000. In their regional approach, the gains for farmers in Argentina are offset by losses to Brazilian producers.

[3] The model used by Qaim and Traxler calculates ceterus paribus area expansion induced by the new technology based on assumed supply and demand elasticities. Trigo and Cap implicitly assume that all new soybean area is due to RR technology. The true area expansion due to RR technology is probably somewhere in between these two estimates.

that 87% of overall benefits from HT soybeans in Argentina accrued to farmers, 9% to sellers of glyphosate and 4% to the seed industry.

HT soybeans had a strong effect on tillage practices and on chemical herbicide use. Glyphosate substitutes for a number of other products, with the result that per hectare herbicide expenditures declined in Argentina even though the average number of herbicide applications and total herbicide use per hectare increased. Herbicides differ in their mode of action, duration of residual activity, and toxicity, so an increase in total herbicide amounts does not inevitably entail negative environmental effects. Glyphosate has essentially no residual activity and is rapidly decomposed to organic components by microorganisms in the soil. According to the international classification of pesticides, glyphosate belongs to toxicity class IV, the lowest class for "practically non-toxic" pesticides (WHO, 1988). Adoption of RR soybeans led to a 93% decline in the use of herbicides belonging to toxicity classes II and III. There are no other herbicides used in soybeans which belong to toxicity class I. The major reason for the rise in the number of herbicide applications is the farmers' conversion to no-till practices that require pre-seeding chemical weed control. While 42 percent of the farmers in the sample used no-till for conventional soybeans, 80 percent of them use this practice on their RR plots.[4] On average, the technology reduced the number of tillage operations by one passage per field, reduced the number of machinery hours by 20 percent, and led to fuel savings of almost 10 liters per hectare (Qaim and Traxler, 2005).

7.2.2 Insect-Resistant Cotton

Bt cotton is highly effective in controlling caterpillar pests such as pink bollworm (*Pectinophora gossypiella*) and cotton bollworm (*Helicoverpa zea*), and is partially effective in controlling tobacco budworm (*Heliothis virescens*) and fall armyworm (*Spodoptera frugiperda*). These Lepidoptera pests comprise a major pest control problem in many cotton-growing areas, but other cotton pests such as boll weevil are not susceptible to Bt and continue to require the use of chemical pesticides (James, 2002). As a

---

[4] RR technology has similarly increased adoption of reduced tillage and no-till in the US.

result, the effect of the introduction of Bt cotton on pesticide usage varies from region to region depending on the local pest populations. Qaim and Zilberman (2003) argue that the relative performance of Bt cotton is likely to be highest when used by developing country small farmers because of the large pest losses suffered by these farmers. Bt cotton varieties have been rapidly accepted by farmers in areas where Lepidoptera pests are the primary pest problem, particularly when resistance to chemical pesticides is high. When boll weevils or other pest populations are high, farmers achieve coincidental control of the BBWC with the use of broad-spectrum chemicals, or pesticide mixtures, reducing the value of Bt control. Bt cotton adoption has been rapid in China and India, but low and restricted to large-scale farmers in Argentina due to the large price premium charged for transgenic seeds (Qaim and De Janvry, 2005). Adoption has varied widely across growing regions in Mexico because infestation levels vary widely (Traxler et al., 2003).

Field-level studies of the performance of Bt cotton have been completed in five developing countries: Mexico (Traxler et al., 2003), Argentina (Qaim and De Janvry, 2003), South Africa (Bennett et al., 2003; Gouse et al., 2004, 2006; Ismael et al., 2002; Kirsten and Grouse, 2003; Thirtle et al., 2003), China (Pray et al., 2001), and India (Bennett et al., 2004; Morse et al., 2005; Qaim, 2003; Qaim et al., 2006; Qaim and Zilberman, 2003). The studies have found that the benefits from biotechnology innovations have been widely shared among consumers, producers and industry. Yields were higher for Bt than for conventional cotton in all five countries, while insecticide use fell by between 33% and 77%. The average farmer share of total benefits was 65% and farmers received a larger share of benefits than industry in all countries except for Argentina. The change in consumer surplus was assumed to be zero in these studies because the increase in the supply of cotton relative to total world production is small.

7.2.3 Bt Maize

Bt yellow maize was first planted in Argentina in 1998/1999 and by 2004/2005 had reached a total of approximately two million ha (60% of maize area) planted (Asociación Semilleros Argentinos). Trigo et al. (2002)

simulate benefits from the adoption of Bt yellow maize. In their model they assume a five percent yield advantage of Bt maize over conventional varieties. They estimate total benefits of about $132 million in 2003. Of the total benefits, 79% accrue to industry and 21% to farmers. The output increase is assumed to not affect world prices, so the change in consumer surplus is zero.

Transgenic crop varieties have delivered large economic benefits to farmers in some areas of some LAC countries over the past ten years. Although the environment benefits have not been detailed here, a number of the studies report strongly positive environmental benefits from HT soybean and Bt cotton. Insecticide use on Bt cotton is significantly lower than on conventional varieties and glyphosate has been substituted for more toxic and persistent herbicides in RR soybeans. Furthermore, reduced tillage has accompanied RR soybeans and cotton in many cases. Negative environmental consequences, while meriting continued monitoring, have not been documented in any setting where transgenic crops have been deployed to date. Although the transgenic crops have been delivered through the private rather than the public sector, the benefits have been widely distributed among industry, farmers and final consumers. This suggests that the monopoly position engendered by intellectual property protection does not automatically lead to excessive industry profits. Finally, the available evidence indicates that transgenic varieties are scale-neutral with regard to both speed of adoption and per hectare benefits. This evidence is from Argentina (Qaim and De Janvry, 2005), Mexico (Traxler *et al.*, 2003), China (Pray *et al.*, 2001), South Africa (Bennett *et al.*, 2003; Gouse *et al.*, 2006) and India (Qaim *et al.*, 2006), and suggests that small farmers have had no more difficulty than larger farmers in adopting the new technologies.

7.3   Research Roles, Financial Resources, and Scientific Capacity in LAC

A simple model of a system for generating and delivering biotechnology research in developing countries might appear as in Figure 7.1. The figure depicts the research process as starting with basic research activity,

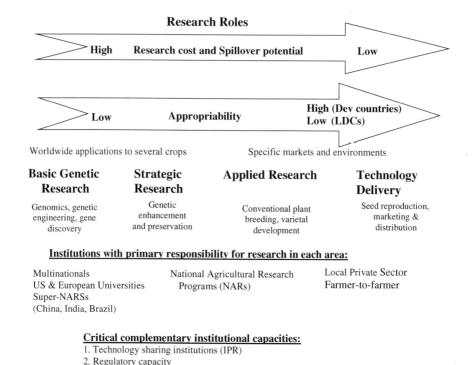

Figure 7.1:   Research roles

proceeding through strategic and applied research, and resulting in the delivery of an improved technology. The diagram suggests a linear path from basic research to technology delivery, with generally reduced levels of spillover potential and research cost and sophistication as the research becomes embodied in farm technologies. Basic, and some strategic, research has worldwide applications, while applied research is often specific to a target market or agroclimatic location.

Basic research findings are routinely published in international journals and presented at international conferences, facilitating knowledge spillovers. Appropriability is generally low for this type of research. Historically, scientists at universities and non-profit research institutes in developed countries have done the bulk of the world's basic research. In recent years, private sector firms have made large investments in upstream research as they search for strategic advantage in developing biotechnology products. A few developing countries have a modest basic science capacity, but are not yet on the scale of the larger developed countries. The next two research stages in Figure 7.1 are broad categories that translate basic research discoveries into technologies usable by farmers. Technology delivery is presented in the diagram to emphasize the importance of institutional development in that area. The process is illustrated as a one-way continuum, but clearly there are many feedback loops that are not shown.

It is clear that countries can benefit from advances in technology without possessing the indigenous capacity to perform all research functions in-country. Research spillovers among countries are pervasive (Alston, 2002; Byerlee and Traxler, 2001; Traxler and Byerlee, 2001), but some capacity in all research areas is required in order to access spillovers. The next section of this chapter reports empirical indicators of relevant LAC scientific and institutional capacity.

7.4   Agricultural Research Expenditures in LAC and Other Developing Countries

Public sector agricultural research expenditures in developing countries have increased steadily over the past decades (Table 7.2). Between 1981 and 2000, the average rate of increase of expenditures for developing countries was nearly three times that of developed countries (Pardey et al., 2006). In 1981, developing countries were spending just 81% as much as developed countries on public sector agricultural research. By 2000 they were spending 26% more than developed countries. There are two important caveats to this good news, though. First, growth in research expenditures has not been uniform across countries or regions. Expenditures have grown rapidly in some of the large countries, while expenditures in many smaller countries have not kept pace with inflation. Expenditures grew at an average annual rate of 8% between 1981 and 2000 in India, China, and Brazil, compared to a rate of 2% in the remaining developing countries. LAC was the LDC region with the slowest expenditure growth rate.

Table 7.2:   Agricultural research expenditures and growth rates by region

Expenditures (million 2000 international dollars)

	1981	2000
Latin America and the Caribbean	1,897	2,454
Sub-Saharan Africa	1,196	1,461
China	1,049	3,150
Asia and Pacific	3,047	7,523
Middle East and North Africa	764	1,382
Developing countries	6,904	12,819
Developed countries	8,293	10,191
Total	15,197	23,010
Annual growth rates (percent per year)	**1981–2000**	
Latin America and the Caribbean	2.0%	
China	4.9%	
Asia and Pacific	4.2%	
Middle East and North Africa	3.4%	
Developing countries	3.1%	
Developed countries	1.1%	
Total	2.1%	

Source: Pardey *et al.*, 2006.
Note: Data are provisional estimates and exclude Eastern Europe and countries of the former Soviet Union.

The second qualification on the good news about increased research expenditures is the absence of private sector interest in agricultural research in developing countries. In 2000 the private sector accounted for just 6% of agricultural research expenditures in developing countries, compared to 54% of expenditures in developed countries (Table 7.3). As a result, total (private and public) agricultural research expenditures were 62% higher in developed than in developing countries (Pardey *et al.*, 2006). This is a gap of more than $11 billion/yr, with the potential to create an enduring difference in rates of technological advance. Of course, spillovers are large from some types of private sector research. Innovations such as pesticides or machinery, while created through expenditures in developed countries, are likely to be effective in developing countries, somewhat overstating the importance of the effective private sector research investment gap.

Table 7.3:   Estimated global public and private agricultural R&D investments, circa 2000

Region/country	Expenditures (million 2000 international dollars)			Share of spending	
	Public	Private	Total	Public	Private
Asia–Pacific	7,523	663	8,186	92%	8%
Latin America and the Caribbean	2,454	124	2,578	95%	5%
Sub-Saharan Africa	1,461	26	1,486	98%	2%
Middle East and North Africa	1,382	50	1,432	97%	4%
Developing-country total	12,819	862	13,682	94%	6%
Developed-country total	10,191	12,086	22,277	46%	54%

Source: Pardey *et al.*, 2006.

However, the lack of private sector research is an important obstacle to the access of developing country farmers to improved crop varieties and biotechnology. The private sector has been the main source of improved varieties in the US and other developed countries for many crops. Also, with the exception of China, the private sector has been the source of GMO technology in all areas where it has diffused. The private sector has accounted for 70% of global investment in agricultural biotechnology, and virtually all of that investment has occurred in developed countries (Table 7.4).

The information on agricultural research expenditures for LAC comes from the IFPRI Agricultural Science and Technology Indicators (ASTI) data base. The detailed information dates from the mid-to-late 1990s. Expenditures have increased more slowly in LAC than in LDCs over-all over the past two decades, but countries in the LAC region have generally given greater support to agricultural research than other developing country regions. LAC has the highest research intensity ratio of any developing country region whether measured as research expenditures as a share of agricultural GDP, expenditures per capita, or expenditures per economically active agricultural population (Table 7.5). Nonetheless, the research intensity measures are less than one-third the average

Table 7.4: Estimated global R&D expenditures on crop biotechnology, 2001

	$ millions	
Private (70%)	3,100	
Public (30%)	1,120	
Industrial Country Total (96%)		**4,220**
China	115	
India	25	
Brazil	15	
Others	25	
Developing Country Total (4%)		**180**
World Total		**4,400**

Source: James, 2002.

Table 7.5: Selected public research intensity ratios, 1976–1995

	Expenditures as a share of AgGDP			Expenditures per capita			Expenditures per economically active agricultural population		
	1976	1985[a]	1995[a]	1976	1985[a]	1995[a]	1976	1985[a]	1995[a]
	(percent)			(1993 international dollars)					
Latin America	0.55	0.72	0.98	3.4	4.0	4.6	26.0	36.0	45.9
Sub-Saharan Africa	0.91	0.95	0.85	3.5	3.0	2.4	11.3	10.6	9.4
China	0.41	0.42	0.43	0.7	1.3	1.7	1.8	3.1	4.1
Other Asia	0.31	0.44	0.63	1.1	1.7	2.6	3.8	6.1	10.2
Developing countries	0.44	0.53	0.62	1.5	2.0	2.5	4.6	6.5	8.5
Developed countries	1.53	2.13	2.64	9.6	11.0	12.0	238.5	371.0	594.1
All countries	0.83	0.95	1.04	3.3	3.8	4.2	12.9	15.3	17.7

Source: Beintema and Pardey, 2001.
[a] Three-year averages centered on 1985 and 1995.

of developed countries. Direct support with government funds (i.e., block grants) was still the prevalent form of financing public research in the early 1990s, averaging 66% of total funding for the countries for which data are available (Table 7.6). Argentina and Chile are the only two countries

Table 7.6:   Source of funding for public agricultural research

Country	Year	Government subsidy	Sales produce and services	Earmarked taxes	Donors	Private	Other
			(percentage share)				
Argentina	1991	21	1	67	0	0	12
Brazil	1991	95	4	0	0	0	1
Chile	1994	41	26	0	8	5	21
Colombia	1991	80	14	0	2	4	0
Ecuador	1991	58	21	0	12	0	9
Guatemala	1991	71	3	0	1	0	25
Mexico	1991	88	5	2	4	0	1
Panama	1986	62	2	0	5	0	31
Venezuela	1987	82	17	0	0	0	1
Sample average		66	10	8	4	1	11

Source: Cremers and Roseboom, 1997.

with less than 50% of funding coming from a direct government grant.[5]

Immense inter-country differences exist in size and scientific capacity. Brazil accounts for about 50% of total LAC expenditures. Adding the budgets of Argentina and Mexico to Brazil's brings total agricultural research expenditures of these three countries to more than 85% of the LAC total. The majority of LAC agricultural R&D systems, however, are small (Figure 7.2). Twenty-five of the 32 LAC countries have less than 200 researchers. The total size of these systems is less than that of a large Land Grant university in the US. The 12 countries of the Central America and Caribbean region together spent just $39 million (again, about the budget of an average size Land Grant university in the US).

More than 13,500 full-time equivalent (FTE) researchers were employed by public sector institutions in 1996 (IFPRI). Of that total, Brazil employed nearly 5,000 researchers (36% of LAC total), and together,

---

[5] In the case of INTA in Argentina, a special tax on several commodities was the major source of income, while in the case of INIA in Chile, research contracts were an important funding source.

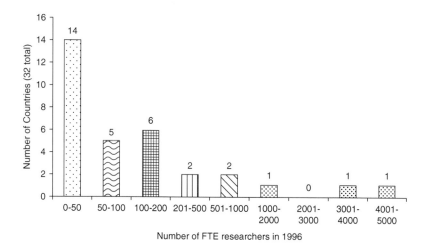

Figure 7.2:   Size distribution of agricultural research systems in LAC region

Argentina and Mexico employed about another 5,000 researchers, bringing the share of LAC total in these three countries to 73%. Differences in the level of training of researchers and in expenditure per researcher are also large (Beintema and Pardey, 2001; Cremers and Roseboom, 1997). While 82% of Brazilian researchers hold graduate degrees, just 20% of the Guatemalan and 27% of the Honduran researchers do. Only Brazil and Mexico have more than half of their researchers with graduate degrees; only Brazil and Chile have 20% or more holding a Ph.D. The educational level of LAC researchers increased steadily between the early 1970s and 1996. There was a six-fold increase in the share of researchers holding a Ph.D., and the share holding an MSc degree more than doubled, while the proportion holding a BSc degree fell from 77% to 33%. These figures for the region are strongly affected by the inclusion of the progress that Brazil and Mexico have made in training researchers. Excluding these two countries, the share of LAC researchers with graduate degrees falls to 55%, with just 18% holding a Ph.D.

Most of the National Agricultural Research Institutions (INIAs) that form the backbone of the National Agricultural Research Systems (NARS) in LAC are public autonomous institutions created in the 1950s, 1960s, or early 1970s. The involvement of alternate suppliers of agricultural research such as NGOs, universities, and the private sector is of recent origin in most countries.

Despite ongoing efforts to reform and restructure agricultural research in LAC, the most common structure remains the INIA model in the bigger LAC countries and the ministerial department model in the smaller LAC countries. A number of other agricultural research suppliers can now be found in most countries, but the quality of these institutes varies widely and there is often a lack of coherence and cohesion among the efforts of the various research providers. The average share of national public agricultural research capacity of the principal agricultural research agencies (either an INIA or a ministerial research department) is 46%. The university research share is significant, at 28.1%, but tends to be lower in the smaller countries. In developed countries, about 43% of the public research was done by universities in the mid-1990s and only 10% in Africa in 1991 (Beintema and Pardey, 2001). Latin American countries have moved in the direction of the developed countries, with universities playing a greater role in agricultural innovation. The share of agricultural research conducted by non-profit agencies is small, at just 4.6%, but is much higher in a few of the smaller countries.

7.5 Basic Science and Agricultural Science Capacity in Latin America

Nowhere is the diversity of the region more evident than in the capacity for scientific research. Given the diversity of LAC countries, the role of modern biotechnology in this effort is likely to vary greatly among countries in the region.

Advances in biotechnology, like other areas of science, require a balance of basic and applied research effort. Basic science research need not be focused on agricultural applications to be important to agriculture, and is conducted in institutions both within and external to the formal agricultural research system. No measure of investments in basic science research in LAC is available. However, good measures of basic research output are available through the use of online bibliometric tools. Bibliometric methods have progressed rapidly over the past decade, particularly with the advent of online databases such as *Social Science Citation Index, Science Citation Index* and *Scopus*. These databases include citation information for manuscripts published in books, journals, conference proceedings and other scientific and popular publications. Using the online tools, publication counts for individual scientists, for faculties at a given university, or for other aggregations can be generated.

I used the *Scopus* database to compile counts of the number of journal articles published by scientists in each LAC country. The *Scopus* database contains articles published in more than 15,000 peer-reviewed journals, including 3,400 journals in the Life Sciences area. Journals from all geographical regions are covered, including non-English titles when English abstracts are provided with the articles. About 36% of the journals covered are published in North America and 3% in South America.

To measure basic science output, I searched for all journal articles published in the areas of "Biochemistry, Genetics and Molecular Biology" (BGMB) from 1997 to 2006 by scientists affiliated with institutions in each LAC country. The *Scopus* database was also used to generate counts of the number of articles published in the area of "Agricultural and Biological Sciences" (ABS). The results are displayed in Table 7.7.

A total of 46,350 BGMB and 7,937 ABS articles were published by LAC scientists. Scientists working in Brazilian institutions generated 45% of total LAC publications in both the BGMB and ABS areas. Argentina and Mexico were next with roughly similar numbers of publications, followed by Chile, Venezuela, Cuba, Colombia, Uruguay, Costa Rica and Peru. More than half of the region's countries had 50 or less BGMB articles, and 15 or less ABS articles. Totals for the other IICA members, Canada, the US and Spain are included in the table as well.

The review of scientific output suggests that Brazil is capable of becoming an important international source of both basic and agricultural science, though it must be recognized that it still has only about 30% of the basic science output and 45% of the agricultural science output of Canada, and less than 4% of the basic science output and less than 9% of the agricultural science output of the US. Canada and the US are the two countries where the most GMOs have been developed. Argentina and Mexico also show significant output in both areas, though not on Brazil's level, and Chile, Venezuela, Cuba, Colombia, and Uruguay also

Table 7.7: Number of articles published by scientists at institutions in LAC countries, 1997–2006

		Biochemistry, Genetics and Molecular Biology	LAC total	Agricultural and Biological Sciences	LAC total
1	Brazil	20,939	45%	3,570	45%
2	Argentina	8,908	19%	1,327	17%
3	Mexico	7,126	15%	1,256	16%
4	Chile	3,143	7%	449	6%
5	Venezuela	1,393	3%	398	5%
6	Cuba	1,359	3%	145	2%
7	Colombia	995	2%	210	3%
8	Uruguay	798	2%	135	2%
9	Costa Rica	328	1%	92	1%
10	Peru	319	1%	84	1%
11	Panama	206	0%	102	1%
12	Jamaica	178	0%	40	1%
13	Ecuador	144	0%	32	0%
14	Trinidad/Tobago	129	0%	26	0%
15	Bolivia	105	0%	26	0%
16	Guatemala	50	0%	15	0%
17	Paraguay	39	0%	4	0%
18	El Salvador	36	0%	8	0%
19	Barbados	35	0%	6	0%
20	Nicaragua	28	0%	4	0%
21	Dom. Rep.	22	0%	1	0%
22	Honduras	21	0%	4	0%
23	Grenada	21	0%	0	0%
24	Bahamas	7	0%	2	0%
25	Guyana	6	0%	0	0%
26	Haiti	5	0%	0	0%
27	Belize	5	0%	1	0%
28	St. Kitts/Nevis	3	0%	0	0%
29	Dominica	2	0%	0	0%
30	Suriname	0	0%	0	0%
31	St. Vincent/ Grenadines	0	0%	0	0%
32	St. Lucia	0	0%	0	0%

(Continued)

Table 7.7:   (Continued)

		Biochemistry, Genetics and Molecular Biology	LAC total	Agricultural and Biological Sciences	LAC total
33	Antigua/Barbuda	0	0%	0	0%
	Total	**46,350**	**100%**	**7,937**	**100%**
	Canada	66,815		6,336	
	US	554,180		42,001	
	Spain	45,452		5,072	
	China	53,397		5,812	
	India	32,325		4,604	

Source: SCOPUS database.

show some limited capacity. Scientific capacity in the remaining countries is quite small. Two-thirds of the region's countries produce less than 10 basic science articles and less than 3 agricultural science articles per year. This calls into question whether there is now, or will be in the foreseeable future, enough trained scientists to even staff competent biosafety regulatory institutions. Establishing regional, rather than individual national, biosafety committees would appear to be the more logical option, though political issues will not be easy.

LAC national agricultural research capacity falls into three groups. The first group includes the 25 smallest LAC agricultural research systems. These are about the size of a single US Land Grant University, but they are at a large disadvantage to US universities in terms of the training of their scientists, most of whom hold BS or MS degrees. The second group of medium-size countries has an increased capacity across the research spectrum, but has large areas of limited expertise. This group includes Costa Rica, Uruguay, Colombia, and Chile. Finally, there are the three "giants" of the region — Brazil, Mexico, and Argentina — that have significant basic research capacity, a higher number of Ph.D. trained scientists, several well-staffed universities, and scientists that regularly participate in international scientific congresses.

The small systems not only lack human capital to conduct basic research, but must also be borrowers of virtually all kinds of research, including finished technologies. These countries are incapable of adequately staffing research for even important agricultural commodities with a full range of required research disciplines. A significant challenge for these countries is to increase the level of training of their agricultural researchers, and to retain the scientists with advanced degrees in the research sector. The low numbers of Ph.D. and MS-level scientists leave many countries below the threshold level of scientific talent needed even to competently screen and adapt technologies developed elsewhere. But it is clear that the bulk of useful agricultural technologies will be developed abroad and adapted to local conditions. In other words, the focus of these countries must be on accessing direct technology spillovers, from whatever source.

The second-tier countries are in a much better position to take advantage of spillovers because their higher numbers of researchers with advanced training are able to screen foreign technologies when given access. These countries will still be dependent on imported technology in many areas, but they are able to perform adaptive research. They should also be capable of carrying out strategic research and some basic research in nationally important commodities.

The top tier countries are able to mount credible research programs in all areas, including basic research. A significant number of their scientists are tied to the international scientific community, and the number of researchers is adequate to cover all important commodities and disciplines. Nonetheless, efforts to take advantage of spillovers are a key component of technical change in the future.

7.6   Capacity to Regulate Agricultural Biotechnology

Twenty countries in the region have signed and ratified the Cartagena Protocol on Biosafety (CPB) (Table 7.8). Another nine have signed but not ratified the CPB, leaving just Guyana and Suriname as countries that have not moved forward on the CPB. While nearly all countries have signed the CPB, the majority of countries are still in the process of passing specific biosafety legislation (Table 7.9).

Table 7.8: Status of action on Cartagena Protocol on Biosafety (CPB)

Parties to the Cartagena Protocol on Biosafety (CPB)		
Antigua and Barbuda	Dominica	Paraguay
Bahamas	Ecuador	Peru
Bolivia	Guatemala	St. Lucia
Brazil	Mexico	Grenada
Colombia	Nicaragua	Trinidad & Tobago
Cuba	Panama	Belize
St. Vincent and the Grenadines	St. Christopher and Nevis	
Countries that have signed but not ratified the CPB		
Argentina	Costa Rica	Jamaica
Venezuela	Haiti	Uruguay
Chile	Honduras	
Countries that have not signed the CPB		
Guyana	Suriname	

Source: Tewolde, 2006.

Seven LAC countries have approved one or more events for food, feed, the environment and planting (Table 7.10). All approved events were developed by the multinational private sector, so the approvals indicate that a country possesses the scientific capacity to staff biosafety regulatory mechanisms, and the political climate to see the process through, rather than national biotechnology research capacity *per se*. The political and public support for biotechnology has been volatile in all countries except for Argentina. In Brazil, for example, RR soybeans were approved for planting by the national regulatory committee in 1998, but a moratorium on the sale of GMO seeds was then imposed until 2005. The approval process in Brazil remains highly political and uncertain. All countries in the region have found it difficult to move events through the biosafety process. The result has been that there has been no increase over time in the number of events approved in the region.

7.7 Intellectual Property Rights in LAC

Issues of the protection of property rights in agriculture have received significant attention in the recent literature (Anonymous, 2006; Byerlee

Table 7.9:   Status of biosafety legislation by country

Specific Biosafety Legislation	Related Legislation	No Information/No Access to Legislation
Argentina	Belize*	Antigua and Barbuda
Brazil	Bolivia*	Bahamas
Mexico	Chile	Barbados
	Costa Rica*	Dominica
	Ecuador	Guyana
	El Salvador*	Haiti
	Guatemala	St. Lucia
	Grenada	St. Christopher and Nevis
	Honduras	St. Vincent and the Grenadines
	Jamaica*	Suriname
	Nicaragua*	Trinidad & Tobago
	Panama	
	Paraguay	
	Peru**	
	Dominican Republic	
	Uruguay	
	Venezuela	

Source: Tewolde, 2006.
*In the process of generating and/or modifying laws.
**Law pending official publication.

and Fischer, 2001; Moschini and Lapan, 1997). The emphasis is the result of the increased importance of the private sector as a research provider as well as interest in the effect of changes in IPR laws and practices that have resulted from new international agreements such as the Convention on Biological Diversity, the International Treaty on Plant Genetic Resources for Food and Agriculture, and requirements arising from the TRIPS Agreements. Relatively little attention is paid to the issue of enforcement in the existing literature, yet the inability to protect IP even when legislation exists has been a critical constraint on private sector investment in crop improvement and in GMOs for developing countries. Plant variety protection (PVP) and other laws are only a first step towards effective protection of IP, as pointed out in a recent

Table 7.10:   Biosafety approvals by type of approval, 1996–2006

Country	Environment — Number of events approved (year of first approval)	Planting — Number of events approved	Food — Number of events approved (year of first approval)	Feed — Number of events approved
Argentina	10 (1996)	10	10 (1998)	10
Brazil	2 (1998)	2	2 (1998)	3
Colombia	4 (2000)	3	5 (2002)	5
Honduras	1 (2002)	1	1 (2002)	1
Mexico	4 (1996)	4	36 (1996)	2
Paraguay	1 (2004)	1	1 (2004)	1
Uruguay	5 (1997)	5	3 (1997)	3
Year				
1996	3	3	8	2
1997	2	2	1	1
1998	5	5	6	5
1999	1	1	2	0
2000	3	3	1	0
2001	1	1	5	2
2002	2	1	5	1
2003	2	2	7	2
2004	4	4	12	5
2005	2	2	5	4
2006	2	2	5	0
Total	**27**	**26**	**57**	**22**

Source: James, 2006.

World Bank publication:

"PVP can be expected to have only a modest impact on the direction of domestic commercial seed markets, given that most PVP systems in developing countries cannot control farmer seed saving and possess very limited enforcement capabilities (because of inadequacies in legal systems, insufficient regulatory staff, and insufficient experience in the companies themselves). The protection of transgenic crops has proven particularly difficult in developing countries. An IPR regime, on its own, is not likely to provide the incentives that elicit the emergence of a robust plant breeding and seed sector; attention to other institutions and the provision of an enabling environment are also necessary." (Anonymous, 2006, pp. xv–xvi)

Table 7.11 summarizes some aspects of IPR legislation among the larger LAC countries. All of the listed countries except for Peru and Costa Rica have adopted UPOV 1978 rules for protection of plant varieties. Trinidad-Tobago, Panama and Nicaragua have also adopted UPOV 1978. The existence of legislation covering other important aspects of IP protection is spotty, and largely untested in court. It appears that the majority of countries are aware of the IP issues involved with biotechnology, but all are

Table 7.11:   IPR protection in agricultural biotechnology related areas in LAC

Country	Discovery	Biol. Process	Plants[a]	Plant Varieties[b]	Animals (Breeds)	Genes
Argentina	No	Yes	Yes	Yes	Yes	Yes
Chile	No	Yes	?	Yes	Yes[c]	?
Brazil	No	Yes	No	Yes	No	No
Uruguay	No	No	No	Yes	No	No
Paraguay	No	No	No	Yes	No	?
Bolivia*	No	No	No	Yes	No	?
Peru*	No	No	No	No	No	?
Ecuador*	No	No[d]	No	Yes	No	Yes
Colombia*	No	No	No[e]	Yes	No	?
Venezuela*	No	No	No	Yes	No	Yes
México	No	No	Yes	Yes	No	?
Costa Rica	No	No	No	No	No	?

Source: Trigo et al., 2002.
*Legislation is under the scope of Decision 344 of the Cartagena Agreement.
[a]Genetic modification.
[b]UPOV 78.
[c]Animal races are explicitly excluded from patentability (law 19.039, Art. 37b), but not animals as such.
[d]Yes to obtain plant varieties, no for animals.
[e]Not defined. WIPO document reports no exclusion for plants from patentability, but it does not appear to be possible to obtain a patent for a plant *per se*.

struggling with the complexity of passing legislation that meets national needs while conforming to international obligations. The degree to which case law has supported enforcement of IP protection is unknown.

7.8 Piracy and the Enforcement of IPR

The difficulty in protecting intellectual property has been a serious concern of the private sector in nearly all developing countries. To date, the private sector's experience with generating revenue from the sale of GMOs in developing countries has not been encouraging. Table 7.12 lists the developing countries and crops where GM crops have been marketed.

Table 7.12:   Piracy in GMO crops in developing countries

Country	GMO Area 2006 (million ha)	Crop	Degree of Piracy
Argentina	15.9	Soy	Near Complete
Argentina	1.8	Maize	Low
Argentina	0.37	Cotton	Low
Brazil	11.5	Soy	Complete
Brazil	0.3	Cotton	Complete
India	3.8	Cotton	High (50%–66%)[a]
China	1.4	Cotton	High (87%)
Paraguay	2.0	Soy	Complete
South Africa	1.4	Maize	Low
South Africa	na	Cotton	Low
South Africa	na	Soy	Unknown
Uruguay	0.4	Cotton	Low
Mexico	0.1	Maize	Unknown
Philippines	0.2	Cotton	Unknown
Colombia	<0.1	Maize	Unknown
Honduras	<0.1		
Total GM area	37		
Area affected by piracy	33		
% area affected by piracy	89%		

Source for total area: James, 2006.
[a] Pray et al., 2001; Anonymous, 2006.

Table 7.13: RR soybean area (million ha) and estimated technology fee collections ($m), 1996–2006

Country	1996	1997	1998	1999	2000	2001	2002	2003	2004	2005	2006	All Years
Argentina	0.1	0.4	1.8	4.9	6.9	8.8	10.4	11.8	13.1	14.4	15.9	88
Brazil	—	—	—	—	—	—	—	3.0	5.0	9.4	11.5	29
Paraguay									1.2	1.8	2.0	5
GM area	0.1	0.4	1.8	4.9	6.9	8.8	10.4	14.8	19.3	25.6	29.4	122
Tech value[a]	$1.5	$5.4	$26	$71	$100	$128	$152	$216	$281	$374	$429	$1,784
Collected[b]	$0.3	$1.2	$6	$16	$9	$11	$13	$15	$16	$18	$20	$125
Lost revenue	$1.1	$4.2	$21	$56	$92	$117	$139	$201	$265	$356	$409	$1,659

Source for area estimates: James, 2006.
[a]Valued at US technology fee rate of $16.00/ha.
[b]Argentina estimates based on Trigo and Cap, 2003; Brazil & Paraguay assumed to be 0.

A rough estimate is that nearly 90% of the area currently sown to GMOs in developing countries is affected by significant levels of seed piracy. The loss of revenue has been most severe in the South Cone, where little revenue has been collected from the planting of a total of nearly 120 million ha of RR soybeans (Table 7.13). Technology fees have been collected on a greater proportion of maize and cotton area than on soybean area. The most consistent collection of fees is on the sale of hybrid maize seed, where it appears that piracy has been a relatively minor problem. Collections have also been high in Bt cotton in Mexico and South Africa, but low in China and India, despite the fact that hybrids are used in India.

The most common form of seed piracy occurs through farmers saving and reselling harvested seed. The size of the legitimate seed market is reduced not just by farmers saving seed for their own use, but by resale of saved seed to other farmers. Often, those selling seed are not just farmers selling seed to their neighbors, but businessmen who market brown bag seed over wide areas, possibly even across national borders. This type of piracy is widespread in the South Cone and is probably present on some scale in all countries. Farmer-to-farmer sales are difficult to detect and expensive to prosecute through the legal system. Prosecution would require courts and juries to rule against a local farmer in favor of a multinational corporation.

Monsanto also found with the Canadian case against Percy Schmeiser that even winning a piracy case in the court of law may entail losses in the court of public opinion. The high level of piracy in cotton in India has occurred despite the fact that available varieties are hybrids.

Monsanto has had few enforcement problems in the US. One of the key elements has been the use of contracts to prohibit seed savings. This allows them to prosecute violators for breach of contract, rather than IP protection. Since 1997, Monsanto has filed similar lawsuits 90 times in 25 states, including North Dakota, against 147 farmers and 39 agriculture companies (Elias, 2005). Monsanto uses a "tipline" that can be used anonymously to report farmers who are illegally using its seeds, and it settles many of those cases before a lawsuit is filed. It has gone to trial five times and has never lost a legal fight against an accused pirate. Protection of IP is far more difficult and uncertain in developing countries.

In the face of difficulties in collecting revenues at the point of sale of soybean seed, Monsanto has proposed a type of endpoint royalty system in Paraguay, Argentina and Brazil. Monsanto has been able to initiate negotiations on the endpoint royalty system because it holds patents on the Roundup Ready technology in many markets. Patents are in place in many countries including Australia, the European Union, Brazil, Belarus, Canada, Switzerland, Japan, Kazakhstan, the Netherlands, Russia, Sweden, Ukraine, Uzbekistan, US, Denmark, Israel, New Zealand, and South Africa. The system has been operating in Brazil and Paraguay since the 2005/2006 growing season, but Monsanto has been unable to reach an agreement with farmers and grain merchandisers in Argentina. In 2005 and 2006, Monsanto used legal actions to halt Argentine soy shipments in Spain, Britain, Denmark, and the Netherlands (Haskel, 2006). The Argentine government and producers have countersued Monsanto, but with no resolution to either the legal issues or the collection of royalties. In January 2004 Monsanto announced that it would cease seed operations in Argentina. Argentina operates under UPOV 1978, which allows farmers to save seed though not to sell or trade saved seed.

Under the endpoint royalty system, farmers who are unable to provide a sales receipt for the purchase of soybean seed from a licensed dealer are required to pay an "indemnity fee" that is paid at the elevator when they sell their harvest. The elevators receive a commission as compensation for handling the fee. The fee is distributed among Monsanto and its seed partners, with an additional percentage allocated to public sector research, or to a foundation that funds research grants.

In Paraguay the fee for the 2006/2007 growing season was $3.09/ton, but is slated to increase to $6.00/ton over time. US farmers pay a technology fee of approximately $5.50/ton for the use of RR soybeans. Royalties in Paraguay are distributed as:

- 53% Monsanto
- 17% Seed companies
- 8% Grain handlers (50 firms)
- 10% Public research
- 12% Administrative expenses.

In Brazil a royalty agreement has been implemented for the 2006/2007 season, but details are not available.

7.9 Summary

This paper has reviewed the experience of LAC countries with the use of GMOs, and has assessed their scientific and institutional capacity to access biotechnology. Several conclusions emerge from this review of biotechnology in Latin America. First, where employed, GMOs have rendered large financial and environmental benefits that have been widely shared among farmers, industry and consumers. The second observation is the extreme diversity of scientific, commercial and technical capacity in the region. The gulf between the three most advanced countries and prospects for the majority of the region's countries is very large. To date there has been little success in developing regional mechanisms for intra-country coordination of biosafety or IPR management, yet such action would appear to be vital for small countries to access biotechnology innovations.

Finally, the use of GMOs has little momentum in the region. The area under GMOs has expanded rapidly, but the number of applications has been stagnant and the process of obtaining approvals has not become more predictable or less costly. Only HT and Bt varieties of soybean, cotton and maize are being grown. All of these have been available since 1996. The rate at which national biosafety committees are approving new events is stagnant, averaging just 2.5 approvals per year for the entire region (Table 7.10). There has been forward movement in putting biosafety and IPR legislation in place, but the rate at which the new laws have been put to use and tested has been very slow. It is likely to be a decade or more before any countries in Central America or the Caribbean see significant impact from biotechnology, and there may also be a loss of momentum in the larger countries.

The greatest obstacle to the spread of GMOs may be the difficulty that industry has had in protecting intellectual property. The private sector has been the source of 100% of the farm use of GMOs to date. It could be the driving force behind future progress as well, but there will be no private sector investment until there is radical improvement in their ability to appropriate the benefits of their investment. The attempt to implement an endpoint royalty scheme is an experiment that has promise as a way forward, but governments, farmers and other parts of the agribusiness sector have been resistant to implementing such a system.

Bibliography

Alston, J. M. (2002). "Spillovers." *Australian Journal of Agricultural and Resource Economics* 46 (3): 315–346.

Anonymous (2006). "Intellectual Property Rights: Designing Regimes to Support Plant Breeding in Developing Countries." Agriculture and Rural Development Department 35517-GLB. The World Bank, Washington, DC.

Asociación Semilleros Argentinos, A. "La Biotecnología En Argentina." http://www.asa.org.ar/bio.asp.

Beintema, N. M. and P. G. Pardey (2001). "Recent Developments in the Conduct of Latin American Agricultural Research." Paper presented at the ICAST Conference on Agricultural Science and Technology, Beijing, 7–9 November.

Bennett, R., *et al.* (2003). "Bt Cotton, Pesticides, Labour and Health — a Case Study of Smallholder Farmers in the Makhathini Flats, Republic of South Africa." *Outlook on Agriculture* 32 (2): 123–128.

Bennett, R. M., *et al.* (2004). "Economic Impact of Genetically Modified Cotton in India." *AgBioForum* 7 (3): 96–100.

Brookes, G. and P. Barfoot (2005). "GM Crops: The Global Economic and Environmental Impact — the First Nine Years 1996–2004." *AgBioForum* 8 (2&3): 187–196.

Byerlee, D. and K. Fischer (2001). "Accessing Modern Science: Policy and Institutional Options in Developing Countries." *IP Strategy Today* 1: 1–27.

Byerlee, D. and G. Traxler (2001). "The Role of Technology Spillovers and Economies of Size in the Efficient Design of Agricultural Research Systems," pp. 161–186, in eds. J. M. Alston, P. G. Pardey, and M. J. Taylor, *Agricultural Science Policy: Changing Global Agendas.* Johns Hopkins University Press.

Chudnovsky, D. (2005). "The Diffusion of Biotech Crops in the Argentine Agriculture Sector." Socio-economic issues of agricultural biotechnology in developing countries: making GM crops work for human development, Bellagio, Italy, 30 May–4 June.

Cremers, M. W. J. and J. Roseboom (1997). "Agricultural Research in Government Agencies in Latin America: A Preliminary Assessment of Investment Trends." ISNAR Discussion Paper 97–7. ISNAR, The Hague.

Elias, P. (2005). "Enforcing Single-Season Seeds, Monsanto Sues Farmers." *USA Today*/Associated Press, 13 January.

Falck-Zepeda, J. B., G. Traxler, and R. G. Nelson (2000). "Rent Creation and Distribution from Biotechnology Innovations: The Case of Bt Cotton and Herbicide-Tolerant Soybeans in 1997." *Agribusiness* 16 (1): 21–32.

Gouse, M., C. Pray, and D. Schimmelpfennig (2004). "The Distribution of Benefits from Bt Cotton Adoption in South Africa." *AgBioForum* 7 (4): 187–194.

Gouse, M., *et al.* (2006). "Three Seasons of Subsistence Insect-Resistant Maize in South Africa: Have Smallholders Benefited?" *AgBioForum* 9 (1): 15–22.

Haskel, D. "Argentina to Take Legal Action against U.S. Biotech Giant Monsanto in Spain." CropChoice news, June 1, 2006. Accessed April 15, 2006 at http://www.cropchoice.com/leadstrygmo060106.html

Ismael, Y., R. Bennett, and S. Morse (2002). "Farm-Level Economic Impact of Biotechnology: Smallholder Bt Cotton Farmers in South Africa." *Outlook on Agriculture* 31 (2): 107–111.

James, C. (2006). "Executive Summary of Global Status of Commercialized Biotech/GM Crops: 2006." ISAAA Briefs 35. ISAAA, Ithaca, NY. http://www.isaaa.org/

James, C. (2002). "Preview: Global Status of Commercialized Transgenic Crops: 2002." ISAAA Briefs 27. ISAAA, Ithaca, NY. http://www.isaaa.org/

Kirsten, J. and M. Grouse (2003). "The Adoption and Impact of Agricultural Biotechnology in South Africa," in ed. N. Kalaitzandonakes, *Economic and Environmental Impacts of First Generation Biotechnologies.* New York: Kluwer Academic Press/Plenum Publications.

Morse, S., R. M. Bennett, and Y. Ismael (2005). "Genetically Modified Insect Resistance in Cotton: Some Farm-Level Economic Impacts in India." *Crop Protection* 24 (5): 433–440.

Moschini, G. and H. Lapan (1997). "Intellectual Property Rights and the Welfare Effects of Agricultural R&D." *American Journal of Agricultural Economics* 79 (4): 1229–1242.

Paarlberg, R. L. (2003). *The Politics of Precaution: Genetically Modified Crops in Developing Countries.* Baltimore: Johns Hopkins University Press.

Pardey, P. G., *et al.* (2006). "Agricultural Research: A Growing Global Divide?" Food Policy Report 17. International Food Policy Research Institute (IFPRI), Washington, DC.

Pray, C. E., *et al.* (2001). "Impact of Bt Cotton in China." *World Development* 29 (5): 813–825.

Price, G. K., *et al.* (2003). "Size and Distribution of Market Benefits from Adopting Biotech Crops." Technical Bulletin 1906. ERS/USDA, Washington, DC.

Qaim, M. (2003). "Bt Cotton in India: Field Trial Results and Economic Projections." *World Development* 31 (12): 2115–2127.

Qaim, M. and A. De Janvry (2005). "Bt Cotton and Pesticide Use in Argentina: Economic and Environmental Effects." *Environment and Development Economics* 10: 179–200.

Qaim, M. and A. De Janvry (2003). "Genetically Modified Crops, Corporate Pricing Strategies, and Farmers' Adoption: The Case of Bt Cotton in Argentina." *American Journal of Agricultural Economics* 85 (4): 814–828.

Qaim, M. and I. Matuschke (2005). "Impacts of Genetically Modified Crops in Developing Countries: A Survey." *Quarterly Journal of International Agriculture* 44 (3): 207–227.

Qaim, M., *et al.* (2006). "Adoption of Bt Cotton and Impact Variability: Insights from India." *Review of Agricultural Economics* 28 (1): 48–58.

Qaim, M. and G. Traxler (2005). "Roundup Ready Soybeans in Argentina: Farm Level and Aggregate Welfare Effects." *Agricultural Economics* 32 (1): 73–86.

Qaim, M. and D. Zilberman (2003). "Yield Effects of Genetically Modified Crops in Developing Countries." *Science* 299 (5608): 900–902.

Raney, T. (2006). "Economic Impact of Transgenic Crops in Developing Countries." *Current Opinion in Biotechnology* 17 (2): 174–178.

Sobolevsky, A., G. Moschini, and H. Lapan (2005). "Genetically Modified Crops and Product Differentiation: Trade and Welfare Effects in the Soybean Complex." *American Journal of Agricultural Economics* 87 (3): 621–644.

Tewolde, A. (2006). "Biotechnology and Biosafety: Instruments for Achieving Agricultural Competitiveness." *ComunIIca* 3 (July–December): 14–20.

Thirtle, C., *et al.* (2003). "Can GM-Technologies Help the Poor? The Impact of Bt Cotton in Makhathini Flats, Kwazulu-Natal." *World Development* 31 (4): 717–732.

Traxler, G. (2005). "The GMO Experience in North & South America." *International Journal of Technology and Globalization* 2 (1/2): 46–61.

Traxler, G. and D. Byerlee (2001). "Linking Technical Change to Research Effort: An Examination of Aggregation and Spillovers Effects." *Agricultural Economics* 24 (3): 235–246.

Traxler, G., *et al.* (2003). "Transgenic Cotton in Mexico: Economic and Environmental Impacts," in ed. N. Kalaitzandonakes, *Economic and Environmental Impacts of First Generation Biotechnologies*. New York: Kluwer Academic.

Trigo, E., *et al.* (2002). *Genetically Modified Crops in Argentine Agriculture: An Open-Ended Story*. Buenos Aires: Libros del Zorzal.

Trigo, E. J. and E. J. Cap (2003). "The Impact of the Introduction of Transgenic Crops in Argentinean Agriculture." *AgBioForum* 6 (3): 87–94.

Trigo, E. J., *et al.* (2002). "Agricultural Biotechnology and Rural Development in Latin America and the Caribbean." Inter-American Development Bank, Sustainable Development Department, Washington, DC.

WHO (1988). "The WHO Recommended Classification of Pesticides by Hazard and Guidelines to Classification." WHO Document VBC/88.953. World Health Organization, Geneva.

Chapter Eight

ℬiotechnology, Agriculture, and Food Security in Southern Africa: Strategic Policy Challenges and Opportunities

*Steven Were Omamo and Klaus von Grebmer**

8.1 Biosafety

A range of conventional biotechnology-related activities (such as tissue culture and marker-assisted selection) are underway in several countries in southern Africa. But only in South Africa have field-based transformation events attained commercial status (Mnyulwa and Mugwagwa, 2005). Several governments have established interim structures to serve as coordinating and advisory bodies (as well as for enforcement of biosafety regulations), but comprehensive parliamentary bills addressing all aspects of biotechnology have yet to be developed in most countries. The promise of modern biotechnology in spurring agricultural development and food security in the region thus remains only partially exploited. Controversy continues to surround public and scientific discussions of such potential, further slowing progress in policy development and implementation. This paper outlines key strategic issues to be addressed if biotechnology is to

*Steven Were Omamo (UN-WFP) and Klaus von Grebmer (IFPRI).

be shaped in ways that benefit the poor and hungry, not only in southern Africa but also elsewhere in Africa. Those issues are argued to relate primarily to biosafety, trade, and intellectual property rights. Implications for policy are drawn.

Disputes over the acceptability of GM food aid during southern Africa's food crisis of 2001–2002 altered the content and character of the debate over the future direction of policy and investment to spur agricultural development and increase food security in the region. The risks and opportunities opened up by GM products render that debate complex and often polarized. Most countries in the region lack regulatory and scientific assessment structures necessary to take decisive steps on biotechnology. Only three countries in the region — Malawi, South Africa, and Zimbabwe — have legal mechanisms for biosafety. Systems elsewhere are still emerging. Most countries have not prioritized development of biosafety regulatory structures because of the low level of their biotechnology R&D. If lessons from the 2002 regional food crisis are any guide, the countries in the region are best advised to put regulatory and scientific monitoring mechanisms in place, because GM products may enter the region not as products from local research, but from trade in such products developed elsewhere. The food aid controversy underlined the fact that in a globalized economy, the development of biosafety regulations is not a luxury, but a necessity.

In creating biosafety frameworks, regional stakeholders need to consider their respective economic, social, and cultural contexts. They would benefit from critically examining the dominant approaches to biosafety in the world, namely those of the European Union and the United States, the latter of which is used as a model in international development circles. Whereas in the European Union modern biotechnology spurred the development of new regulations, in the United States scientists and regulators relied on the country's existing regulatory structure instead of creating new laws. However, these approaches, while instructive, may not be entirely appropriate for the region. The US experience, for example, illustrates the hazards of developing biosafety frameworks not attuned to local food habits and economic and health conditions. US agencies did not take these considerations into account and so risked implying the untested assertion that GM crops are safe for all populations. The population of southern Africa consumes unique foods, uses unique food processing methods, and relies on staple foods, such as maize, for the majority of their caloric intake. Further-more, the high prevalence of morbidity, malnutrition, and compromised immunity due to HIV needs to be considered when testing GM products in the region.

As more complex GM foods are developed, these contextual factors will require even greater attention. People in the region need assurances that their safety, health, and beliefs have been taken into account as far as possible before new forms of food products are introduced. Key aspects of a biosafety framework would therefore include: (1) legislative frameworks that include provisions to address trade-offs across public agencies in var-ious sectors (e.g., agriculture vs. health vs. environment) and stakeholder groups (e.g., farmers vs. consumers); (2) clear criteria for selecting products to be regulated; (3) unambiguous requirements for transparent state action and enforceable provisions for vigorous public involvement; (4) rigorous risk-benefit assessment and management; and (5) communication with stakeholders on national biotechnology strategies and policies.

8.2 Trade

As participants in world trade, all southern African countries need biosafety policies capable of evaluating GM products entering the country for environmental and food safety. Harmonizing biosafety regulations across countries would be sensible. Regional similarities in economy, ecology, and food habits would ease the process. However, the World Trade Organization (WTO) is putting pressure on countries to harmonize their policies with its own regulations. Compatibility with regional and WTO standards would facilitate trade for these countries, but each country should be able to establish regulations that meet its own needs and goals.

On one hand, introducing agricultural biotechnology provides an opportunity for poorer countries to produce higher yields, lower their pro-duction costs, and source cheap agricultural exports. On the other hand, such benefits may come at the cost of reduced access to key markets, espe-cially in Europe, where consumer sentiment against GMOs is likely to remain high well into the future. Individual countries, and the region as a whole, must find ways to resolve this tension.

Different consumer preferences in the world regarding GM foods —
and, as discussed earlier, the environmental, food-habit, social, and health
conditions in southern Africa — indicate that most southern African countries should endeavor to develop biosafety and trade policies that suit their
respective needs, despite pressure from the WTO to conform to its guidelines. In reality, the contention over the trade in and safety of GMOs
has been caused by lack of international standards. This has given WTO
member countries room to adopt trade-restrictive measures on GMOs. For
example, the WTO recognizes environmental concerns, but thus far these
concerns have not been tested in a legal dispute. Although the Cartagena
Protocol on Biosafety is an international agreement on procedures for safe
transboundary movement of GMOs, it is not clear whether the WTO will
recognize the Protocol's regulations. Finally, the WTO currently focuses
on environmental safety. Safety of GM foods, another vital issue, is one
about which the WTO treaty regulations remain undeveloped.

Harmonization and rationalization of national and regional policies
on biotechnology and biosafety is a goal that the governments and other
stakeholders in the countries of southern Africa should and can achieve,
particularly to facilitate the smooth movement and transit of GM material
within the region, whether for commercial or non-commercial purposes.
First, national guidelines among the different ministries must be clarified.
Countries should then harmonize their policies and procedures for standard
setting and enforcement, risk-benefit assessment and management, prior
informed consent, and information and documentation. A cost-effective
and highly successful initiative in harmonizing seed regulations and policies
in eastern and central Africa could provide valuable lessons on how to pro-
ceed (ECAPAPA, 2002). This relatively modest initiative has yielded concrete trade-enhancing outcomes. Research findings coupled with focused
deliberations among stakeholders drawn from the public and private sectors
led to agreements that reduced the number of quarantined pests from 33 to
3, thereby reducing the period required for issuance of phytosanitary cer-
tificates from two weeks to two days, with major cost savings. Participants
agreed on uniform procedures for variety evaluation, reducing the number of seasons required for National Variety Performance Trials from six to
two. Major rationalization of requirements for seed imports and exports was
achieved in all participating countries, leading in some cases to a one-stop,

one-person process, whereas in the past several people in distant locales would have been involved. National and regional seed trader associations have been created, with much of the impetus coming from private sector participants.

The potential economic benefits that GM crop production might bring to small farmers and food security in the region are not a panacea for broader trade-related difficulties (Mupotola, 2005). If southern Africa fails to address the issue of export subsidies and protected markets in developed countries and their adverse effects on developing countries, little benefit will result. In the era of biotechnology, there is thus added onus on countries such as those in southern Africa to act cohesively and participate fully in areas of mutual interest like these.

8.3   Intellectual Property Rights

If southern African governments start to procure biotechnologies, they should consider conforming to the provisions of the Trade-Related Aspects of Intellectual Property Rights agreement. For their own benefit, they will also need to decide on the desired extent and use of IPRs and determine the cost implications (Olembo, 2005).

A country not currently growing GM crops may decide to do so and will need to choose whether to develop the technologies itself or not. If southern African countries decide to obtain technologies of foreign multinational research companies, they will need greater clarity in their IPR policies. Yet, despite having already acceded to one or more regional or international agreements on IPRs, most countries in the region still lack clear-cut policies. Strong IPRs can provide the incentives private companies require to sell their technologies. Advocates of protective IPRs argue that a country can make advances in agricultural growth and food security as a result of these technologies. Regardless of their choice to go forward independently or to lease technologies from outside, governments will need to articulate clearly the protection to be granted to breeders and to small farmers and resources in the country.

Countries in the region may develop legislation that protects the rights of farmers as well as indigenous knowledge and resources. In response to the

International Union for the Protection of New Varieties of Plants agreement, in 2002 the Organization of African Unity published *The African Model Law* to protect the rights of local communities, farmers, and breeders and to regulate access to biological resources. This document was developed as a model for African national laws, but to date no such laws have been enacted. IPRs should be coherent and balance the rights of the innovators with those of the poor, while also reflecting each country's needs and development goals.

8.4   Implications

There is continued uncertainty about the possibility and seriousness of food safety and environmental problems resulting from expanded application of biotechnology in southern Africa, especially with respect to GM products. At the same time, food insecurity is a major problem in the region. GM crops may help alleviate hunger and malnutrition, but to what extent and how much is unclear, especially if the underlying causes of these problems are not simultaneously addressed. Given these uncertainties, what policies should southern African governments pursue?

Greater investment in regional capacity building is essential. The will to address biotechnology issues must be matched by readiness to strengthen national and regional capacity in scientific research, policy design and implementation, risk-benefit assessment and risk-benefit management, as well as in managing institutional processes that support these activities. Governments and other stakeholders must identify key capacity gaps and determine which ones require immediate attention and which can be addressed later. Improved skills and knowledge will be needed in the areas of scientific research, regulation, legal services, and policy.

Capacity-strengthening strategies will have to be prioritized and realistic. Core scientific capabilities and infrastructure are required for research on GM crops and, regarding biosafety, on biotechnology product evaluation, risk-benefit management, inspection, and monitoring. Given the differences among countries in these areas, there could be benefits to creating regional actions to coordinate cross-border capacity building. SADC is well-poised to provide leadership in this area. Regional coordination of efforts for creating effective regulatory systems, including their harmonization, will also improve regional economic activity and food security.

Critics of biotechnology often point out that a technological solution is being advanced to solve problems that at root have political and economic causes. Non-GM policies to eradicate hunger and malnutrition have been implemented and have shown success when they were designed to suit local contexts, were well-managed, and received the requisite levels of political, institutional, and economic support. There is also concern that with the use of biotechnologies, these basic and necessary policies may be neglected. It is also being increasingly recognized that food security depends on the broader foundation of good governance, peace, rule of law, respect for human rights, and equity in development.

If GM technologies are adopted, their positive impact on malnutrition and food insecurity will depend in part on continuation and expansion of "conventional" programs that have also been implemented to achieve these ends and to improve governance. Improved household food security through GM agriculture — if achieved — will not reduce child malnutrition unless governments also invest in programs for child health, child care, and child feeding, all of which women have difficulty providing due to their own poor health, nutritional status, and knowledge, as well as time demands.

A key problem in the debate over biotechnology is the existence of false information and misrepresentations, causing conflicting claims to arise that only make decision making more difficult. Again, the most critical information for southern African stakeholders and policymakers is on the benefits and risks that biotechnology would bring to their region, and only long-term scientific research can provide answers on these issues. Governments must make requisite long-term investments to facilitate generation of such information.

Concerted efforts to formulate and implement biosafety strategies, policies, and regulatory systems require reliable and sustainable streams of financial resources, especially to meet the heavy burden of capacity strengthening. If southern African countries choose to develop innovations in biotechnology, they will also need to invest in research over a long time frame and in a steady manner, either individually or, better, collectively.

Bibliography

ECAPAPA (Eastern and Central Africa Program for Agricultural Policy Analysis) (2002). *Harmonization of seed policies and regulations in eastern Africa: Results and agreements.* ECAPAPA Monograph Series 4. Entebbe: ECAPAPA.

Mnyulwa, D. and J. Mugwagwa (2005). "Agricultural Biotechnology in Southern Africa: A Regional Synthesis." In *Biotechnology, Agriculture, and Food Security in Southern Africa,* eds., Steven Were Omamo and Klaus von Grebmer. Washington, DC: International Food Policy Research Institute.

Mupotola, M. (2005). "Trade Policy." In *Biotechnology, Agriculture, and Food Security in Southern Africa,* eds., Steven Were Omamo and Klaus von Grebmer. Washington, DC: International Food Policy Research Institute.

Olembo, N. (2005). "Intellectual Property Rights Policy." In *Biotechnology, Agriculture, and Food Security in Southern Africa,* eds., Steven Were Omamo and Klaus von Grebmer. Washington, DC: International Food Policy Research Institute.

Pelletier, D. (2005). "Food Safety and Consumer Choice Policy." In *Biotechnology, Agriculture, and Food Security in Southern Africa,* eds., Steven Were Omamo and Klaus von Grebmer. Washington, DC: International Food Policy Research Institute.

Sengooba, T. (2006). "Status report: GM crop field trial and commercialization activities on the African continent." Slide presentation. Program for Biosafety Systems Eastern Africa Office, Kampala.

Chapter Nine

Developing Country Options under TRIPS: Choices to Maximize Biotech Transfer

William Lesser and Deepthi Kolady*

9.1 Introduction

The TRIPs (Trade-Related Aspects of Intellectual Property Rights),[1] Annex 1C of the World Trade Organization (WTO) agreement, was controversial during negations in the past decade and remains so today, especially within developing countries. Many developing country representatives continue to view the WTO agreement as imbalanced in

---

*William Lesser is the Susan Eckert Lynch Professor of Science and Business, and Department Chair, in the Applied Economic and Management Department at Cornell University. Lesser's research focuses on the implications of agricultural biotechnology products on production costs and the size, structure, and geographic distribution of farming. He also concentrates on the costs, benefits, and structural implications of intellectual property for plants, seed, and animals (http://aem.cornell.edu/profiles/lesser.htm).

Deepthi Kolady is a research collaborator with IFPRI and visiting fellow in the Department of International Agriculture at Cornell University. The chapter was prepared while she was a Post-Doctoral Fellow in the Dyson School of Applied Economics and Management at Cornell University. Deepthi's research interests include agricultural biotechnology, plant IPRs, agriculture markets, and technology adoption in developing countries.

[1]Text available at http://www.wto.org/english/docs_e/legal_e/legal_e.htm#TRIPs; last visited 8/1/07.

construction and more so in execution, particularly as regards a perceived failure to provide enhanced access for agricultural products into developed country markets. In response, as the Doha Round got underway it included an explicit recognition of what seemed to be the "developing country round": "The majority of WTO members are developing countries. We seek to place their needs and interests at the heart of the Work Programme adopted in this Declaration."[2]

As regards TRIPs, in seeming recognition of critiques, the Declaration continues, "We instruct the Council for TRIPS, in pursuing its work programme [ ], the review of the implementation of the TRIPS Agreement under Article 71.1[Review and Amendment] ..."[3] Yet while these efforts are underway to assess and possibly modify TRIPs, it is recognized that TRIPs allows considerable discretion in its implementation which developing countries generally have not availed themselves of: "While the TRIPS agreement left room for maneuver in different areas, this flexibility was not used by many countries. They thus renounced the possibility of tailoring the implementation legislation, to the extent possible, to their own needs and conditions" (Correa, p. 24). Nor is this recognition particularly recent; Sherwood (1997a) writing near the adoption date noted, "... it is critical to observe that various levels of intellectual property protection are possible and that the TRIPs Agreement is far from the highest level."

Article 1.1 of TRIPs makes the existence of that flexibility evident: "Members may, but shall not be obliged to, implement in their laws more extensive protection than is required by this Agreement, provided that such protection does not contravene the provisions of this Agreement." That is, the TRIPs Agreement establishes minimum standards of protection, leaving in most instances the maximal level to the discretion of each member country.[4]

---

[2]Doha WTO Ministerial 2001: Ministerial Declaration T/Min(01)/Dec/1, 20 November 2001, Par. 2. Available at http://www.wto.org/English/thewto_e/minist_e/min01_e/mindecl_e.htm. Last visited 7/3/07.
[3]Ibid., Par. 19.
[4]Members are also left "free to determine the appropriate method of implementing the provisions of this Agreement within their own legal system and practice" (TRIPs Article 1.1,

The distinction between minimal TRIPs requirements and practice can be described in part by examining the "IPR index" developed by Sherwood (1997b). In his case, he used a judgment-based ranking system applied to 18 developing countries, mostly in Latin America. The system is based on a score of 100 points allocated as enforceability (25 points), administration (10 points) and patents (17 points). The TRIPs requirements were awarded a 55, identical to South Korea, the highest ranked of the 18. In contrast, Argentina was given a 39 and Brazil a 49. The IP aspects of NAFTA using the same methods were scored a 68. Of course, the time frame of the study means the study countries were in the pre-compliance period, but the index does suggest that TRIPs sets a rather low "floor" on IP requirements. The "enforcement" and "patent" categories of Sherwood's (1997b) index are the principal sources of the low ranking.

It is of course one matter to have the right to flexibility and another to determine how and when that flexibility can optimally be exercised. The objective of this paper is to identify those areas of TRIPs which are particularly relevant to the transfer of biotechnology and evaluate when alternative (and when relevant) standards more stringent than currently applied would enhance transfer and public welfare. Hence, particular attention is focused on the patent, Geographic Indications and enforcement provisions of TRIPs. Structurally, the paper follows the order of Articles in the Agreement. For the legal interpretation of the Articles, we draw particularly on Correa (2007).

9.2 TRIPs Articles

9.2.1 *Exhaustion (Article 6)*

For the purposes of dispute settlement under this Agreement, subject to the provisions of Articles 3 and 4 nothing in this Agreement shall be used to address the issue of the exhaustion of intellectual property rights.

---

final sentence). However, considering that dimension of flexibility exceeds the purpose of this chapter.

This article refers to what is commonly known as "grey imports" or "parallel imports": the exportation of a protected item to a second (or third) country following the initial sale. TRIPs allows countries to establish by policy either "national exhaustion" which means the holder retains rights to approve or not approve sale in every other country following initial sale, or "international exhaustion." With international exhaustion, the sale of a protected item anywhere in the world ends the rights of the rights holder, permitting subsequent sale anywhere. In short, international exhaustion allows arbitrage, while national exhaustion does not. Of course, rights holders where permitted can use side agreements to control subsequent resale, such as with established exclusive marketing areas, but that possibility does not negate the national option over the form of exhaustion. Parallel imports apply largely to patented and copyrighted products.

As Maskus (pp. 208–216) notes, restrictions on parallel imports always benefit technology developers, which are heavily located in a few developed countries. Perhaps for that reason, parallel imports are generally supported by developing country governments even though products (like pharmaceuticals) lower priced to more elastic developing country demand could be exported to higher priced/lower demand elasticity countries. The consequence would be a higher price in the developing country. The balance of benefits over costs of allowing parallel imports is, as Maskus notes, an empirical issue for which there is little hard information.

Applied to biotechnologies, the products of relevance are predominately gene constructs (i.e., the MON810 technology for corn borer resistance), specific genes (the 35S promoter) or finished products containing the gene constructs (herbicide-tolerant soybeans). Constructs and parts can be and are sometimes sold, although licensing is a more common form of access. However, many developing country scientists had experienced difficulty in negotiating use of the 35S promoter, so that a parallel trade source would have been a welcome option. Yet the outright market for these high-level technologies is severely restricted, so applying international exhaustion is unlikely to have a substantive effect on access.

An entire construct can of course be accessed by growing out the appropriate seeds and transferring the construct to a locally adapted cultivar by traditional breeding practices. Under such circumstances, the seeds would likely have been sold for food, feed or industrial purposes rather than as a technology transfer mechanism. Since the initial sale of the technology in such cases would have conveyed an "implied license" to produce the food, feed or industrial product only and not recreate the product, no exhaustion would have occurred and the distinction between national and international would be irrelevant.

Another dimension of exhaustion must be considered if the technology emanates from a country where no IPR protection was available. Technically, no exhaustion would have occurred as there were no rights available. Nonetheless, Correa (p. 86) cites several European Court of Justice cases where parallel import from just such countries was permitted. For agbiotech, however, the products are frequently locally adapted so that a direct transfer from a second country would not be feasible except in limited instances.

Overall, then, the choice of exhaustion seems to have limited relevance for biotechnology transfer and should be decided in regards to other products. Principal among those would be pharmaceuticals, which indeed were the subject of a special WTO Declaration on Public Health, which in Paragraph 5(d) reiterated the freedom to choose the means of exhaustion.[5] Theoretically, international exhaustion would enhance market efficiency but with the risk of limiting developing country access to lower priced medicines for the more elastic demand conditions prevailing in poorer countries. However, as a practical matter, the true nature of demand in countries where only a small wealthy elite may be able to afford the products is unclear. Indeed, as Correa (pp. 88–89) notes, rigid standards in importing countries and other factors mean that the problem of re-importation of medicines from the poorest developing countries "is still largely theoretical."

9.2.2   *Geographical Indications (Article 22)*

1. Geographical indications are, for the purposes of this Agreement, indications which identify a good as

---

[5]Doha WTO Ministerial 2001: TRIPS "Declaration on the TRIPS agreement and public health," WT/Min(01)/Dec/2, 20 November. Available at http://www.wto.org/English/thewto_e/minist_e/min01_e/mindecl_trips_e.htm. Last visited 7/5/07.

originating in the territory of a Member, or a region or locality in that territory, where a given quality, reputation or other characteristic of the good is essentially attributable to its geographical origin.

2. In respect of geographical indications, Members shall provide the legal means for interested parties to prevent:

   (a) the use of any means in the designation or presentation of a good that indicates or suggests that the good in question originates in a geographical area other than the true place of origin in a manner which misleads the public as to the geographical origin of the good;

   (b) any use which constitutes an act of unfair competition within the meaning of Article 10bis of the Paris Convention (1967).

4. The protection [ ] shall be applicable against a geographical indication which, although literally true as to the territory, region or locality in which the goods originate, falsely represents to the public that the goods originate in another territory.

The concept of Geographic Indications (GIs) is more familiar in the form of appellations of origin, which are limited to wines and spirits. However, the differentiating characteristic of a GI may include "human factors," such as handling and processing techniques, in addition to soil and climatic factors. GIs are similar to but may be used in parallel with trademarks (the mechanism used in the US). The key difference is that a GI does not identify a specific producer or owner, but are rather group or communally owned and managed.

In the Paris Convention (Article 10bis), products are protectable under "unfair competition" legislation, defined in Article 9 as "direct or indirect use of a false indication of the source of the goods or the identity of the producer, manufacturer or merchant" so as to mislead the consumer.

Examples of current non-spirit GIs include Roquefort cheese, Parma hams, Idaho potatoes and onions and, recently, Darjeeling tea. A GI for basmati rice (India) is under consideration. From the country and producer perspective, a GI can enhance prices by reducing competition for other producing areas as well as by providing a mechanism for enhancing quality.

With Darjeeling Tea, for example, output from Darjeeling is 10 million kg, while 80 percent of its production is exported at a premium price (Das, 2006). However, a far larger quantity of inferior quality product is sold as "Darjeeling," diminishing the value of the name. Yet the majority of GIs are of EU origin, and indeed the EU is the major proponent of strengthening the GI legislation. To date, the empirical literature on the economic effects of GIs is essentially non-existent. As with any product, effects under TRIPs will depend largely on supply elasticities and demand elasticities in export markets.

At issue is the proposal under the Doha Round to enhance protection under GI legislation — e.g., apply the TRIPs Article 23 provisions to all products. While supported by a number of countries[6] the principal proponent is the EU, which as noted has the most to gain. The EU (TN/IP/W/11, June 2005) proposal has two components:

- The heightened level of protection presently allowed for wines and spirits to be extended to all products (see below), and
- A list of registered, protected GI names which countries can opt out of only with cause and within a specified time period.

The registration list has been very contentious and will not be evaluated further here. The proposed strengthening of benefits, however, has distinct potential benefits and includes the following:

- No requirement to document that the "quality, reputation or other characteristic of the good is essentially attributable to its geographical origin." That is, a mere demonstration of origin is sufficient.
- No requirement to document that misuse of the GI name will confuse or potentially mislead consumers.
- Terms like "style," "type," "kind" are not allowed as means of preventing misleading the public, nor is the naming of the place of origin if different from that associated with the GI.
- The GI name cannot become generic.

---

[6]Including Bulgaria, the EU, Guinea, India, Jamaica, Kenya, Madagascar, Mauritius, Morocco, Pakistan, Romania, Sri Lanka, Switzerland, Thailand, Tunisia and Turkey. See http://www.wto.org/english/tratop_e/trips_e/gi_background_e.htm#protection; last visited 7/6/07.

Clearly, the proposed "enhanced" GI system provides stronger protection for those countries with applicable products. Developing countries may benefit in general if the enhanced system is adopted by WTO members. The mere removal of requirements to document whether consumers will be misled lifts a significant, complex requirement in importing countries. As the benefits to an international agreement are obviously for export markets, the degree of benefit would depend on the number and acceptance of products in international markets. In that regard, it is no surprise that the EU would be the major beneficiary and is the major supporter. In terms of imports, developing countries are limited consumers of GI products, at least those protected to date, so that the trade consequences would be limited.

Overall then, the economic benefit from stronger GI legislation depends on the number of products with recognized names internationally. In terms of biotechnologies, that consideration does not apply, so GI legislation is neutral in regards to biotechnologies.

9.2.3 *Patentable Subject Matter (Article 27)*

1. Subject to the provisions of paragraphs 2 and 3, patents shall be available for any inventions, whether products or processes, in all fields of technology, provided that they are new, involve an inventive step and are capable of industrial application. Subject to paragraph 4 of Article 65, paragraph 8 of Article 70 and paragraph 3 of this Article, patents shall be available and patent rights enjoyable without discrimination as to the place of invention, the field of technology and whether products are imported or locally produced.

3. Members may also exclude from patentability:

   (b) plants and animals other than micro-organisms, and essentially biological processes for the production of plants or animals other than non-biological and microbiological processes. However, members shall provide for the protection of plant varieties either by patents or by an effective *sui generis* system or by any combination thereof.

This Article incorporates many of the dimensions of flexibility under TRIPs which are most relevant to biotechnology transfer. Due to the extent and range of the options, it is possible here to consider only aspects directly relevant to biotechnology transfer. Countries, in making a determination of applying TRIPs within local law, would of course wish to consider ramifications for other sectors as well as biotechnology. Only those aspects of this Article for which there is a clear economic consideration are evaluated here — as is reflected in only part of the Article being included above.

Note should be made that subsection 27.2 of this Article allows (but does not require) exclusions from patentability "to protect ordre public and morality, including to protect human, animal or plant life or health or to avoid serious prejudice to the environment…" While the exclusions made under this Article can be categorical and thus have substantial potential economic effects, the absence of an agreed definition of *"ordre public"* as well as different perspectives on whether patent offices are equipped to make moral judgments means that the application of this Article is largely based on non-economic criterion and hence is not considered further here. It should be mentioned though that Correa (pp. 287–292) argues the language utilizing words like "serious" and a requirement that the exclusion be based on more than the existence of an exclusionary public law indicate the Article should be invoked only in extreme cases.

a. *Invention*

Under Article 27.1, *"patents shall be available for any invention"* where the interpretation pivots over the definition of "invention," and in particular whether invention necessarily involves a creative aspect or mere discovery if based on insight and effort is sufficient. Definitions of "invention" differ in this regard. The American Heritage Dictionary New College Edition (1979 Edition) defines invention as "A new device or process developed from study and experimentation," while "invent" is described as "To conceive of or devise first; originate." Conversely, Wikipedia defines invention as "an object, process, or technique which displays an element of novelty"[7] with "novelty" being a patent law term meaning previously unknown.

This debate is a reiteration of the long-standing effort under patent law to distinguish "invention" from "mere discovery." Perhaps Edison's quip

---

[7] Available at http://en.wikipedia.org/wiki/Invention. Last visited 7/10/07.

that "invention is 99 percent perspiration and one percent inspiration" captures the distinction best — is focused effort sufficient to differentiate invention from discovery? Under US law, both invention and discovery are considered as sources of patentable subject matter; "Whoever invents or discovers..."[8] The same terminology applies in the case of plant patents (which are limited to asexually propagated plants excluding tuberously propagated ones): "Whoever invents or discovers and asexually reproduces a distinct and new variety of plant..."[9] may obtain a plant patent. In this context, the allowance of "discovery" is critical for many new varieties appear as natural mutants which must be identified and reproduced. On the matter of discovery, US practice differs from that of the European Union (EU). The European Patent Convention defines patentable inventions as follows:

(1) European patents shall be granted for any inventions which are susceptible of industrial application, which are new and which involve an inventive step.
(2) The following in particular shall not be regarded as inventions within the meaning of paragraph 1:

(a) discoveries, scientific theories and mathematical methods.[10]

The issue of invention versus discovery is critical to the treatment of naturally occurring genes. The US allows — and has awarded scores — patents for genes in a purified form. On this there is concurrence with the EU: "Biological material which is isolated from its natural environment or processed by means of a technical process may be the subject of an invention even if it already occurred in nature."[11]

---

[8] 35 U.S.C. 101 Inventions patentable. Available at http://www.uspto.gov/web/offices/pac/mpep/consolidated_laws.pdf. Last visited 7/10/07.
[9] 35 U.S.C. 161 Plant patents, *op. cit.*
[10] Article 52, available at http://www.european-patent-office.org/legal/epc/e/ar52.html. Last visited 7/10/07.
[11] European Directive 98/44/EC on the legal protection of biotechnological inventions. Available at http://europa.eu.int/eur-lex/pri/en/oj/dat/1998/l_213/l_21319980730en00130021.pdf. Last visited 7/10/07.

However, other nations are equally specific in excluding naturally occurring genes, such as Brazil:

Article 10: The following are not considered to be inventions or utility models:

IX. Natural living beings, in whole or in part, and biological material, including the genome of germ plasma of any natural living being, when found in nature or isolated there from, and natural biological processes.[12]

So under TRIPs, (developing) countries can and do exclude naturally occurring genes from patentability. Genes modified in the laboratory would not be statutorily excluded in that way. The issue here then is what effect such an exclusion could have on biotechnology transfer. Certainly, naturally occurring genes are used in biotechnology products, an example being a "gene of a Papaya ringspot virus (PRSV) isolate collected in the State of Bahia, Brazil" for use in preparing a papaya ringspot virus-resistant papaya for growing in Brazil (Souza, Nickel and Gonsalves, 2005). What, though, are the consequences?

Non-patented technologies if anything ease technology transfer, so they have no negative effects on movement. There could be implications for investment in a search for useful genes since without patents, claiming benefit would be very difficult both domestically and in other countries also denying patents to naturally-occurring genes. Countries dependent on the private sector would be more affected than those for which the public sector would be the major research entity. The same comments would apply to pharmaceuticals, but those considerations exceed the purpose here.

On another level, it would be difficult for countries and local/indigenous peoples to claim benefits from naturally occurring genes. The FAO International Treaty on Plant Genetic Resources for Food and Agriculture does not apply to genes as it is restricted to materials containing "functional units

---

[12] Intellectual Property Law Brazil, Patents, Article 10.IX. Available at http://www.araripe. com.br/law9279eng.htm#patsec1. Last visited 7/10/07. Adherence to Articles 1–12 and 19 (1967 text) is required by TRIPs Article 2.1.

of heredity."[13] National access laws could extend to individual genes, but few countries have operable legislation.

b. *Novelty*

Novelty refers to the newness of an invention, absolute novelty meaning the invention was not described in writing or use prior to the submission of the initial patent application. Conversely, countries can adopt various "grace periods" up to one year. The US currently allows a one-year grace period, Japan six months for academic publications only, while the EU adheres to absolute novelty. As TRIPs is silent in regards to novelty, any period up to one year is permissible, that period being set by the Paris Convention for maintaining priority rights in other countries.[14]

Absolute novelty requires very tight control over disclosure and is particularly difficult for universities and other public research institutions to manage. The free exchange of information is also affected to a greater degree than when a novelty period exists. Recognizing that the developing country scientists who typically operate in a limited national group are more likely to rely on international collaboration, the existence of a novelty period would seem to be particularly beneficial in that context.

c. *Scope of Protection*

Patent scope refers to the degree of non-obviousness or inventive step required for a patent grant. Establishing a very high standard makes patenting difficult, and the more so for developing country scientists who typically work with more limited resources. Conversely, very low patentability standards can impede R&D by a thicket of rights to very limited innovations. Protecting and maintaining patents are also costly, so low threshold patents would generate inefficiencies. Narrower patents enhance the opportunity to "invent around" them and thus limit the monopoly power conveyed

---

[13] Available at ftp://ftp.fao.org/ag/cgrfa/it/ITPGRe.pdf. Last visited 7/10/07.
[14] Article 4.C(1), available at http://www.wipo.int/treaties/en/ip/paris/trtdocs_wo020.html #P83_6610. Last visited 7/10/07.

with a grant. TRIPs is silent as regards patentability standards, so countries have considerable discretion in that regard.

Other groups have reached different conclusions regarding optimal patent scope. The UK Commission on Intellectual Property Rights, for example, concluded (Barton *et al.*, 2002, Chap. 6):

> "For developing countries, the currently prevalent low standard of inventive step raises two concerns. The first is that as applied in developed countries, it could hinder research of importance to developing countries. The second concern is that developing countries would be expected to apply a similar standard in their own regimes. We would urge developing countries to think carefully before doing so and to explore whether a different higher standard is more desirable. One suggestion that has been made would be to require the patent applicant to demonstrate that the proposed invention reflects a standard of inventiveness higher than that which is normal in the industry involved."

Those high standards, though, would largely exclude patenting options by developing country scientists. Already the vast majority of applications in developing countries (as well as developed countries, with the exceptions of the US and Japan) are by foreign entities.[15] To concerns that large firms could dominate systems with low standards (Correa, 2007, p. 277), one should note that large firms have the resources to dominate patent systems with high standards as well.

d. *Exclusions from Patentability*

Most countries have chosen to exclude patents for plant varieties, be they products of biotechnology or traditional breeding, choosing instead the *sui generis system* option. *Sui generis* in this context refers to special purpose IP law specific to plant varieties, otherwise known as Plant Variety Protection (PVP). Other *sui generis* systems exist — for example, for mask works for integrated circuit designs. In the US and a limited number of additional

---

[15]WIPO data, available at http://www.wipo.int/ipstats/en/statistics/patents/; last visited 8/6/07.

countries,[16] varieties with Genetically Engineered (GE) traits are eligible for utility patents (that is, are patentable subject matter). A very limited number of countries allow patents for traditionally bred varieties.

The choice of the protection mechanism for plants is the principal aspect under TRIPs of relevance to biotechnology transfer. Key differences between patents and PVP are:

- **Patents for plants:** Patents provide the greatest scope of protection for the rights holder. The use of a patented variety in a breeding program is an infringement, as is using the crop as a seed source for subsequent seasons. Moreover, there is no statutory prohibition on the types of plants for which patent protection can be granted. Conversely, however, it is the absence of the research exemption which is of great concern to the public sector and contributes greatly to the resistance to providing patent protection for plants.
- **PVP:** PVP is generally acknowledged to provide less extensive protection than patents for plants because of the statutory research exemption, known as the breeders' exemption. The research exemption means that a protected variety can be used freely in a breeding program, and if the resultant new variety is non-infringing (which means it must exhibit at least one distinct attribute), it can even be protected in its own right. For GE varieties, the effect is that the transfer of a new conventional trait to a GE variety protected only by PVP means control over the GE trait is now shared. The degree of distinctness required to avoid infringement is a national decision which is difficult to specify country by country.

The dominant worldwide PVP system is the series of conventions from UPOV (International Union for the Protection of New Varieties of Plants, in its French acronym[17]). Since TRIPs does not mention UPOV, UPOV membership is presumably not required but appears to be sufficient to meet the *"effective sui generis system"* requirement of TRIPs. Thus, the UPOV

---

[16]In Australia and Japan, and the EU member states, applications that are applicable to more than a single variety, which is to say GE applications, are patentable.

[17]See www.upov.org.

requirements for protection are a sufficient if perhaps not a necessary standard for describing PVP protection. For reasons which will be clearer later, requirements for both the 1978 and 1991 Acts will be described when they differ in relevant ways. Presently, the 1991 Act is the only one open for new members.

Minimum scope of protection: PBRs cover all genera and species, with certain minimums under the several acts, as follows:

- 1978 Act (Article 4): on adoption, three rising to at least 24 genera or species within eight years.
- 1991 Act (Article 3): for new members on adoption, at least 15 genera or species, rising to all genera and species within ten years.

Initial and dependent varieties: The 1991 Act (Article 14.5) does add a significantly new component: that of essentially derived varieties. This component provides an exception to breeders' rights: protected materials may still be used in a breeding program, but if the resultant variety is judged to be essentially derived, it cannot be commercialized without the permission of the initial variety's owner. Before considering the technical aspects of this article, it is perhaps helpful to consider several justifications. If the background or development breeder spends 15 years breeding disease resistance from a wild relative into a commercial variety, then under the 1978 Act provisions, the resultant variety could be used as a basis of subsequent breeding, and within a few years competitive varieties would appear. The development breeder would then have difficulty recovering the costs of the 15 years of work, meaning that, as a practical matter, background breeding would have to be left to the public sector. The owner of a leading commercial variety would be in a similar situation regarding the insertion of a genetically modified trait by another party. Under the 1978 Act, if herbicide resistance had been produced by cross-breeding patented genes into that leading commercial variety, then the resulting genetically modified herbicide-resistant variety could be commercialized, with nothing owing to the original variety owner. Yet that original variety owner would be prevented from using the patented genes in its breeding program, thus producing a distinct asymmetry of rights. Article 14.5 is intended to correct this imbalance by establishing two levels of protection:

- Initial varieties are those on which essentially derived varieties depend. If the initial variety is protected, these essentially derived varieties can be bred from an initial variety but not commercialized without permission from the variety owner.
- Essentially derived varieties are often referred to informally as *dependent varieties*. If the background-bred variety were an initial variety, any minor derivative varieties would be dependent and, in practice, could expect to pay royalties.

UPOV (Article 14.5(b), 1991 Act) uses terms such as "*predominately derived.*" Other varieties retain the expression of the "*essential characteristics.*" Essentially derived varieties may be produced in a number of ways, including by selection, backcrossing, or transformation by genetic engineering. Several UPOV-associated committees have used words such as "*the preponderance of genetic material.*" Just how initial and derived varieties are distinguished can be quite critical, but this may not be clearly determined until there are actual decisions settling disputes revolving around this issue. Lesser and Mutschler (2004), though, do argue that essential derivation systems are not operational because two forms of innovation, single and multiple gene, are incorporated and no standard can apply to both. We know that many national PBR offices are treating the matter as an infringement; that is, the self-identified initial-variety owner is left to sue the purported dependent-variety holder, and it is up to the courts to resolve the counterclaims. This approach relieves a national office from having to make difficult distinctions, but could prolong the process of identifying operational definitions.

Countries which are selecting the *sui generis* option are sometimes melding parts of the 1978 and 1991 UPOV Acts, most commonly adding the essential derivation clauses to the 1978 Act text. For example, see the Act of Brazil.[18] Since UPOV membership is not a requirement for satisfying TRIPs, this approach seems acceptable.

Countries' principal objection with patents for plant varieties appears to be the lack of access for breeding purposes, at least under most

---

[18] Available at http://www.upov.int/en/publications/npvlaws/brazil/9456.pdf. Last visited 7/13/07.

interpretations of the research exemption. The bar against farmer saved seed is a further concern. These are both significant issues, the lack of breeding access being the more significant long-term. However, disallowing patenting for any form of plant variety including biotechnology while disallowing patents for naturally occurring genes (including the Bt gene) provides very limited protection and is a disincentive for biotechnology transfer. PVP even with essential derivation clauses is decidedly not equivalent to patent protection. Countries could consider allowing patenting with a liberal research exemption, which is not specified under TRIPs. Within PVP, the text of the 1991 Act provides many clarifying rights, which simplifies enforcement. The principal limitation appears to be the requirement to protect all genera and species after a short introductory period. However, PVP with a limited scope of protectable species is likely anyway *effective* under the TRIPs requirements.

e. *Subsection Conclusions*

As regards biotechnology transfer, the significant decisions under Article 27 relate to the granting of patents for naturally occurring genes and a use of narrower standards for the award of a patent. However, it is relevant to note that PVP, even with the incorporation of "essentially derived" stipulations, is not equivalent to a patent. Hence, patents should be considered for genetically engineered varieties but not conventionally bred ones.

9.2.4 *Compulsory Licenses (Article 31 (abbreviated))*

Other Use without Authorization of the Right Holder
Where the law of a Member allows for other use[19] of the subject matter of a patent without the authorization of the right holder, including use by the government or third parties authorized by the government, the following provisions shall be respected:

(a) authorization of such use shall be considered on its individual merits;

---

[19]"Other use" refers to use other than that allowed under Article 30.

(b) such use may only be permitted if, prior to such use, the proposed user has made efforts to obtain authorization from the right holder on reasonable commercial terms and conditions and that such efforts have not been successful within a reasonable period of time;

(c) the scope and duration of such use shall be limited to the purpose for which it was authorized;

(d) such use shall be non-exclusive;

(e) such use shall be non-assignable, except with that part of the enterprise or goodwill which enjoys such use;

(f) any such use shall be authorized predominantly for the supply of the domestic market of the Member authorizing such use;

(g) authorization for such use shall be liable, subject to adequate protection of the legitimate interests of the persons so authorized, to be terminated if and when the circumstances which led to it cease to exist and are unlikely to recur;

(h) the right holder shall be paid adequate remuneration in the circumstances of each case, taking into account the economic value of the authorization;

(i) the legal validity of any decision relating to the authorization of such use shall be subject to judicial review or other independent review by a distinct higher authority in that Member;

(j) any decision relating to the remuneration provided in respect of such use shall be subject to judicial review or other independent review by a distinct higher authority in that Member.

Such compulsory licenses have a long and controversial history in patent law, extending at least as far back as the Paris Convention which in Article 5.A(2) allows:[20]

(2) Each country of the Union shall have the right to take legislative measures providing for the grant of compulsory licenses to prevent the abuses which might result from the exercise of the exclusive rights conferred by the patent, for example, failure to work.

---

[20] Article 5.A(2), available at http://www.wipo.int/treaties/en/ip/paris/trtdocs_wo020.html #P83_6610. Last visited 7/10/07.

Flexibility in the use of compulsory licenses was reiterated in Article 5(b) of the Doha Declaration on public health:[21]

> Each member has the right to grant compulsory licenses and the freedom to determine the grounds upon which such licenses are granted.

Compulsory licenses allow countries to limit the use of the exclusive rights granted through the issuance of a patent, including in cases of non-use, national emergencies, and the cross-licensing of dependent patents. They are controversial simply because they allow the revocation (even if limited and temporary) of the sole right granted by a patent, the right to exclude others from use.

Most countries have statutory allowances for compulsory licensing. Brazil, for example, in Article 68 states:[22]

> A patentee will be subject to having its patent compulsorily licensed if he exercises rights resulting therefore in an abusive manner or by means of abuse of economic power proven under the terms of the law by an administrative or court decision.
>
> §1 The following may also result in a compulsory license:
>
> I. Non-exploitation of the subject matter or the patent in the territory of Brazil, by lack of manufacture or incomplete manufacture of the product or, furthermore, by lack of complete use of a patented process, except in the case of non-exploitation due to economic unfeasibility, when importation will be permitted; or
> II. Commercialization that does not meet the market needs.

The same does not apply to US law, even though the US is one of the principal users of court-directed compulsory licensing to resolve antitrust concerns.

---

[21] Doha WTO Ministerial 2001: TRIPS "Declaration on the TRIPS agreement and public health," WT/Min(01)/Dec/2, 20 November. Available at http://www.wto.org/English/thewto_e/minist_e/min01_e/mindecl_trips_e.htm. Last visited 7/5/07.

[22] Intellectual Property Law Brazil, Patents, Article 68. Available at http://www.araripe.com.br/law9279eng.htm#patsec1. Last visited 7/10/07.

Under TRIPs, member states have complete discretion over when to apply compulsory licenses, being subject only to procedural restrictions such as an allowance for prior good faith negotiation on the part of the applicant and allowance for termination of the agreement once the underlying circumstances cease to exist. However, the terms of such licensing are slightly more restrictive, being limited by the requirement for "adequate remuneration" for the right holder. Interestingly, licensing is "*predominately*" for the domestic market, opening the possibility of parallel exporting at least on a limited scale (see above).

The considered application of compulsory licenses would seem to have particular applicability for biotechnology transfer for several reasons:

• With the exception of a few major agricultural countries (China, Brazil, Argentina, India, South Africa), developing countries are secondary markets for international biotech firms. That means the profit potential is lower and the transfer process delayed. Indeed, many developing country scientists have complained of great delays in negotiating agreements.

• With a limited profit potential, biotech firms will be motivated by the potential for the loss of control over the technology more than the earnings potential. This point is emphasized by the "pirate" Bt cotton seeds which have taken a large market share in both China and India (http://www.biotech-info.net/illegal_cotton_India.html).

Under this line of reasoning, however, compulsory licenses are set up as a compensating mechanism for poor enforcement practices (see below), which creates a double incentive for major biotechnology firms to avoid developing country markets. At the same time, developing countries are highly dependent on those same firms as the major source of commercialized biotechnologies and the principal storehouse of knowledge of application. Further, for small farmer access, developing countries are typically dependent on the private sector to fund the costly biosafety reviews. These matters are typically addressed under the heading of "humanitarian donations" (see, for example, Kolady and Lesser, 2006).

The preceding applies to licenses for products, but access to patented processes is a legitimate concern for developing countries as well. When the process applies to a research technology like the "gene gun," the issue can have significant relevance for countries. The use of compulsory licenses would seem appropriate in these instances, as needed.

In short, continuing access to biotechnology products requires more of an ongoing partnership for which a heavy reliance on compulsory licensing can be antithetical for most countries. Rather, compulsory licenses applied to products would seem to be better used very judiciously and as an incentive to reach mutually agreeable negotiated terms. However, in the case of very small markets for biotechnology products within a country where an ongoing relationship is unlikely, the use of compulsory licenses could seemingly be freer without additional future consequences. Licenses as regards patented processes could have broad implications for the conducting of research and would seem to be relevant for the application of a compulsory license when reasonable negotiations were unsuccessful.

9.2.5 *Enforcement (Articles 41, 42, 44 and 45 (abridged))*

1. Members shall ensure that enforcement procedures as specified in this Part are available under their law so as to permit effective action against any act of infringement of intellectual property rights covered by this Agreement, including expeditious remedies to prevent infringements and remedies which constitute a deterrent to further infringements. These procedures shall be applied in such a manner as to avoid the creation of barriers to legitimate trade and to provide for safeguards against their abuse.

2. Procedures concerning the enforcement of intellectual property rights shall be fair and equitable. They shall not be unnecessarily complicated or costly, or entail unreasonable time-limits or unwarranted delays.

3. Decisions on the merits of a case shall preferably be in writing and reasoned. They shall be made available at least to the parties to the proceeding without undue delay. Decisions on the merits of a case shall be based only on evidence in respect of which parties were offered the opportunity to be heard.

4. Parties to a proceeding shall have an opportunity for review by a judicial authority of final administrative decisions.

5. It is understood that this Part does not create any obligation to put in place a judicial system for the enforcement of intellectual property rights distinct from that for the enforcement of law in general.

Members shall make available to right holders[23] civil judicial procedures concerning the enforcement of any intellectual property right covered by this Agreement. Defendants shall have the right to written notice which is timely and contains sufficient detail, including the basis of the claims. Parties shall be allowed to be represented by independent legal counsel, and procedures shall not impose overly burdensome requirements concerning mandatory personal appearances.

- The judicial authorities shall have the authority to order a party to desist from an infringement, *inter alia* to prevent the entry into the channels of commerce in their jurisdiction of imported goods that involve the infringement of an intellectual property right, immediately after customs clearance of such goods.
- The judicial authorities shall have the authority to order the infringer to pay the right holder damages adequate to compensate for the injury the right holder has suffered because of an infringement of that person's intellectual property right by an infringer who knowingly, or with reasonable grounds to know, engaged in infringing activity.

Effective enforcement is the *sina non quo* of effective IPR systems. Enforcement as noted received the highest weighting in the Sherwood (1997b) IPR system weighting system, as it did for the Lesser and Lybbert (2004) scale, where enforcement is proxied by the Corruption Perception Index.[24] As Barton *et al.* (p. 163) note, "IPRs are valuable to rights holders only if they are well enforced, which implies that legal systems need to be effective." Empirically, effective enforcement was found to be critical to the functionality of PVP in Argentina (Jaffe and van Wijk, Chap. 2), and in China firms "cite perceived weak enforcement possibilities as a reason for refraining from introducing elite material in the Chinese market or in investing in major breeding programs (with partners)" (Louwaars *et al.*, p. 90).

In the context of TRIPs, however, enforcement has a specific focus on enforcement against infringement. Note should also be made that the mandate is to "*permit effective action against any act of infringement*" in

---

[23]For the purpose of this Part, the term "right holder" includes federations and associations having legal standing to assert such rights.

[24]Available at http://www.transparency.org/policy_research/surveys_indices/cpi/2005. Last visited 8/2/07.

contrast to preventing/discouraging future infringement. That is, damages are to be "*adequate to compensate for the injury the right holder has suffered*" rather than requiring, say, punitive damages (treble damages as is common in the US). Requirements are to have procedures in place, while considerable discretion is allowed in determining what is "adequate" and "effective." Meanwhile, the authority to grant injunctive relief is allowed but never mandated.

Developing countries likely will recognize that effective enforcement exceeds beyond the issue of infringement, for example, penalties for falsifying a patent application. For infringers, if the penalty is the imposition of a royalty rate which would have applied had an agreement been reached with the right holder, there is little incentive to negotiate.

Countries are not required to "put in place a judicial system for the enforcement of intellectual property rights distinct from that for the enforcement of law in general." Yet as a practical matter, the technical complexity of many infringement cases may necessitate just such a specialized court. A standardized court also limits "venue shopping" as prevailed in the US prior to the establishment of the Court of Appeals for the Federal Circuit as the patent court. The Barton *et al.* (p. 165) recommendation that relief be sought through "administrative action and through the civil rather than criminal justice system" applies as regards the use of civil actions, but the TRIPs requirement for judicial review limits the scope of administrative action, at least as regards infringement.

9.3 Conclusions

The TRIPs requirements are minimum IPR standards for WTO member countries to meet, and a low standard according to the judgment of many knowledgeable observers. This means there exists considerable latitude for countries in determining just which policies and procedures to adopt. This article examines which enhanced forms of IPR legislation by developing countries would benefit the international transfer of agricultural biotechnologies to developing countries. Further complicating the analysis is the limited information available on the significance of IPR in enhancing technology transfer. Agricultural biotechnologies are especially difficult to assess because, when available in the form of seeds, they are notoriously difficult to limit unapproved access and use.

Under these conditions, the number of effective enhancements to the minimal TRIPs requirements are indeed limited, as is set out here. More specifically, the following conclusions are reached:

- Discovered genes should be allowed as patentable subject matter. Among other considerations, developing countries are likely sources of such genes.
- Compulsory licenses are potentially significant for access to biotech process technologies, but are less relevant for biotech products.
- PVP systems are incomplete substitutes for patents for genetically modified varieties. Countries likely, though, will wish to disallow patents for conventional varieties, and in any case allow for a research exemption allowing for research use for any patented variety.
- The opportunity for developing country scientists to patent developments will be enhanced if minimal patent scope is moderate and a grace period is allowed.
- An effective enforcement system is a major requirement of an operational IPR system, and considerable resources and judicial independence will be required to achieve the needed level of enforcement. In that regard, the TRIPs requirements are indeed minimal.

Bibliography

Barton, J. H., et al. (2002). "Integrating Intellectual Property Rights and Development Policy." London, The Commission on Intellectual Property Rights, September. Available at http://www.iprcommission.org/graphic/documents/final_report.htm; last visited 8/2/07.

Correa, C. M. (2007). Trade-Related Aspects of Intellectual Property Rights: A Commentary on the TRIPS Agreement. Oxford: Oxford University Press.

Das, K. (2006). "International Protection of India's Geographical Indications with Special Reference to 'Darjeeling Tea'." The Journal of World Intellectual Property, 9 (5): 459–495.

Jaffe, W. and J. van Wijk (1995). "The impact of plant breeders' rights in developing countries." U. Amsterdam, Inter-American Institute for Cooperation on Agriculture, October.

Kolady, D. and W. Lesser (2006). "Who Adopts What Kind of Technologies? The Case of Bt Eggplant in India." *AgBioforum*, 9 (2): 94–103.

Lesser, W. and T. Lybbert (2004). "Do Patents Come Too Easy?" *IDEA: The Journal of Law and Technology*, 44 (3): 381–409.

Lesser, W. and M. A. Mutschler (2004). "Balancing Investment Incentives and Social Benefits when Protecting Plant Varieties: Implementing Initial Variety Systems." *Crop Science*, 44: 1113–1120.

Louwaars, N. P., *et al.* (2005). "Impacts of Strengthening Intellectual Property Rights Regimes on the Plant Breeding Industry in Developing Countries: A Synthesis of Five Case Studies." Wageningen, U. Wageningen, Center for Genetic Resources, February.

Maskus, K. E. (2000). *Intellectual Property Rights in the Global Economy*. Washington, DC: Institute for International Economics.

Sherwood, R. M. (1997a). "The TRIPS Agreement: Implications for Developing Countries." *IDEA*, 3: 491–544.

Sherwood, R. M. (1997b). "Intellectual Property Systems and Investment Stimulation: The Rating of Systems in Eighteen Developing Countries." *IDEA*, 3: 261–370.

Souza, J., O. Nickel, and D. Gonsalves (2005). "Development of virus-resistant transgenic papayas expressing the coat protein from a Brazilian isolate of papaya ringspot virus (PRSV)." *Fitopatologia Brasileira*, 30: 357–365.

PART III

FOREIGN DIRECT INVESTMENT

Chapter Ten

*W*hat Matters to African Firms? The Relevance of Perceptions Data

Alan Gelb, Vijaya Ramachandran, Manju Kedia Shah and Ginger Turner*

10.1 Introduction: Firm Perceptions of the Investment Climate

In common with many other surveys, the Investment Climate Surveys conducted by the World Bank collect both quantitative data on firm performance and perceptions-based data on the severity of a number of

*Vijaya Ramachandran is a senior fellow at the Center for Global Development. She works on private sector development in Africa and oversees CGD's work program on fragile states. Most recently, Vijaya's research has focused on the analysis of enterprise survey data in Africa, identifying the constraints to doing business from the perspective of the private sector; this work was published as a CGD book entitled *Africa's Private Sector: What's Wrong with the Business Environment and What to Do About It*. Vijaya served as rapporteur to the Africa Progress Panel in 2008 and continues to serve as a consultant to the Panel. Prior to joining CGD, Vijaya taught at Georgetown University and also worked at the World Bank and in the Executive Office of the Secretary-General of the United Nations. Her work has appeared in several media outlets including the *Washington Post*, *Voice of America*, and the *Huffington Post*. Vijaya earned her Ph.D. in Business Economics from Harvard University in 1991.

Alan Gelb is a senior fellow at the Center for Global Development. He had previously been Director of Development Policy at the World Bank, and prior to this, Chief Economist potential constraints facing the firm. Perceptions-based data are sometimes used in economic analysis, but there has been some debate on their value for assessing constraints. Firms' benchmarks may differ by country — much as a poor family in an OECD country may feel "poorer" than a more deprived one in a low-income country, a firm in South Africa may see corruption as a more serious problem than a firm in, say, Nigeria even if corruption is more endemic in the latter country. Benchmarks may be influenced by waves of pessimism and euphoria reflecting adverse or favorable trends. Since firms and entrepreneurs enter and exit in response to opportunities and constraints, they are endogenous to the investment climate and their opinions may not accurately reflect the severity of constraints as perceived by potential or discouraged entrants.

How seriously a firm rates a particular "external" investment climate constraint could also be influenced by its severity relative to other constraints. Whether studies should rate or rank constraints is a live issue, particularly in the light of efforts to find the "binding constraint" to growth (Hausmann, Rodrik and Velasco, 2005). Firms may not recognize the origin of their problems — for example, slow customs clearance could reflect an "external" difficulty (corruption, slow procedures) or factors internal to the firm (inability to provide proper documentation).

Despite these shortcomings, views on the severity of investment climate constraints are widely used to frame priorities for reforms and investments. They are increasingly complemented by "Doing Business" indicators based on expert surveys (World Bank, *Doing Business*, 2004–2007). The latter provide a more comparable cross-country perspective across a detailed range of regulation, but not a firm-level view of the *de facto* severity of regulatory and infrastructural obstacles. In principle, such approaches are

---

for the Africa Region and Staff Director for the 1996 World Development Report, *From Plan to Market*. His main recent areas of work have included the special development challenges of resource-rich countries, aid and development outcomes, the transition from planned to market economies, and Africa, including directing a major study, *Can Africa Claim the 21st Century?*.

The authors are grateful to George Clarke, Michael Clemens, William Cline, Benn Eifert, Alan Hirsch, Alvaro Gonzalez, Giuseppe Iarossi, Jean Michel Marchat, David Roodman, and seminar participants at the Center for Global Development and the World Bank for helpful suggestions.

complementary, but combining approaches is only valuable if each supplies some useful information.

The objective of this chapter is therefore to provide an initial analysis of firms' perceptions of business climate constraints, as reported across a number of World Bank Investment Climate Surveys, with special emphasis on Africa.[1] How does the reported severity of these constraints compare across countries and across different types of constraints, such as macroeconomic management and governance, regulation, factor markets and infrastructure? Does the probability that a firm rates a constraint as serious appear to vary systematically by type of firm as well as across countries? Do the firms' ratings conform to patterns expected from other survey data, where available? Do the cross-country patterns conform to other cross-country evidence?

In this chapter, we look at perceptions of firms regarding the investment climate across 26 African countries where similar questions have been included — Burundi, Democratic Republic of Congo, Ethiopia, Malawi, Guinea-Bissau, Eritrea, Uganda, Gambia, Madagascar, Mozambique, Tanzania, Mali, Burkina Faso, Zambia, Benin, Kenya, Mauritania, Senegal, Lesotho, Angola, Cape Verde, Swaziland, Namibia, South Africa, Mauritius, and Botswana. These surveys encompass almost 5,000 firms. The surveys were carried out between 2002 and 2006 by the Africa Private Sector Group of the World Bank.

In Section 10.2 we review some existing literature on firm perceptions, including studies bearing on the choice of whether to ask firms to rank or to rate constraints. Section 10.3 provides a picture of how views on constraints differ across countries, and also considers whether cross-country perception patterns are reasonably consistent with other data. Section 10.4 shifts towards firm-level analysis — we offer a simple conceptual model of firms' responses and test this using Probit regressions, to see whether factors such as size, ownership and exporter status drive firm perceptions as expected. We also test whether firms' views actually reflect their experience, as evidenced by responses to other questions in surveys. Section 10.5 concludes.

---

[1] More information on the World Bank's Investment Climate Surveys can be found at www.enterprisesurveys.org

10.2   What Do Perceptions Tell Us? A Review of the Literature

10.2.1   *Rankings versus Ratings*

Any study of perception-based data needs to start off with a clear under-standing of what is being measured. As shown by many studies, including those referenced in Iarossi (2006), responses are sensitive to how the ques-tion is framed. One debate is whether ratings or rankings are preferable for measuring "values" or other opinion-based variables. Krosnick and Alwin (1987) find that rating and ranking choices can produce different results, but that the difference is eliminated when "non-discriminating" respon-dents — that is, those who rate most items similarly — are removed from the sample. To reduce the incidence of low discrimination, McCarty and Shrum (2000) suggest that first asking respondents to pick their least and most important values, and then to rate all values, provides more robust differentiation than using rankings alone. Alwin and Krosnick (1985) also analyze comparisons of ranking and rating. They conclude that ranking may be preferred as forcing stronger expression and relationships. But they include an important caveat — forcing a ranking may induce spurious dif-ferentiation for respondents who genuinely do not have major preferences among different choices. One way of interpreting this literature is that, while the choice of ranking and rating will depend on the precise question at hand, elements of ranking and rating may need to be combined to allow responses that are less constrained yet discriminating.

This has implications for investment climate analyses which usually include coverage of many potential constraints. Whether a single "bind-ing constraint" exists is an empirical question. In this case, rating would therefore seem preferable, to allow responses to reflect an essential degree of flexibility. In addition, simply asking firms to rank constraints provides no information on whether the top-ranked constraint is serious or not. But what is the benchmark against which firms in a given country are expected to rate the severity of a particular constraint? Except possibly for multinationals active in many economies, firms will have no "absolute" scale against which the effect of individual constraints can be assessed. Further, any simple quantitative criterion (how much could sales increase if a particular constraint is relaxed?) can mislead in cases where constraints bind firms simultaneously. In such cases, even if all constraints together are important, no one constraint may be important on its own, and we might expect to see a cluster of constraints identified.

There is no simple answer to such questions. Firms' responses are likely to embody a blend of ratings and rankings — constraints will be stressed if seen as seriously problematic, and particularly if seen as serious relative to other constraints experienced by the firm. To help firms discriminate in this way, without forcing an absolute ranking, the procedure advocated by McCarty and Shrum (2000) seems the most appropriate. First, introduce a "showcard" with all alternatives to help firms to consider the most and least important ones, then ask for ratings. The Investment Climate Surveys discussed below do not formally use the showcard method. However, we understand that in practice, managers are usually informed about the list of constraints before being asked to rate their importance, so that the procedure in general conforms to the McCarty–Shrum recommendation.[2]

Another important issue raised by Iarossi (2006) and others concerns the ordering of alternatives. This has been shown by studies to potentially influence responses. One approach to this problem could be to randomize the order of options. This is not done in the ICA surveys; however, the ordering of the options is the same across all countries, so that differences in response cannot be ascribed to order changes.[3] Finally, Bourguignon (2006) notes the importance of distinguishing between the perception of a constraint and the impact on performance if this constraint is relaxed. This bears on how the question should be framed and the importance of confirming opinion-based indicators with behavioral evidence. The present paper does not go as far as this, but focuses on the factors shaping the opinions and what they suggest about investment climate priorities in Africa.

---

[2] From discussions with World Bank staff fielding survey instruments, it is clear that in some cases, enumerators are instructed to show managers the entire list. In other cases, they may do so anyway in order to speed up the response process.

[3] Informal discussions with Alvaro Gonzalez and a review of his work on the correlations between perceptions is also worth noting — Gonzalez shows that perceptions are highly correlated in some countries but not in others, possibly identifying a "country effect" when firms answer perception questions.

10.2.2   *Some Previous Studies*

Most firm surveys request qualitative views on aspects of the business environment, but few studies provide cross-country information comparing their patterns and their relationships with "objective" constraints. Two of the few are Hellman *et al.* (2000) and Fries, Lysenko and Polanec (2003), which use BEEPS (Business Environment and Enterprise Performance) data to assess changes in the business climate across a number of countries in Central and Eastern Europe. The former paper focuses on governance, corruption and state capture. Among other results, it concludes that there is little evidence pointing to "country perception bias" associated with the use of different benchmarks. The latter paper concludes that qualitative measures of the business environment appear to provide reasonably accurate measures of its quality and of changes over time. It also shows relationships between these qualitative measures and quantitative behavioral variables, such as firms' investment and growth rates.[4]

The question of whether firms' perceptions of the severity of constraints are reflected in actual behavior is more contentious, however, particularly in the area of finance. Ayyagari, Demirguc-Kunt and Maksimovic (2006) assess evidence on the severity of constraints from the World Business Environment survey on firm-specific sales growth rates. They find considerable differences between the relative severity of constraints as described by firms and the factors that appear to be most correlated with differences in growth. In particular, recent growth rates appeared to be strongly influenced by whether firms considered access to finance as a serious constraint even when finance was not widely identified as a key binding constraint. Some analysts have argued the converse. Although access to credit is often flagged by firm managers as a constraint in African surveys, Teal (1998), Raturi and Swamy (1999) and others suggest that evidence does not support the argument that limited credit is the main reason why firms are not investing more in their own operations, even though some firms may be credit constrained. This could be because marginal returns to investment

---

[4] Conversations with Alvaro Gonzalez and discussions of his informal analysis of perceptions data have highlighted the importance of country-level clustering of perceptions; we discuss this issue in our estimations in subsequent sections of our paper.

are well below the average and therefore act as a disincentive to expansion, even when firms have retained earnings.

A recent, comprehensive paper on firm perceptions looks at the issue of finance as well as several other key components of the investment climate across a very large set of countries (Carlin, Schaffer and Seabright, 2006). Carlin *et al.* find that small firms complain about finance while large firms complain about almost everything else. Their result raises an interesting question: if small firms' concerns about finance are not related to their actual credit constraints, could it be the case that large firms' perceptions are spurious as well? In particular, are large firms complaining about actual constraints or are they complaining about other things because they do not have a problem with access to finance? We address this issue in our econometric analysis, by looking at the pairwise correlations between firm perceptions and quantitative measures of the investment climate, across small, medium and large firms in our data sample.

In an overview of subjective data that relies on a wide range of empirical literature, Bertrand and Mullainathan (2001) argue that subjective data must be treated with skepticism. They argue that subjective data should not generally be used as dependent variables because of a host of problems related to measurement errors. But they also note that these data can be used as explanatory variables as long as caution is exercised with regard to causality. The authors also argue that changes in answers to questions do not appear to be useful in explaining corresponding changes in behavior, based on their review of studies conducted in the US.

In our analysis, although we consider correlations between subjective and objective measures, we do not yet have panel data and are as yet unable to assess whether these correlations are the same or different over time.

10.3 Constraints in Investment Climate Surveys

10.3.1 *Country Profiles and Country-Level Differences in Firm Perceptions*

Many Investment Climate Surveys ask firms the following question:

> Please tell us if any of the following issues are a problem for the operation and growth of your business. If an issue poses a

problem, please judge its severity as an obstacle on a five-point
scale where:

0 = No obstacle, 1 = Minor obstacle, 2 = Moderate obstacle,
3 = Major obstacle, 4 = Very severe obstacle, DK = Don't
know, NA = Not applicable

A) Telecommunications
B) Electricity
C) Transportation
D) Access to land
E) Tax rates
F) Tax administration
G) Customs & trade regulations
H) Labor regulations
I) Skills/education of workers
J) Business licensing & operating permits
K) Access to finance (e.g., collateral)
L) Cost of finance (e.g., interest rates)
M) Economic & regulatory policy uncertainty
N) Macroeconomic instability (inflation, exchange rates)
O) Corruption
P) Crime, theft, disorder
Q) Anti-competitive or informal practices

We begin our analysis by looking at five constraints — electricity, access
to finance, corruption, macro-instability, and labor regulations — which
are fairly representative of the range of infrastructure, factor-market, governance and regulatory constraints that firms typically face. We also widen
our analysis, as we go along, to consider a slightly larger set of constraints
that are related to the five mentioned above.

Table 10.1 shows the percentage of firms ranking each of these constraints to be major or severe, in the 26 countries used in this analysis.[5]

---

[5] Additional calculations available from the authors show the perceptions of firms with
regard to the five constraints for individual countries, as well as the results for all constraints,
by country and by aggregated groups.

Table 10.1:   Percentage of firms ranking a constraint as major or severe

	Per capita income	Electricity	Corruption	Access to finance	Macro instability	Labor regulations
Low Income						
Burundi	100.0	79.10	14.93	67.91	47.01	2.24
DRC	120.0	84.78	15.22	67.39	63.59	16.85
Ethiopia	160.0	42.45	39.00	42.82	35.28	4.57
Malawi	160.0	60.51	46.79	42.04	75.80	12.74
Guinea-Bissau	180.0	73.77	29.51	86.89	54.10	4.92
Eritrea	220.0	36.76	1.52	54.39	80.88	5.8
Uganda	280.0	87.63	20.97	62.90	21.51	1.61
Gambia	290.0	72.95	14.75	68.03	27.05	3.28
Madagascar	290.0	41.72	45.99	59.06	64.71	14.98
Mozambique	310.0	64.02	63.74	79.33	62.84	38.25
Tanzania	340.0	57.92	50.97	49.03	42.86	12.26
Mali	380.0	22.56	49.25	56.49	11.81	3.73
Burkina Faso	400.0	68.63	54.90	76.47	35.29	17.65
Lower Middle Income						
Zambia	490.0	37.71	47.70	54.60	76.00	17.14
Benin	510.0	69.02	85.08	74.32	49.71	36.41
Kenya	530.0	48.22	74.41	44.31	52.80	22.87
Mauritania	560.0	46.51	27.91	53.49	18.60	8.14
Senegal	710.0	31.65	40.43	55.98	26.50	14.89
Lesotho	960.0	35.62	36.11	39.44	40.00	17.57
Angola	1350.0	62.03	35.44	62.45	24.05	13.5
Cape Verde	1870.0	70.45	13.64	47.73	13.64	13.64
Upper Middle Income						
Swaziland	2280.0	18.09	27.66	36.17	15.96	13.83
Namibia	2990.0	13.04	25.55	36.33	24.64	14.49
South Africa	4960.0	9.28	16.32	12.89	33.51	33.39
Botswana	5180.0	9.38	25.78	42.19	35.16	10.16
Mauritius	5260.0	13.00	36.73	33.33	39.70	28.14

Figures 10.1a–10.1c show spider charts with the percentages of firms rating constraints as major or severe across three income groups. These suggest a pattern, with constraints such as power and finance dominating at low income levels, corruption becoming a more serious problem at middle

Low Income: GDP per capita upto $400
(Burundi, DRC, Ethiopia, Malawi, Guinea-
Bissau, Eritrea, Uganda, Gambia, Madagascar, Mozambique,
Tanzania, Mali and Burkina Faso)

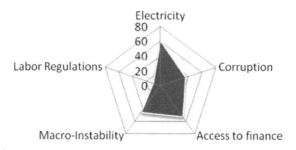

Figure 10.1a: Percentage of firms ranking a constraint as major or severe in countries with income up to $400 per capita

Lower Middle Income: GDP per capita >$400 upto $ 2000
(Zambia, Benin, Kenya, Mauritania, Senegal, Lesotho, Angola,
and Cape Verde)

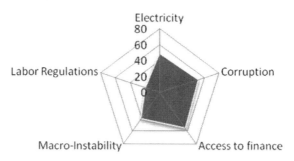

Figure 10.1b: Percentage of firms ranking a constraint as major or severe in countries with income between $400 and $2,000 per capita

income levels, and a decline in perceived problems at high income levels except for labor regulation.

To illustrate the evolution of constraints in a more dynamic way, Figures 10.2a–c show three sets of constraint perceptions by income, together with fitted polynomial trend-lines. Figure 10.2a shows the set of constraints that decrease in perceived severity with income. Of primary

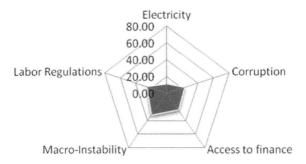

Upper Middle Income: GDP per capita > $2000
(Swaziland, Namibia, South Africa, Mauritius, and Botswana)

Figure 10.1c: Percentage of firms ranking a constraint as major or severe in countries with income above $2,000 per capita

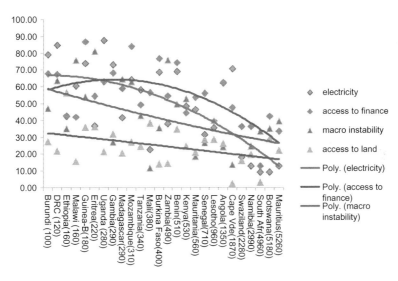

Figure 10.2a: Percentage of firms ranking the constraint as major or severe by GDP/capita — "elemental" constraints that decline with income

concern is electricity — almost 70 percent of African firms at the lowest end of the income scale complain about the lack of power or unreliable power. Also important in this class are macroeconomic instability and access to finance. Of lesser importance but still declining in severity with income

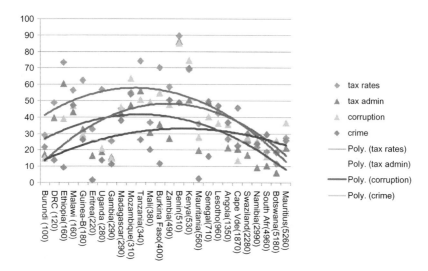

Figure 10.2b: Percentage of firms ranking the constraint as major or severe by GDP/capita — "governance" constraints that peak in the middle of the income range

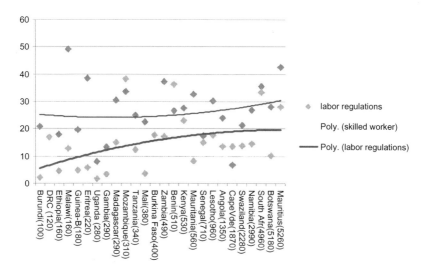

Figure 10.2c: Percentage of firms ranking the constraint as major or severe by GDP/capita — constraints rising with income: labor regulations and shortage of skills

is access to land. Since Africa is land-rich, this does not reflect actual scarcity in a physical sense; rather, it refers to shortages of serviced, industrial premises, which tend to be closely associated with deficient infrastructure. Power, finance, land and the ability to plan are basic requirements for a dynamic business; we therefore term these *elemental* constraints.

Figure 10.2b shows the set of constraints that are particularly problematic for firms in the middle of our income range. These include corruption, tax rates and administration, and crime. Concerns about corruption follow a path similar to concerns about taxes and crime, *but with a slight lag* — it is as if firms take a little longer to be convinced that corruption is decreasing. These constraints tend to be related to the quality of *governance and state effectiveness*.

Figure 10.2c shows the set of constraints that peak at the upper end of the income scale — labor regulations and skill shortages. These problems tend to be perceived as more serious once the basic elements are present for the firm to do business, and once the most pressing governance-related problems are attenuated by improvements in state capacity. They reflect the need for skilled labor, especially in more sophisticated economies.[6] They also reflect the fact that, as the regulatory capacity of the state strengthens, business will be but one constituency among many, and that it will need to compete with other interests, including organized labor and possibly environmental and other constituencies. These impediments to business are more likely to be of a *policy* nature rather than related to infrastructure or governance.

Figures 10.2a–c suggest an approach to classifying constraints and the way in which firms' perceptions of their difficulties are likely to vary with income level. At the low end of the scale, manufacturing firms are most likely to be concerned about the most elemental constraints to doing business. Is there a reliable power supply? Can finance and premises be secured? Can the firm plan ahead, or does macroeconomic instability make this impossible? In some countries, individual constraints can be at a level where they can be considered as truly binding. Electricity tariffs in Uganda

---

[6] Skills shortages are seen as more serious than labor regulations in almost all countries in the sample.

would have to increase to almost \$0.29 per kWh if the consumer were to bear the full costs of electricity including the expensive thermal generation used in attempts to plug capacity gaps. The cost of load-shedding to the economy is significant, and expensive back-up generation has impacted the competitiveness of industrial production. The cost of unserved energy has been estimated at about US\$0.39 per kWh excluding multiplier effects.[7] Not surprisingly, 87% of Ugandan firms considered electricity as a major or severe constraint in 2006. These constraints do not die away completely as the business climate improves — in South Africa, for example, macroeconomic instability is rated as a serious problem by many exporters concerned about the volatility of the Rand. But their relative importance declines once these basic requirements for doing business are established.

Moving up the scale to lower-middle-income, firms must confront a number of problems caused by weak governance and low administrative and bureaucratic capacity. These include the tax system (rates and administration), corruption and the control of crime and violence. Poor governance may, of course, be responsible for some of the elemental constraints (corruption means that investments in power generation do not go ahead), but the firms do not experience these effects directly. Some aspects of regulation will be less troubling to firms in these settings — even if labor laws are stringent, the weak capacity of the state to enforce them means that they are less likely to be perceived as a serious problem.

Moving further up to middle-income, unless higher income is due to "exogenous" factors such as large hydrocarbon deposits, the state tends to become more capable. Civil society may become better organized, and checks and balances stronger, causing corruption to be less of a serious problem. Concerns about infrastructure, access to finance, and access to land also decrease considerably; even concerns about crime fall off relative to perceived difficulties in the "low-middle" category. But business will not be the only constituency — labor is also exercising its voice. Policies become more serious determinants of the business climate at this stage, largely because the state has stronger capacity to implement them.

---

[7] Power Planning Associates (2007).

The shortage of skilled labor is regarded as a more serious constraint than labor regulations over the entire spectrum of countries. While it is more frequently cited in the higher income group of countries, this does not prove that the skills constraint is actually more serious. Skills may be cited because concerns over many of the other constraints have declined to low levels. However, within individual economies, it is also the case that larger and more technically advanced firms express greater concerns over labor skills than smaller, low-productivity firms (see discussion below, in Table 10.3), and this provides some support to the proposition that skills shortages become more acute constraints in relatively sophisticated, high-productivity economies.

10.3.2 Country Profiles and Other Country-Level Indicators

Having developed a picture of how constraints are perceived to bind at different levels of income, we consider whether the incidence of complaints aligns with cross-country indicators of the investment climate. Tables 10.2a and 10.2b contain a summary of some comparisons.

The intensity of perceived constraints is reasonably well-correlated with the country-level indicators. Governance and macroeconomic perceptions compare with *Institutional Investor* ratings and Kaufmann–Kraay (KK) governance measures — the former is statistically significant, while the latter is not. Firms' concerns about corruption are correlated with the KK measure "Control of Corruption" and perceptions of crime also correlate with the KK measure of "Rule of Law"; these correlations are not statistically significant but are of the right sign and of reasonable magnitude.

Concerns over access to finance are very strongly correlated with macro-level indicators, being less frequent in countries with high ratios of private credit/GDP, better quality credit information and higher *Institutional Investor* ratings, while concerns over the cost of finance are strongly correlated with country-level interest-rate measures. One concern over using access to finance as an indicator of the quality of the business climate is that access will be endogenous and weaker firms are most likely to complain. While this may be true, the strength of the cross-country relationship suggests that finance is likely to be an economy-wide constraint in the sense

Table 10.2a: Correlations of selected constraints with external indicators

Perception area (Investment climate data and selected comparators)	Pearson's correlation coefficient (P>|r|)
Macro-instability	Government effectiveness (KK) −0.32 (0.12)
Corruption	Control of corruption (KK) −0.28 (0.17)
Crime and theft	Rule of law (KK) −0.07 (0.72)
Political and economic uncertainty	Investor rating (*Institutional Investor*) −0.47 (0.02)***
Political and economic uncertainty	Regulatory quality (KK) 0.48 (0.12)***
Labor regulation	Difficulty of firing (*Doing Business*) −0.15 (0.46)
Cost of finance	Interest rate (IMF) 0.72 (0.001)***
Access to finance	Domestic credit to the private sector (% of GDP, 2004) −0.69 (0.003)***
Access to finance	Investor rating (*Institutional Investor*) −0.65 (0.005)***

Note: Figures in parentheses represent levels of confidence.

Table 10.2b: Correlations between *Doing Business* and firm perceptions

Number of licensing procedures vs. Business license perception	−0.06*** (<0.0001)
Days to get a license vs. Business license perception	−0.20*** (<0.0001)
Strength of legal rights index vs. Economic instability perception	−0.01 (0.41)
Strength of legal rights index vs. Corruption perception	−0.11*** (<0.0001)
Depth of credit info index vs. Access to finance perception	0.22*** (<0.0001)
Investor protection index vs. Economic instability perception	0.13*** (<0.0001)
Investor protection index vs. Corruption perception	0.05*** (0.0002)
Number of tax payments vs. Tax administration perception	−0.12*** (<0.0001)
Time to pay taxes vs. Tax administration perception	−0.06*** (<0.0001)
Trading cost for exports vs. Customs and trade perception	0.03 (0.06)
Trading cost for imports vs. Customs and trade perception	0.03 (0.04)
Property registration (days) vs. Access to land perception	−0.02 (0.14)
Difficulty of firing index vs. Labor regulation perception	−0.15 (0.46)

Note: Figures in parentheses represent levels of confidence.

that deeper financial markets facilitate access by firms that would be unable to access credit in shallower financial markets.

Correlations with *Doing Business* indicators, reported in Table 10.2b, are strong in some cases and less so in others.[8] Correlations between *Doing Business* measures of the time and cost to get a business license are strongly aligned with relevant perceptions of firms, as are indices of the strength of legal rights, the depth of credit information and investor protection. Measures of the burden of taxes are also strongly correlated with firm complaints about tax rates and tax administration.

The lower correlations in some areas are likely because those indicators focus on very detailed regulatory areas and are generally representing the rules that govern business rather than firm experiences. Firing cost, for example, is only one element of labor regulation, and it may not be the main problem for all firms even if they see labor regulation as a severe constraint. Also, compliance rates may be low at lower levels of income because rules are simply not enforceable. In general, cross-country comparison of perceived constraints indicates that the patterns are credible.

10.4 Firm-Level Analysis

10.4.1 *A Model of Firm Responses*

We now consider the determinants of responses at firm level, and whether these relate to more "objective" measures of the business climate. The probability that a particular firm considers a particular constraint to be severe could be expected to depend on a number of factors. Some constraints might impact differently on large versus small firms, on exporting firms versus those selling locally, on foreign-owned versus domestic firms, or on firms in different sectors. Perceptions are also likely to reflect individual experience, for example, of power outages, of costs of security, or of the need to pay bribes. Also, as noted above, ratings are likely to reflect a mixture of relative and absolute perceptions of severity.

---

[8] Additional correlations with other external indicators not shown here, are available from the authors.

A rating in one area is therefore likely to depend on ratings in other areas. In particular, the perceived severity of constraints "external" to the firm is likely to be inversely related to the severity of "internal", firm-specific constraints reflecting limited capabilities. The distinction is conceptually clear but may be blurred in practice. For example, the costs imposed by crime may impact on all firms similarly, but a reported constraint in access-ing credit could partly reflect firm-specific factors, such as limited collateral, a weak order book, or incapacity or unwillingness to produce adequate busi-ness plans and audited financial statements. Many studies have found the level of education of entrepreneurs to be a significant determinant of SME performance. We would expect internal constraints to be more serious for smaller firms less able to access the range of skills and technology avail-able to their larger counterparts. In Africa, many larger firms are owned by expatriates or networked ethnic groups able to increase access to a range of inputs and skills (Biggs and Shah, 2006; Ramachandran and Shah, 2007).

To more systematically frame the determinants of firm perceptions, we construct a simple model. Profits reflect revenues less costs; they can also fall below potential profits because of business-climate related losses, such as those due to power outages and theft.[9] Costs and losses are assumed to reflect a mix of external and internal constraints faced by the firm. A profit-maximizing manager will rate each constraint based on how it is expected to impact on the profit function. Firm-specific determinants of the rating can include characteristics such as size, ownership and export status, as well as the experiences of the firm itself.[10] Other determinants will include sector or country-fixed effects. Based on this approach, we carry out maximum likelihood estimation of a set of Probit regressions.

Therefore, for firm i and constraint j:

$$Y_{ij}^* = F(\mathbf{X}'\beta) + u,$$

---

[9] For estimates of losses due to power outages and their impact on total factor productivity, see Eifert, Gelb and Ramachandran (2005).

[10] It is worth noting that a manager's perceptions may be driven by the expected cost rather than the actual cost. For example, the perception of crime may be driven by events in the neighborhood rather than the individual's own experience. We still expect that this perception will be related to a quantitative measure, i.e., in this case, it would be the expenditures on security systems, guards, etc.

where

Y_{ij}^* = underlying probability that firm i considers constraint j to be
major or severe;

Y_{ij} = observed dummy that is set to 1 if $Y_{ij}^* > 0$.

Independent variables (vector **X**) include:

- size of firm (number of employees)
- ownership of firm (domestic or foreign)
- export status of firm (whether an exporter)
- sector fixed effect
- country groups fixed effect
- experience indicator of constraint j as reported in survey by firm i
- u_{ij} = error term.

We expect that perceptions of some constraints will be positively correlated with size. Larger firms have greater internal capabilities; they typically contract at greater distance for inputs and sales, and therefore are more dependent on well-working transport and logistics systems; they will also be more visible to those implementing labor and other regulations. Conversely, we might expect small firms to be more concerned about constraints that reflect scale economies in providing services and weaker internal capabilities, such as access to finance. Certain aspects of the investment climate, such as finance, are likely to affect domestic firms more, whereas foreign firms are likely to complain about customs regulations or other regulatory barriers. Exporting firms may have particular concerns, such as macroeconomic instability, as evidenced by large swings in exchange rates.

Surveys include a number of variables that reflect firms' experience of some of the constraint areas. For electricity supply, these include days and sales lost to power outages; for corruption, informal payments as a percentage of sales; for crime, theft and disorder, the cost of security as a percentage of sales (the cost includes wages to security guards, alarm systems, etc.); for tax administration, days lost due to inspectors' visits; and for customs and trade regulation, the number of days to clear exports. Views on the cost of finance can be compared with the interest rate paid by the individual firm (as derived from the surveys) and whether the firm has a loan or overdraft, while views on access to finance can be tested against whether a firm has a loan or overdraft and whether its accounts are audited.

Many other drivers of perceptions are not captured in the model — e.g., popular opinion about the investment climate (whether the media is reporting heavily about corruption) or whether firms feel able to speak freely to evaluators about sensitive areas. To the extent that all firms within a country are influenced uniformly by this type of event or if firms in some sectors are influenced more than others, the country or sector dummies will capture these effects. However, if individual firms across sectors are influenced unevenly, or if perceptions are driven by the moods of individual managers, the effect would be captured in the residual.[11] As a first approximation, we assume that the firm-specific indicators pick up the main factors causing responses to different constraints to be related, and thus that error terms are independent across equations.

Probit regressions are run for the countries in our sample, with the middle-income countries as the default country group and "other" as the default sector. The dependent variable is a 0/1 dummy, set to 1 if the firm ranks a constraint as major or severe. Table 10.3 presents the results. In every regression, firm perceptions are correlated with experience; and the coefficients on the experience dummies are both significant and of the correct sign.

Firm characteristics drive perceptions of some constraints but not others. Firm size does not particularly drive concerns about electricity; firms across the board in low-income and low-middle-income Africa complain about the severity of this constraint.

Governance, as measured by corruption, is of more concern to larger firms. Foreign-owned firms are also more concerned about corruption, perhaps due to their visibility and need to make informal payments to ease the burden of regulation. Tax administration is seen as more serious problems by exporting firms, suggesting that the *ad hoc* nature of enforcement means that such firms often find themselves vulnerable (Emery, 2003).

---

[11] Firm-specific effects (such as unobservables related to managerial quality) can be measured only with panel data, which we do not yet have for our sample of countries.

Table 10.3: Econometric estimations

	Electricity	Labor regulation	Corruption	Cost of finance	Access to finance	Access to land	Tax admin	Skilled labor	Customs and trade regulation
Intercept	-1.6228***	-1.33***	-1.0491***	-0.84***	-0.1047	-0.7290***	-1.4697***	-1.14***	-0.9006***
	(0.1004)	(0.098)	(0.083)	(0.113)	(0.083)	(0.093)	(0.09)	(0.08)	(0.129)
Lwork	0.0096	0.102***	0.0470***	-0.0218	-0.1259***	-0.0768***	0.0221	0.13***	0.025
	(0.015)	(0.017)	(0.014)	(0.018)	(0.015)	(0.016)	(0.015)	(0.01)	(0.028)
Exportd	0.0007	0.05	0.0391	-0.0185	-0.0216	-0.0580	0.1142*	0.009	-0.1000
	(0.061)	(0.06)	(0.054)	(0.06)	(0.055)	(0.063)	(0.061)	(0.05)	(0.09)
Fgnown	-0.0121	-0.025	0.2682*	-0.1897**	-0.1324***	-0.063	-0.0214	-0.06	0.07
	(0.055)	(0.058)	(0.042)	(0.062)	(0.051)	(0.057)	(0.056)	(0.05)	(0.089)
Days lost	0.0037***	—	—	—	—	—	—	—	—
	(0.0003)								
Maj. union	—	0.016**	—	—	—	—	—	—	—
		(0.058)							
Bribe pmt	—	—	0.2682***	—	—	—	—	—	—
			(0.042)						
Overdraft	—	—	—	0.2329***	—	—	—	—	—
				(0.053)					
Audit	—	—	—	0.0655	-0.1591***	—	—	—	—
				(0.058)	(0.046)				

(Continued)

Table 10.3: (*Continued*)

	Electricity	Labor regulation	Corruption	Cost of finance	Access to finance	Access to land	Tax admin	Skilled labor	Customs and trade regulation
Ownland	—	—	—	—	—	-0.4112*** (0.045)	—		—
Daytax	—	—	—	—	—	—	0.0113*** (0.002)		—
Training								0.10** (0.04)	
Exp clear	—	—	—	—	—	—	—		0.0148*** (0.005)
Low income	1.2532*** (0.0696)	-0.483*** (0.06)	0.40*** (0.05)	1.0087*** (0.0718)	0.6204*** (0.0538)	0.4901*** (0.0606)	0.9305*** (0.0666)	-0.15*** (0.05)	0.4708*** (0.105)
Low middle income	1.0765*** (0.0725)	-0.047*** (0.063)	0.72*** (0.06)	1.3470*** (0.0747)	0.7152*** (0.0578)	0.5241*** (0.0676)	1.0763*** (0.0690)	-0.10 (0.10)	0.49*** (0.114)
N	4326	4858	4863	3193	4659	4717	4273	4898	2028
Log likelihood	-2538.99	-1942.49	-3048.85	-1990.26	-2980.14	-2451.96	-2536.36	-2704.8	-1226.77

Large firms also complain more about labor regulations and skill shortages; the coefficient on size is both positive and significant at the 1 percent level of confidence.

Domestic and small firms complain significantly more about the access to finance and its cost than do large firms and foreign firms. Smaller firms also complain more about access to land. These results are robust to variations in econometric specification; however, we do note that these represent correlations in our data rather than causal relationships.

These results suggest that smaller African firms tend to work within more restricted markets. They may be less visible to regulators and less appealing targets for predatory officials. They may also require fewer licenses and use less technologically sophisticated production processes that demand fewer skilled workers. They will therefore not be as strongly affected by many investment climate problems, but will face additional internal constraints — a shortage of managerial or accounting skills or collateral. The investment climate may pose an increasing challenge to firms as they seek to become larger and more capable. A firm looking to expand will need to weigh potential revenues against the higher costs that include uncertainty over the supply of key inputs, such as power and public services, as well as the greater exposure to regulatory predation that comes with increased size and visibility.

All of the experience variables produce significant coefficients of expected sign, even after eliminating fixed effects, so that firms' experience shapes their ratings. Days lost due to power outages is a significant determinant of the ranking of electricity as a major or severe constraint. Another regression, not reported here, shows that sales lost is also significant. Similarly, the rate of unionization drives perceptions of labor regulations, bribes paid affect perceptions about corruption, days to clear exports are tied to complaints about customs, etc. None of these results are surprising — for example, firms with access to overdrafts are more likely to view high interest rates as a constraint. The results on access to finance are also interesting. After netting out for fixed effects (which include the size factor), having accounts audited substantially decreases the probability that a firm considers access to finance as a serious constraint. This suggests the importance of including measures to increase access to accounting and auditing services in programs to widen financial access.

It is worth reflecting on why the experience variables are significant at all when fixed effects are included in regressions. If firms are responding to country-level differences in, say, security or power supply, differences should simply appear as fixed effects at the level of country/income groups. The fact that Table 10.3 shows many significant coefficients suggests high levels of arbitrariness and dispersion in the investment climates of Africa, so that some firms suffer from much greater power outages or slow customs clearances more than others. This may be because such public services are delivered on an *ad hoc* basis, or because certain individual firms are more vulnerable to predation while others have formed political relationships to improve service delivery.

10.4.2 *Camels and Hippos*

Before we move to our concluding section, it is worth considering the issue raised by Ricardo Hausmann on camels and hippos (Hausmann and Velasco, 2005). The argument is that if you are in the desert and you interview camels about the investment climate, you would get a very different idea about what the main problems are of living/working in a desert (probably heavy loads or mean camel riders) than if you could interview hippos who do not live there. Hausmann argues that the really interesting thing to look at is therefore the underlying industrial structure (i.e., the camel to hippo ratio), from which you can infer what the real problem is (no water).[12]

It is certainly true that the mix of firms surveyed reflects a degree of self-selection, whether for regulatory/governance issues or others. For example, one would not expect to find many hi-tech computer firms in Burundi, or shipbuilding in Botswana.[13] However, there are also several indications

---

[12] We are grateful to George Clarke for discussions on this subject (see Clarke *et al.*, 2007).
[13] The approach taken by the World Economic Forum in their annual competitiveness report does try to adjust for country differences by weighting different constraints differently at different levels of development. It is also implicit in arguments that comparative advantage is shaped by costs of non-traded goods and services, as well as factor proportions. In extreme cases, the economy will consist of only subsistence farming and offshore oil rigs or, as in rural Niger, cattle.

from our results which suggest that in practice, these differences do not dominate:

- Within countries, responses are relatively uniform across types of firm, including foreign-owned firms which are presumably able to compare across countries. Deviations in the firms' responses are appreciable only where expected (for example, foreign firms are less constrained by finance).

- Cross-country, we find correlations between the intensity of complaints and other country indicators (for example, complaints about finance are far more prevalent in countries with low financial depth). On the Hausmann argument, firms in countries with low financial depth should be self-selected accordingly, and not see this as a particular constraint.

Perhaps the most convincing evidence is generated by looking at firms that have adjusted to a constraint. Our results show quite clearly that firms are not passive in the face of constraints. Where possible they will adjust to them, and the question arises whether the ability to adjust means that the constraint is no longer recognized as serious. To answer this question, we take one example — whether perceptions about the electric power constraint are affected by ownership of a generator (Figure 10.3). The

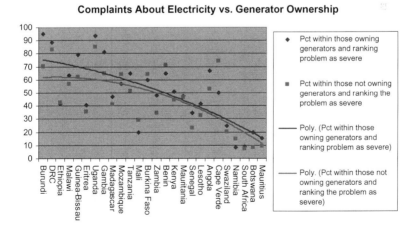

Figure 10.3: Perceptions regarding electricity, disaggregated by generator ownership

results show that firms do not identify absent or unreliable power as less constraining when they own a generator. Firms with generators actually complain slightly more about electricity in many countries; this may reflect the fact that generator power costs some three times more than power from the grid.

The evidence on the lack of effect of generator ownership on the perception of whether power is a severe constraint suggests that firms recognize a constraint even when they can adapt to it. Indeed, the Hausmann argument can be turned around. If the self-selection process for firms is incomplete (as suggested by the above), the constraints identified will likely be seen as even more serious by those firms that have not chosen to enter. Alleviating Uganda's power constraint could thus bring in a multiple of new business as well as improve conditions for established firms. If even camels would like to have more water (as we are sure camels in general do in deserts), this suggests that a host of other animals will come in if the water constraint is alleviated.

10.5   Conclusion

Just as household perceptions of well-being may not correlate perfectly with objective measures of income or consumption, so firms' perceptions of critical investment climate constraints may not always correspond fully to "objective" reality. Nevertheless, this analysis of the patterns of firms' responses across African countries suggests that they do not complain indiscriminately, but exercise judgment and choice in indicating a number of constraints as serious. Response patterns correlate reasonably well with other country-level indicators related to the investment climate. Responses at firm level also reflect the experience of firms, for example, of the problems posed by erratic power supply, or the costs of bribes or security. Firms can sometimes mitigate investment climate problems. For example, faced with unreliable grid power they can purchase generators. But mitigation is costly, and does not mean that firms cease to recognize the severity of the problem.

Firms in most African countries tend to see many areas of the investment climate as serious constraints to business. Some constraints seem to be independent of scale, but larger firms complain more frequently about many constraints. These may discourage firms' growth and their progression towards greater visibility, more sophisticated technology and wider market reach in terms of both inputs and sales. Finance and access to land are particular areas of concern to smaller firms, while firms across the board are concerned about infrastructure and corruption. Notwithstanding these differences, firm-effects appear to be less powerful than country-effects in shaping the pattern of responses. Almost all firms in South Africa are better off than almost any firm in low-income Africa, for almost all of the constraints examined in this paper. The only exceptions are labor regulations and availability of skilled labor, which appear to become binding constraints as GDP per capita rises.

What do these results tell us about "binding constraints" to business? Contrary to the proposition of Hausmann–Rodrik that a single or few binding constraints can be identified for any given country, we find that firms tend more to identify groups of constraints as posing serious problems. At least in Africa, there may be systematic relationships between countries' level of development or income and the types of constraints most often seen as binding.

At the lowest level, the most serious constraints as seen by the firms tend to be those closely related to the ability to plan work and produce at all — macroeconomic stability, electric power, and finance. Concerns in these areas decline as income rises, to be replaced by a second set of constraints. These new constraints relate to the quality of governance and the capability of the state to provide important services. These include corruption, the level of taxation and quality of tax administration, and security. These in turn ease as countries move to middle-income status and governments develop greater capacity and regulatory competence. But this opens the way to a third set of obstacles — business will not be the only political constituency. Organized labor may be powerful in some countries. In others, business might feel constrained by environmental regulations. Moreover, in these countries the state has stronger capacity to implement regulation, so that policies in these areas may have more impact on business than they would in many low-income countries.

Individually-binding constraints are therefore more likely at the two ends of the income spectrum. At the low end, easing some specific infrastructural constraint may have a large payoff in terms of business opportunities. At the higher end, surveys may distinguish a few policy areas of particular concern to business. Things are more difficult in the middle of the spectrum, where weak governance and low state capacity cause business to experience a wide range of business climate impediments.

But even in cases where particular constraints emerge as serious, there is no magic bullet. Efforts to improve the business climate will need to be implemented across a broad front, with physical investments in infrastructure complemented by regulatory reforms and also by careful monitoring of service delivery to increase pressure for actual changes on the ground. Firms' views can help to prioritize reforms across broad areas — with finer prioritization requiring analysis of the specific concerns in each priority area, including through *Doing Business*-type indicators. In this way, perceptions data can kick off the business-government consultative process; further quantitative assessments can deepen this dialogue and lead to specific reforms.

Bibliography

Alwin, D. F. and J. A. Krosnick (1985). "The Measurement of Values in Surveys: A Comparison of Ratings and Rankings." *Public Opinion Quarterly* 49 (4): 535–552.

Ayyagari, M., A. Demirguc-Kunt and V. Maksimovic (2006). "How Important Are Financing Constraints? The Role of Finance in the Business Environment." WPS 3820, The World Bank.

Bertrand, M. and S. Mullainathan (2001). "Do People Mean What They Say? Implications for Subjective Survey Data." MIT Working Paper 01-04, January.

Biggs, T. and M. K. Shah (2006). "African Small and Medium Enterprises, Networks, and Manufacturing Performance." World Bank Policy Research Working Paper No. 3855, February.

Bourguignon, F. (2006). "Economic Growth: Heterogeneity and Firm-Level Disaggregation." Unpublished Note, The World Bank.

Carlin, W., M. Schaffer and P. Seabright (2006). "Where Are the Real Bottlenecks? A Lagrangian Approach to Identifying Constraints on Growth from Subjective Survey Data." CEPR Discussion Paper Series No. 5719, June.

Clarke, G. *et al.* (2007). *South Africa: An Assessment of the Investment Climate* (Washington, DC: The World Bank).

Country Credit Ratings (2006). *Institutional Investor.*

Eifert, B., A. Gelb and V. Ramachandran (2005). "Business Environment and Comparative Advantage in Africa: Evidence from the Investment Climate Data." Center for Global Development Working Paper 56.

Emery, J. (2003). In *Beyond Structural Adjustment: the Institutional Context of African Development*, eds., Van de Walle, Ball, and Ramachandran (Palgrave Macmillan).

Fries, S., T. Lysenko and S. Polanec (2003). "The 2002 Business Environment and Enterprise Performance Survey: Results from a Survey of 6100 Firms." Working Paper No. 84, November.

Hausmann, R., D. Rodrik and A. Velasco (2005). "Growth Diagnostics." Manuscript.

Hausmann, R. and A. Velasco (2005). "Slow Growth in Latin America: Common Outcomes, Common Causes." Manuscript.

Hellman, J., G. Jones, D. Kaufmann and M. Schankerman (2000). "Measuring Governance and State Capture: The Role of Bureaucrats and Firms in Shaping the Business Environment." Working Paper No. 51, June.

Iarossi, G. (2006). *The Power of Survey Design* (The World Bank).

Kaufmann, D., A. Kraay and M. Mastruzzi (2006). "Governance Matters V: Governance Indicators for 1996–2005."

Krosnick, J. A. and D. F. Alwin (1987). "An Evaluation of a Cognitive Theory of Response-Order Effects in Survey Measurement." *Public Opinion Quarterly* 51 (2): 201–219.

McCarty, J. A. and L. J. Shrum (2000). "The Measurement of Personal Values in Survey Research: A Test of Alternative Rating Procedures." *Public Opinion Quarterly* 64: 271–298.

Power Planning Associates (2007). Report on *Bujagali II* for the International Finance Corporation.

Ramachandran, V. and M. K. Shah (2007). "Why Are There So Few Black-Owned Businesses in Africa." Center for Global Development Working Paper #104, January.

Raturi, M. and A. V. Swamy (1999). "Explaining Ethnic Differentials in Credit Market Outcomes in Zimbabwe." *Economic Development and Cultural Change* 47 (3): 585–604.

Teal, F. (1998). "The Ghanaian Manufacturing Sector 1991–1995: Firm Growth, Productivity and Convergence." Working Paper 98-17, CSAE, Oxford University.

World Bank (2004–2007). *Doing Business*, annual publication.

$\mathcal{M}$aking the Most out of FDI in Africa

Norbert L. W. Wilson and Malick Diarrasouba*

11.1 Introduction

Governments of developing countries especially in Africa are giving attention to the potential role of foreign direct investment (FDI) in their
economies. In spite of the abundance of natural resource in Africa, the
continent is the poorest region in the world. FDI may be one of many ways
out of this poverty.

The purpose of this chapter is to set forth some ways in which investment can be attracted to Africa. The kind of investment that is needed
is investment that has a positive effect on the host country. This chapter
explores the benefits of FDI and the reasons for the limited amount of FDI
in Africa. With these limits, we consider the quality of FDI. We explore

*Wilson and Diarrasouba are assistant professor and graduate student at Auburn University
in the Department of Agricultural Economics and Rural Sociology. The authors thank
participants at the Symposium for their comments and suggestions.

Contacts: Auburn University, Department of Agricultural Economics and Rural
Sociology, 100 C Comer Hall, Auburn University, AL 36849, USA, +1 334 844 5616,
WilsonL@auburn.edu

quality issues with three case studies of FDI into Africa. We consider two international mechanisms which may help increase the quantity and quality of FDI into Africa: the Investment Climate Facility and the United Nations' Global Compact. In the review, we also posit a way to go beyond these two mechanisms.

11.2   FDI May Promote Growth

While other chapters in this book address the role of FDI in economic development, we want to look briefly at this literature and connect it to the concerns of Africa. Economists have long recognized the importance of investment in wealth creation. Earlier growth theories of Solow and others identified three potential sources — increasing capital stock, population and technical efficiency — suggesting that investment is the key to growth. In this line of reasoning, countries that are unable to generate sufficient saving to finance desired investment rely on other countries mainly in the form of foreign debt and FDI for economic growth.

Lin and Sosin suggest that the benefit of foreign debt is to purchase advanced equipment and technology in order to allow the country to raise the efficiency production which can help sustainable growth. On the other hand, the cost of foreign debt is the repayment of principal and interest. In addition, since foreign debt is denominated in foreign currencies, there is a high risk of exchange rate volatility which can impede the payment of the loan (Tarzi).

In contrast, FDI can be a valuable source of capital because it allows the introduction of new technology, completes domestic investment, improves the competitiveness of firms and provides managerial skills and access to global markets, hence FDI may be an engine for growth. Moreover, Choong, Yusop and Soo argue that FDI, via technology transfer and spillover efficiency, can stimulate a country's economic performance which in turn may alleviate poverty.

The evidence suggesting that FDI is important in the development process has led to a number of studies of the determinants of FDI. Perkins and Neumayer mention that the way new technology can improve growth is if certain conditions are met. New technologies diffuse faster under conditions of openness to international trade and investment. Based on neoclassical theories, they argue that market liberalization brings with it technological efficiency, productivity and competitiveness. Since the literature on FDI-led economic growth is based on the endogenous growth model, FDI, to generate growth, has to be associated with other factors such as trade policy, human capital development, and export-oriented policies; in other words, absorptive capacities (Choong, Yusop and Soo). de Mello argues that the absorptive capacity of the recipient country tends to affect the volume of FDI, which in turn depends on institutional factors such as trade regime legislation and political stability. Furthermore, Balasubramanyam, Salisu and Sapsford claim that countries with an export-oriented regime will attract FDI, because of openness. The presence of a free market, which is allowed by openness, turns out to provide a better environment for investment.

Asiedu (2001) supports this finding, but points out that African countries show a weaker connection between openness and FDI. She argues that sub-Saharan Africa (SSA) receives less FDI than other developing countries based solely on geographic location. Based on rates of return, African countries do not benefit the same as other developing countries. Additionally, Asiedu (2004) argues that relative to other developing countries, African countries have fallen behind in receiving FDI because African countries have fallen behind in terms of infrastructure development, openness to trade and investment and institutional quality. While African countries have made absolute improvements in these areas, the extent of reform has been substandard compared to other regions. Thus, Africa as a region has become less attractive as a host of FDI.

Hermes and Lensink point out that, in order to attract FDI, the host country needs to develop its financial system. A well-developed financial system allows the efficient allocation of resources and improves the absorptive capacity. A poor financial institution obscures investment opportunities. Choong, Yusop and Soo, in turn, put forward that to benefit from the technological transfer embodied in FDI, the development of the domestic financial sector is a key to mobilize savings better, which turns out to improve resource allocation and boosts technological innovation. Therefore, FDI has a positive effect on economic growth if the financial sector of the host country has a minimum level of development.

In addition to financial institutions, some scholars believe that market size, the availability of skilled labor, political stability, availability of good infrastructure, return on investment and exchange rate are positively related to FDI (Sumner). Asiedu (2006) supports this claim by arguing that small countries in terms of natural resources or market size can increase FDI if they promote infrastructure development, education of the labor force, macroeconomic stability, openness to FDI, market openness (less corruption) and political stability.

As an example, Lesotho, despite its geographic location and small size, had been able to attract FDI due to its macroeconomic stability, political regime and low volatility of its currency. These conditions enabled Lesotho to create employment and boost exports of apparel due to the presence of foreign investment (Lall). The problem with this example is that FDI to Lesotho dropped dramatically after the dismantling of the Multi-Fiber Agreement in 2005 (*WIR*, 2006). The example illustrates the complex interactions of domestic policies and the effects of exogenous factors, such as international policy shifts.

Moss, Ramachandran and Shah provide a different perspective on the reasons for the low FDI into Africa, particularly sub-Saharan Africa. Among the common reasons Africa receives little of the world's FDI, namely small market size measured in GDP, political and social uncertainty and limited market openness, Moss, Ramachandran and Shah argue that African countries are skeptical of FDI. The connection of FDI with colonialism and imperialism, post-colonial exposure to the former Soviet Union and its ideological bias against foreign (especially Western) capital, economic nationalism and the questions of the purported benefits to FDI as brought by researchers, NGOs and observers has fed the skepticism of Africa of FDI. The skepticism may have led to now former policies that shunned FDI. Though African governments may have eliminated many of the anti-FDI policies of the past, skepticism of FDI, in some countries, may still inform ideology and rhetoric leading to a belief that FDI is harmful. Thus, African countries are in a challenging position as suggested by the data of FDI in the region.

11.3 Africa Lags Behind

Africa lags behind the rest of the world when it comes to FDI. In terms of inward FDI stock,[1] the *entire continent* of Africa has received less FDI than either Brazil (in 2001 and 2005) or China (see Figure 11.1). As suggested in the literature, market size is one of many factors contributing to FDI. A comparison of FDI stock relative to GDP shows that African countries, as a group, have been similar to other countries (see Table 11.1). Because the African share of global GDP has been small, it is not surprising to see that Africa has had a small share of global FDI stock (see Table 11.2). Not only has the African share of global FDI been small, it has been growing at a rate less than the global FDI growth rate. When compared to FDI growth

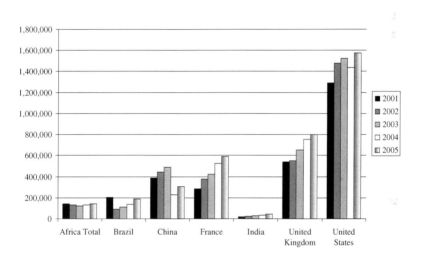

Figure 11.1:   Inward FDI stock in real terms
Source: Authors' calculations, *WIR* (2000–2006) and World Bank *World Development Indicators*.

---

[1] UNCTAD defines FDI stock as the following: "FDI stock is the value of the share of capital and reserves (including retained profits) attributable to the parent enterprise, plus the net indebtedness of affiliates to the parent enterprise. Data on FDI stocks is presented at book value or historical cost ..., reflecting prices at the time when the investment was made."

Table 11.1:   Percent of FDI inward stock relative to GDP in select countries or country groupings

	2001	2002	2003	2004	2005
Africa Total	28.00%	26.16%	24.40%	26.51%	27.58%
Brazil	43.14%	21.89%	25.39%	25.00%	25.27%
China	29.83%	30.81%	30.56%	12.71%	14.23%
France	21.57%	26.52%	24.08%	25.98%	28.25%
India	4.67%	5.00%	5.12%	5.56%	5.62%
United Kingdom	38.48%	36.16%	37.22%	36.19%	37.14%
United States	13.11%	14.45%	14.23%	12.62%	13.09%

Source: Authors' calculations, *WIR* (2000–2006) and World Bank *World Development Indicators*.

Table 11.2:   Percentage share of global GDP for select countries and regions

	2001	2002	2003	2004	2005
Africa Total	1.69%	1.59%	1.41%	1.30%	1.20%
Brazil	1.55%	1.32%	1.24%	1.42%	1.74%
China	4.26%	4.56%	4.51%	4.60%	5.05%
France	4.31%	4.49%	4.99%	5.15%	4.90%
India	1.52%	1.54%	1.64%	1.70%	1.81%
United Kingdom	4.60%	4.81%	4.95%	5.31%	5.06%
United States	32.29%	32.32%	30.20%	28.95%	28.32%

Source: Authors' calculations and World Bank *World Development Indicators*.

in developing countries like Brazil and China, the African growth rate has been extremely low (see Figure 11.2).

While African countries overall receive limited amounts of FDI, some African countries have been doing relatively well. Table 11.3 suggests that South Africa, Nigeria and Angola have done well in attracting inward FDI stock. Angola and Nigeria are similar because a large portion of the FDI to these countries has been in the oil industry. FDI into South Africa has been more diverse with investments into banking, telecommunications

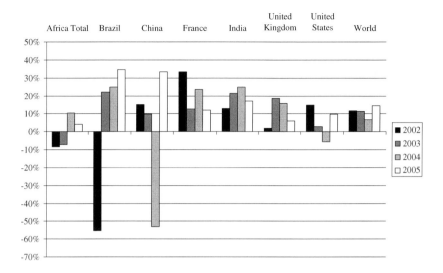

Figure 11.2: Percentage growth of real inward FDI stock
Source: Authors' calculations, *WIR* (2000–2006) and World Bank *World Development Indicators*.

Table 11.3: Percent of FDI in Africa in 2000–2005

	2000	2001	2002	2003	2004	2005
Angola	5.40%	6.35%	7.90%	8.00%	8.19%	5.24%
Nigeria	16.10%	13.35%	15.15%	14.42%	14.82%	13.59%
South Africa	29.41%	31.51%	19.87%	18.43%	21.85%	27.08%
North Africa	28.86%	28.89%	33.68%	34.01%	30.93%	30.49%
Rest of SSA	20.24%	19.91%	23.40%	25.14%	24.21%	23.61%

Source: Authors' calculations and *WIR* (2000–2006).

and other non-primary goods. These three countries have represented 40 to over 50 percent of FDI stock into Africa for the years 2000–2005. Given the share of FDI that has gone to North Africa, Angola, Nigeria and South Africa, the remaining 45 African countries, which are from sub-Saharan Africa, have received only 20 to 25 percent of the relatively small FDI into Africa.

In terms of inflows[2] of FDI, 2005 was a great year for African countries. Overall the continent experienced a 78 percent increase in inflows,
which is much larger than the 28 percent increase in the rest of the world.
However, the increase was primarily attributed to the boom in the global
commodity markets. Therefore, the inflow increase was in the primary sector. Despite the gain, the African share of global FDI inflows fell, even
below the shares attained in the 1970s and 1980s. WIR (2006) attributes
this falling share to limited increases in production capacity and diversification. African countries that received the least FDI inflows, which were
also the least developed countries, were those that "have limited natural
resources, lack the capacity to engage in significant manufacturing and as
a result, are among the least integrated into the global production system"
(WIR, 2006, p. 40).

Even this cursory review of the data and the literature indicates that
Africa, in terms of FDI, is behind and the reasons for this state of affairs.
While the amount of FDI matters, another branch of the literature points
out that the quality of the FDI also matters in terms of reaping the benefits of
FDI. WIR (2006) states: " ... [Africa] continues to exhibit weaknesses that
constrain its ability to attract quality FDI of the kind that would generate
broader beneficial effects in its economies" (p. 40). In a review of the FDI
literature, Sumner argues that for FDI to be beneficial for the poor, FDI must
have a net positive effect on the country's national account. More relevant
for this discussion, he argues that "good" FDI must have positive impacts on
employment, income and wages and income inequality. FDI must generate
net positive transfers to government revenue. Also, the type of FDI, its
mode of entry and the condition of the host country can influence the
quality of the FDI, which is the ability of the FDI to promote growth and

---

[2] UNCTAD defines FDI inflows as the following: "For associates and subsidiaries, FDI flows
consist of the net sales of shares and loans (including non-cash acquisitions made against
equipment, manufacturing rights, etc.) to the parent company plus the parent firm's share
of the affiliate's reinvested earnings plus total net intra-company loans (short- and long-
term) provided by the parent company. For branches, FDI flows consist of the increase in
reinvested earnings plus the net increase in funds received from the foreign direct investor.
FDI flows with a negative sign (reverse flows) indicate that at least one of the components
in the above definition is negative and nót offset by positive amounts of the remaining
components."

improve the livelihood of the people in the host country. In a study of OECD countries, Alfaro and Charlton provide evidence that the growth effects of FDI are positively and significantly related to the characteristics of the quality of FDI. The researchers do not explicitly investigate the pathways that FDI leads to growth, but implicit in their analysis is the idea that FDI permits, among other things, technology transfers.

11.4   Case Studies of FDI in Africa

For illustrative purposes, we provide three brief case studies of FDI in Africa. These cases reflect the diversity of FDI into Africa and the perceived benefits and costs of FDI. The examples provided are not intended to promote or deride the companies or countries noted.

Blue Skies Company: Blue Skies Company is a privately-held joint venture of British and Ghanaian interests. The company cuts and processes fresh fruit from Ghana (and imports from Brazil, Egypt, Kenya, South Africa and the UK during supply gaps) and sells them to markets in Europe. Wilson and Cacho state that Blue Skies meets EUREPGAP[3] standards. Blue Skies enables its growers to meet these standards through free training and support. The company has brought in experts from Europe and South Africa to help its farmers learn the standards and the production practices to meet the standards. In response to consumer demand, Blue Skies also adopted and surpassed a code of conduct for socially responsible business practices as reflected by permanent employment contracts, medical insurance and social security benefits for employees (Dannson, Gallat and Röttger).

Dunavant Ltd.: Dunavant is a privately-owned, American cotton broker. In 1999, Dunavant bought the Anglo-African company Lonrho to expand cotton production in Zambia. And like the expansion into Uganda, Dunavant maintained the same local management (Zachary). The company has distinguished itself because of how ingrained it is in

---

[3] EUREPGAP is an initiative of retailers of the Euro-Retailer Producer Working Group to establish standards and procedures for global certification of good agricultural practices (EUREPGAP, 2005).

Zambia. According to Zachary, Dunavant is "so well-connected to farmers off the beaten track that social welfare agencies have begun to partner with the company to provide services to remote refugees uprooted by civil war in northern Uganda and to Zambia's rural HIV and AIDS sufferers" (p. 2). Because of these connections and work in the community, Dunavant was recognized as a finalist of the 2004 US Secretary of State's Award for Corporate Excellence. Martin Brennan, US Ambassador to Zambia, stated: "[Dunavant recognizes] that we must make investments in people and communities as well as in goods and services. Dunavant's commitment to fighting HIV/AIDS in Zambia demonstrates its enlightened understanding that the best way to do well is to do good" (Embassy of the United States Lusaka Zambia). In another investment, Dunavant was reported to spend in 2006 $2 million to train 100,000 farmers in a yield productivity-enhancing program (*Times of Zambia*).

Chambishi Mines Zambia: In 1998, the state-owned China Non-Ferrous Metals Mining and Construction Company (NFC) purchased the Chambishi copper mine in Zambia. The mine in Chambishi had been out of service for several years, and the NFC brought it back into production. Since the mine has been in operation, a number of concerns have been expressed. Zambians have not typically been appointed to the management of the mine. The Zambian community has expressed concerns over labor practices at the mine (Trofimov). The concerns, based in part on the deaths of miners in 2005, led to a violent protest where several workers were shot (*The Economist*). While not specific to the Chambishi mine, the Chinese have built a 1,160-mile railroad from Lusaka, Zambia to the port in Dar es Salaam, Tanzania. While the project was completed ahead of schedule, the Zambians and Tanzanians are still dependant on the Chinese for technical assistance to run the train. As *The Economist* laments, "African hopes of technology transfer may be over-optimistic" (p. 54).[4]

---

[4] Over the last several years, substantial investment has come from China and other Asian countries into Africa. The news media about this investment has intimated concerns about the effects of this investment. This case study suggests some of the concerns, but it is by no means a thorough discussion of the complex issues related to the expansion of investments by China or other Asian countries into Africa. For more on Asian (specifically Chinese and Indian) investments, see Broadman.

11.5   At Least Two Ways Forward[5]

We have tried to establish the challenges that Africa faces as it relates to FDI: low quantity and variable quality. African countries have attempted a number of policies to rectify both issues such as investment promotion agencies (Wilson and Cacho). A review of the numerous efforts to promote FDI in individual countries could be useful. However, we have decided to consider two international mechanisms that are in place that could improve FDI quality and quantity into Africa because these mechanisms have the potential to affect many countries in Africa. As this review has attempted to cover the entire African continent, we felt the best approach was to consider multilateral mechanisms.

11.5.1   *The Investment Climate Facility (ICF) for Africa*

Formally launched at the World Economic Forum in 2006, the ICF is a fund and a private-public partnership to bring about change in the investment climate in Africa for Africa. Early on, the ICF received endorsements or approvals from the 2005 G8 Gleneagles Meeting, Tony Blair's Africa Commission, the British Department for International Development (DfID), the New Partnership for Africa's Development (NEPAD) and the African Union (Moss and Rose). The plan is to raise $550 million[6] over the seven-year life of the program. The monies are to come from donor countries and the private sector, which are to contribute $2.5 million (DfID).

The ICF will use its fund to achieve the following objectives:

• Build the environment for investment climate reform

   o Encourage, develop and work with coalitions for investment climate reform and support business government dialogue.

---

[5] This section was greatly influenced by comments made at the Symposium where an earlier version of the material of this chapter was presented.

[6] The $500 million is to come from sovereign nations and international institutions, and $50 million is to come from corporations (FitzGerald, 2006b).

- Get the investment climate right

    o Support governments in creating a legal, regulatory and adminis-
    trative environment that encourages business at all levels to invest,
    grow and create jobs.

- Encourage business to respond

    o Improve Africa's image as an investment destination through a
    coordinated effort to publicize improvements in the investment
    climate (ICF).

The ICF operates by funding proposals that have the greatest rate of
return in improving the investment climate. Projects that will improve the
environment for small businesses and reduce poverty, especially through
job creation, are the most highly favored (DfID). The proposals are
screened by the ICF Secretariat, and the Board of Trustees accepts or
rejects the projects (smaller projects are evaluated by a sub-committee
of the Board).

The Board of Trustees is composed of African business and political
leaders. In particular, one of the co-chairs is former Tanzanian president
Benjamin Mkapa. The ICF reports that it evolved with consultations with
key stakeholders. The NEPAD Heads of Government and African trade
ministers have accepted the priority areas as ones that are critical for
Africa to address (ICF). Ideally, this level of African political and business involvement will help the ICF, which is housed in Tanzania, to have
more traction than other projects not based in the region.

As a way of improving the likelihood of successful projects, the countries eligible to receive ICF funding are those countries that have agreed to
participate in the African Peer Review Mechanism (APRM) of NEPAD.
Ideally, countries that are willing to go through APRM are serious about
improving their governance and are sufficiently flexible to permit the
changes that ICF projects may suggest.[7]

---

[7] The African Peer Review Mechanism is a voluntary review process sponsored by NEPAD.
The five-staged process reviews the policies of countries and makes recommendations
to reviewed countries. For a description of the APRM, see http://nepad.org/2005/files/
aprm.php. For an assessment of the APRM see Kanbur, where he highlights a significant

Moss and Rose question whether the US government should donate money to the ICF. The authors argue that the ICF has a number of strengths, namely: timeliness of a critical issue; credible, respected leadership; available money[8]; selectivity (only APRM countries); and an exit strategy. However, they question how the ICF will use the money, the conceptualization of the problems African countries face and the independence of the ICF.[9] In response, Niall FitzGerald, the co-chair of ICF, argues that the ICF projects are ones that come from Africa and reflect the needs of stakeholders, particularly African governments and businesses with inputs from investors, donors and others (FitzGerald, 2006b).

FitzGerald suggests that the ICF has the potential not only to increase the quantity of FDI into Africa, but also that ICF-funded projects could have spillover effects like high-quality FDI can. He states: "What I'm suggesting ... is that being successful in Africa requires an entrepreneurial attitude and a willingness to help create the market and infrastructure around it, not just enter it. An understanding that operating in Africa may entail investment in the wider environment, such as in the supply chain, distribution channels and in the workforce, in terms of training and health care. Such investments not only enable business, they also help society as a whole" (FitzGerald, 2006a).

11.5.2   *The UN Global Compact*

The ICF is structured to help improve the investment climate in African countries, thus increase investment into African countries. The UN Global

---

passage of the APRM providing support for countries to make changes suggested by the APRM.

[8] At the time of their report, the ICF had $90 million. The UK government has offered $30 million, with money also coming in from the World Bank's International Finance Corporation, the Irish and Dutch governments and several corporations (Anglo-American, Royal Dutch Shell, SAB Miller and Unilever). FitzGerald (2006b) states that by August 2006, the ICF has raised $117.4 million. Coca-Cola, Celtel and Standard Bank were added to the list of companies that have contributed to the ICF.

[9] As we have found, part of the reason for the criticism by Moss and Rose is the limited information available on the ICF. FitzGerald (2006b) notes that the first round of projects has been funded. However, no information (ICF web page, Lexis/Nexis, internet searches, etc.) is readily available on the projects.

Compact (GC) is to help improve the behavior of firms throughout the world. Ultimately, the GC may help improve the actions of signatory firms such that the investments of these multinational firms are beneficiary to the host country. This corporate social responsibility may provide high-quality FDI that will contribute to the economic well-being and growth of developing economies, like those in Africa.

Former UN Secretary-General Kofi Annan at the 1999 World Economic Forum introduced the GC. "Through the power of collective action, the Global Compact seeks to promote responsible corporate citizenship so that business can be part of the solution to the challenges of globalization. In this way, the private sector — in partnership with other social actors — can help realize the Secretary-General's vision: a more sustainable and inclusive global economy" (GC).

The GC is a voluntary program. By signing to the GC, firms are agreeing to adjust their behavior so as to promote the core values, known as the Ten Principles, of the GC (see Box 1). However, the GC is not a legally binding contract, a monitoring or regulatory body or a code of conduct (GC). But, the GC establishes networks for firms and other stakeholders and forums for sharing best practices (Williamson). Georg Kell, the executive head of the GC, views it as a principles-based initiative that begins with the commitment of a CEO. The job of the CEO is to communicate to all employees the Ten Principles as core values. Taking on these core values, the employees are to implement them throughout the organization and explain the actions of the firm to society via corporate documents (PriceWaterhouseCoopers). The documents are called the Communications of Progress (COP).

The Ten Principles point to ways that the GC can potentially help improve the quality of FDI. As Sumner argues, good FDI should have an impact on employment, wages and income inequality. If applied correctly, the GC could encourage firms to have positive effects on employment and wages. The other literature recognizes that good FDI transfers technology, which may contribute to the economic growth of the host country. The environmental components of the GC can help firms disseminate technologies and encourage host countries to find better ways to avoid practices that harm the environment. A common reason for the limited amount of FDI in Africa is the concern of corruption. By adhering to the Ten Principles, a firm can discourage corruption.

Box 1. The Ten Principles of the Global Compact

The Global Compact asks companies to embrace, support and enact, within their sphere of influence, a set of core values in the areas of human rights, labor standards, the environment, and anti-corruption:

Human Rights

Principle 1: Businesses should support and respect the protection of internationally proclaimed human rights; and

Principle 2: make sure that they are not complicit in human rights abuses.

Labor Standards

Principle 3: Businesses should uphold the freedom of association and the effective recognition of the right to collective bargaining;

Principle 4: the elimination of all forms of forced and compulsory labor;

Principle 5: the effective abolition of child labor; and

Principle 6: the elimination of discrimination in respect of employment and occupation.

Environment

Principle 7: Businesses should support a precautionary approach to environmental challenges;

Principle 8: undertake initiatives to promote greater environmental responsibility; and

Principle 9: encourage the development and diffusion of environmentally friendly technologies.

Anti-Corruption

Principle 10: Businesses should work against corruption in all its forms, including extortion and bribery.

Source: http://www.unglobalcompact.org/AboutTheGC/ TheTenPrinciples/index.html.

Nevertheless, uncertainty abounds with the GC. Savitz and Choi suggest that Ban Ki-Moon, the new Secretary-General of the United Nations, has not provided strong support of the GC. They suggest that two camps exist: some critics believe that the GC will falter without the strong support of the Secretary-General; other observers argue that the GC is well-imbedded in corporate life and can stand alone without the support of the Secretary-General (Savitz and Choi).

In terms of reach, the GC is limited. Savitz and Choi state that only 5 percent of multinationals are signatories, and 345 companies have been de-listed for failing to report their progress on the Ten Principles. As of 2005, only 70 US firms had signed onto the GC. Kell believes that the low numbers are because of uncertainty of what the GC is and the litigiousness of US society. By signing onto the GC, some fear that CEOs could be legally bound to certain actions, which according to Kell they are not (PriceWaterhouseCoopers).

In a critique of several guidelines or codes of corporate social respon-sibility for multinationals, Paine *et al.* state: "The codes and guidelines promulgated by business, government, and civic groups in recent years contain a lengthy and confusing menu of possibilities" (p. 123). The GC is one of the guidelines mentioned in the review. Relating the GC to the issue of "good" FDI, the Ten Principles are very broad and may not necessarily encourage "good" FDI.

Between two challenging groups is where the GC lies. On the one side, civil society organizations (CSOs) see the voluntary guidelines of the GC as an eroding of the possible oversight that the UN could have over multinationals that perform poorly. Some CSOs worry that multina-tional firms are simply "blue washing," that is, taking on the UN prin-ciples with little change in their behavior. On the other side are the multinationals that see the creation of the GC as the first step in greater oversight of their operations by an international body (Williamson). It is in this tension of appearing to do too little or appearing to be over-bearing that, according to Kell, the GC is innovative because the GC is to encourage a change in the values of the firm, not laws. Kell sees the change in core values as having a systemic change in the firm. He states that "the company must have its values correct everywhere, irrespective of where they operate. They must have a common ethical framework" (PriceWaterhouseCoopers, p. 14).

If this idea holds, then we could see the GC having positive effects around the world through the subsidiaries of signatories of the GC. For example, Nestlé is recognized as a company that uses the GC to bring about good investing. In China, the food company is noted to have attempted to improve life in communities around its factories in Northeast China by improving local cattle breeding, road systems and livestock feed (Nash).

The Investment Climate Facility and the Global Compact have great potential to effect change in Africa by improving the quantity and quality of FDI into Africa. But, are these two mechanisms the best way to bring about the needed changes in Africa?

11.6   What about Africa?

As suggested earlier, both the ICF and the GC have problems. Clearly, African countries have substantial limitations in terms of resources to bring about the changes that the ICF could provide. The work of the GC could bring about a shift in corporate values that encourages investments into Africa which uplifts and not exploits. As mentioned earlier, the small size of the GC list of signatories means that the benefits of the GC are limited. The GC has as its core output the COP, a self-assessment of adherence to the Ten Principles. For firms to do such an exercise may be all that can be expected. As it stands, neither governments nor CSOs can have a say in the development of the COPs. They may critique the report after the exercise. The self-assessment is limited by the biases that the firm has of itself and its desire to avoid controversy. Also, the self-assessment is of all activities of the firm, not specifically of the FDI of the firm. For a large multinational, a proper assessment of all of the firm's activities is a tremendous task in addition to running the business. Maybe the self-assessment is not the best use of resources for these firms. A critical, independent review of the FDI that goes into countries at the host country level may be better.

At its core, the ICF is still a foreign-aid program, though there is support from multinationals. Also, the ICF has substantial direction from African business and political leaders, particularly through the Board of Trustee members from the African Union and NEPAD. However, from the evidence reviewed, African CSOs were not involved in the formal creation process nor are they involved in the granting process. For the ICF to influence governments (and ultimately the citizens) to improve the investment climate, a sense of ownership must be established. Otherwise, the civil servant at the port or the tax office has little incentive to implement the changes suggested by programs sponsored by the ICF. Without this sense of ownership, financial incentives or regulations to bring about changes to improve the investment climate will only bring about temporary adjustments or lead to rent seeking.

Two assumptions of these mechanisms pervade: Africa needs money to improve the investment climate, and outsiders must make changes for Africa to receive good FDI. However, not every challenge that Africa faces is one that money or outsiders can resolve.

We put forth another way. We consider a review process that critically assesses FDI that comes into Africa to ensure the quality of the FDI and at the same time encourages greater FDI. The review process would look like the peer reviews of NEPAD or OECD countries with the additional feature of true collaboration amongst business, governments (including international organizations) and CSOs at every stage of the review. This review could be done in collaboration with the APRM. Like the other peer reviews, international and local experts would contribute to the reviews. Most importantly, the reviews would not take place at the headquarters alone; rather, the reviews would include assessments at the subsidiary in the host country. The publicized review would explore where the firm has done well and where the firm could improve given the context of the country. Such a review could really hold firms accountable not only to the local needs but also to those of the world community. In addition, the review would also consider how the local government and society have helped or hindered the progress of the firm. The review would consider how the community has partnered with the firm to ensure that the firm and the community prosper. Non-pecuniary issues like how the firm, community and government have communicated and shared their core values and experiences could be an important part of the review.[10]

The only way that such a review process could take place is with voluntary cooperation from the firm, governments and communities under review. While at this stage such a review may be beyond reach, if the will exists, then all parties will respond to demands of the review.

---

[10] The idea that we propose here has roots at the Organization for Economic Cooperation and Development (OECD). In a 2005 special project for young professionals at OECD, Wilson with several other colleagues discussed a peer review process for FDI. The proposed idea discussed here pushes that idea forward with a greater emphasis on FDI in Africa and consideration of CSOs and governments.

Unlike the ICF, the proposed mechanism incorporates the voices of CSOs and is not about creating projects. The proposed mechanism is about creating learning opportunities for the three agents involved. In the review, firms could exert soft pressure on the community to encourage actions that better prepare workers for the firms. By the same token, CSOs could suggest ways to engage workers and the local community that will permit more efficient interactions of the firm with the community.

The proposed mechanism differs from the GC because the review takes place at the level of the firm's contact with the host country. The community and the government have a say in how well the firm is doing based on a core set of principles that are derived from an African perspective. Because of the community and government review, the firm actually gets a say at how the firm has been treated. As a review that comes from those affected, greater participation, acceptance and response to the recommendations are possible.

11.7 Concluding Remarks

Our proposed mechanism is not meant to dismiss the ICF or the GC. Much good could come from both mechanisms. Rather, our hope is for provocation. We hope to urge business, political and social leaders on the African continent to bring about changes that will reverse the trends of low quantity and variable quality FDI in their region. International partners will have a role to play in improving the investment climate and encouraging high quality FDI into the region. However, to bring about change, local people, not just political and business leaders, will have to get involved in the process. Indigenous ideas will have to come forward as a way to bring about the change. A collaboration of business, social and political leaders, both African and non-African, will develop the solutions to improve FDI in Africa and ultimately economic development.

Bibliography

Alfaro, L. and A. Charlton (2007). "Growth and the Quality of Foreign Direct Investment: Is All FDI Equal." NBER Working Paper 072.

Asiedu, E. (2001). "On Determinants of Foreign Direct Investment to Developing Countries: Is Africa Different?" *World Development* 30 (January): 107–119.

—. (2004). "Policy Reform and Foreign Direct Investment in Africa: Absolute Progress but Relative Decline." *Development Policy Review* 22: 41–48.

—. (2006). "Foreign Direct Investment in Africa: The Role of Natural Resources, Market Size, Government Policy, Institutions and Political Stability." *World Economy* 29 (January): 63–77.

Balasubramanyam, V. N., M. A. Salisu and D. Sapsford (1996). "Foreign Direct Investment and Growth in EP and IS Countries." *Economic Journal* 106: 92–105.

Broadman, H. (2007). *Africa's Silk Road: China and India's New Economic Frontier.* World Bank, Washington, DC.

Choong, C. K., Z. Yusop and S. C. Soo (2004). "Foreign Direct Investment, Economic Growth, and Financial Sector Development: A Comparative Analysis." *ASEAN Economic Bulletin* 21: 278–289.

Dannson, A., S. Gallat and A. Röttger (2007). "Blue Skies Company Ltd." Linking Farmers to Markets Food and Agriculture Organization (FAO), http://www.fao.org/ag/ags/subjects/en/agmarket/linkages/pvtco.html. Accessed April 18, 2007.

de Mello, L. R., Jr. (1999). "Foreign Direct Investment-Led Growth: Evidence from Time Series and Panel Data." *Oxford Economic Papers* 51: 133–151.

Department for International Development (DfID) (2006). "Africa Opening for Business: Prime Minister Confirms UK Support for Africa's Investment Climate Facility (ICF)." Press Release DfID, http://www.dfid.gov.uk/news/files/pressreleases/investment-climate-facility.asp, (November 17). Accessed May 3, 2007.

The Economist (2006). "Never Too Late to Scramble." 381 (October 28): 53–56.

Embassy of the United States Lusaka Zambia (2005). "U.S. Government Recognizes Dunavant Zambia Limited for Good Business Practices." Press Release US Embassy Zambia, http://zambia.usembassy.cgov/zambia/pr011205, (January 12). Accessed February 6, 2007.

EUREPGAP (2005). "What is EUREPGAP?" http://www.eurep.org/languages/english/about.html. Accessed September 23, 2005.

FitzGerald, N. (2006a). "Africa Post-Gleneagles: Threats and Opportunities" (or "Will A Year of Talk Be Followed by a Year of Walk?"). Speech at the Federation of British Industry, January 16, 2006, www.cbi.org.uk. Accessed May 16, 2007.

—. (2006b). "Why the Investment Climate for Africa Deserves U.S. Support — A Response to the CGD Note: The Investment Climate Facility for Africa: Does it Deserve U.S. Support?" http://www.cgdev.org/doc/commentary/ICFResponseCGDNote.pdf. Accessed May 16, 2007.

The Global Compact (GC) (2007). http://www.unglobalcompact.org. Accessed May 10, 2007.

Hermes, N. and R. Lensink (2003). "Foreign Direct Investment, Financial Development and Economic Growth." *Journal of Development Studies* 40: 142–161.

The Investment Climate Facility for Africa (ICF) (2007). http://www.investmentclimatefacility.org/index.htm. Accessed May 12, 2007.

Kanbur, R. (2004). "The African Peer Review Mechanism (APRM): An Assessment of Concept and Design." *Politikon* 31 (November): 157–166.

Lall, S. (2005). "FDI, AGOA and Manufactured Exports by a Landlocked, Least Developed African Economy: Lesotho." *Journal of Development Studies* 41: 998–1022.

Lin, S. and K. Sosin (2001). "Foreign Debt and Economic Growth." *The Economics of Transition* 9 (November): 635–655.

Morgan, M. (2006). "Foreign Investment Failing Us." *The Statesman* (Ghanaian Newspaper), www.thestatesmanonline.com/pages/news_detail.php?newsid=1060&section=1, (October 20). Accessed May 22, 2007.

Moss, T. J., V. Ramachandran and M. K. Shah (2004). "Is Africa's Skepticism of Foreign Capital Justified? Evidence from East African Firm Survey Data." Working Paper No. 41, Center for Global Development, June.

Moss, T. and S. Rose (2006). "Africa's Investment Climate Facility: Does it Deserve U.S. Support?" CGD Note, Center for Global Development, www.cgdev.org, (August). Accessed May 1, 2007.

Nash, P. (2003). "Global Compact Challenges Firms." *Business Weekly*, www.chinadaily.com.cn, (April 8). Accessed May 23, 2007.

New Partnership for African Development (NEPAD) (2003). http://nepad.org/2005/files/aprm.php, (September 16). Accessed May 12, 2007.

Paine, L., R. Deshpande, J. D. Margolis and K. E. Bettcher (2005). "Up to Code: Does Your Company's Conduct Meet World-Class Standards?" *Harvard Business Review* 83 (December): 122–133, 154.

Perkins, P. and E. Neumayer (2005). "The International Diffusion of New Technologies: A Multitechnology Analysis of Latecomer Advantage and Global Economic Integration." *Annals of the Association of American Geographers* 95: 789–808.

PriceWaterhouseCoopers (2005). "The UN Global Compact: Moving to the Business Mainstream." *The Corporate Responsibility Report* 2 (Winter): 12–16.

Savitz, A. and M. Choi (2007). "The Future of the Global Compact: Does the New UN Secretary General Have the Commitment — and Corporate Experience — to Drive the Compact?" *The Corporate Responsibility Officer*, www.thecro.com, (March 6). Accessed May 25, 2007.

Solow, R. M. (1956). "A Contribution to the Theory of Economic Growth." *Quarterly Journal of Economics* 70: 65–94.

Sumner, A. (2005). "Is Foreign Direct Investment Good for the Poor? A Review and Stocktake." *Development in Practice* 15 (June): 269–286.

Tarzi, S. (2005). "Foreign Direct Investment Flows into Developing Countries: Impact of Location and Government Policy." *Journal of Social, Political and Economic Studies* 30 (Winter): 497–516.

Times of Zambia (2005). "Dunavant to Spend $2m on Training." http://www.times. com.cm/news/viewnews.cgi?category=12&id=1128880204. Accessed February 6, 2007.

Trofimov, Y. (2007). "New Management: In Africa, China's Expansion Begins to Stir Resentment; Investment Boom Fuels 'Colonialism' Charges; A Tragedy in Zambia." *The Wall Street Journal*, New York, N.Y., (February 2): A.1.

United Nations Conference on Trade and Development (UNCTAD) (2002). http://www.unctad.org/Templates/Page.asp?intItemID=3165&lang=1. Accessed June 1, 2007.

Williamson, H. (2003). "Signing Up to Corporate Citizenship Social Responsibility: The UN's Global Compact Initiative is Encouraging Companies to Commit to Their Wider Role in a Fair Society." *The Financial Times*, London, (February 12): 12.

Wilson, N. and J. Cacho (2007). "Linkages between Foreign Direct Investment, Trade and Policy: An Economic Analysis with Application to the Food Sector in OECD Countries and Case Studies in Ghana, Mozambique, Tunisia and Uganda." OECD Trade Policy Working Paper, No. 50, Organization for Economic Cooperation and Development, Paris.

World Investment Report (WIR) (2000). United Nations Conference on Trade and Development (UNCTAD), Geneva.

World Investment Report (WIR) (2001). United Nations Conference on Trade and Development (UNCTAD), Geneva.

World Investment Report (WIR) (2002). United Nations Conference on Trade and Development (UNCTAD), Geneva.

World Investment Report (WIR) (2003). United Nations Conference on Trade and Development (UNCTAD), Geneva.

World Investment Report (WIR) (2004). United Nations Conference on Trade and Development (UNCTAD), Geneva.

World Investment Report (WIR) (2005). United Nations Conference on Trade and Development (UNCTAD), Geneva.

World Investment Report (WIR) (2006). United Nations Conference on Trade and Development (UNCTAD), Geneva.